Birmingham Archaeology Monograph Series 4

A Romano–British Livestock Complex in Birmingham

Excavations 2002-2004 and 2006-2007
at Longdales Road, King's Norton, Birmingham

by

Alex Jones, Bob Burrows, C. Jane Evans, Annette Hancocks and Josh Williams

with contributions from

Emily Bird, Erica Macey-Bracken, Val Fryer, Pam Grinter, Kay Hartley, John Halsted, Rob Ixer, Paul Mason, Jane Timby, Felicity Wild and Steven Willis

Illustrations by Nigel Dodds and Bryony Ryder

BAR British Series 470
2008

Published in 2016 by
BAR Publishing, Oxford

BAR British Series 470

Birmingham Archaeology Monograph Series 4
A Romano-British Livestock Complex in Birmingham

ISBN 978 1 4073 0362 8

© Birmingham Archaeology and the Publisher 2008

The authors' moral rights under the 1988 UK Copyright,
Designs and Patents Act are hereby expressly asserted.

All rights reserved. No part of this work may be copied, reproduced, stored,
sold, distributed, scanned, saved in any form of digital format or transmitted
in any form digitally, without the written permission of the Publisher.

BAR Publishing is the trading name of British Archaeological Reports (Oxford) Ltd.
British Archaeological Reports was first incorporated in 1974 to publish the BAR
Series, International and British. In 1992 Hadrian Books Ltd became part of the BAR
group. This volume was originally published by Archaeopress in conjunction with
British Archaeological Reports (Oxford) Ltd / Hadrian Books Ltd, the Series principal
publisher, in 2008. This present volume is published by BAR Publishing, 2016.

Printed in England

PUBLISHING

BAR titles are available from:

        BAR Publishing
        122 Banbury Rd, Oxford, OX2 7BP, UK
EMAIL info@barpublishing.com
PHONE +44 (0)1865 310431
FAX   +44 (0)1865 316916
        www.barpublishing.com

Contents

Chapter 1: Summary and Introduction — 1

Summary — 1
Introduction by Alex Jones and John Halsted — 4
    Background — 4
    Longdales Road fieldwork 2002–2007 — 6
    Aims — 8
    Methodology (Fig. 4) — 8
    Arrangement of report — 9

Chapter 2: Area A, the Double-Ditched Enclosures (Field 2) — 13

Results by Alex Jones and Josh Williams — 13
    Phasing — 13
    Phase 1: First double-ditched enclosure (Enclosure A1), AD 120–mid 2nd century (Figs 7–9, Plates 4–6) — 13
        Description of Phase 1 features — 13
        Finds and dating evidence from Phase 1 features — 17
        Interpretation of Phase 1 features — 17
    Phase 2: Second double-ditched enclosure (Enclosure A2), late 2nd–3rd century (Figs 7, 10–11) — 19
        Description of Phase 2 features — 19
        Finds and dating evidence from Phase 2 features — 21
        Interpretation of Phase 2 features — 21
    Phase 1–2 features (not illustrated in detail) — 21
        Description and interpretation — 21
    Phase 3: Later Romano-British activity, 3rd-early 4th century (Figs 7, 12–13) — 24
        Description of Phase 3 features — 24
        Interpretation of Phase 3 features — 24
    Phase 1–Phase 3 features (Figs 7, 13–15) — 26
        Description of Phase 1–Phase 3 features — 26
        Finds and dating evidence from Phase 1–Phase 3 features — 27
        Interpretation of Phase 1–Phase 3 features — 27
    Phase 4: All post-Roman activity — 27
Finds — 27
    Small finds by Erica Macey-Bracken with Rob Ixer (Fig. 16) — 27
        Catalogue — 27
    Romano-British pottery by Annette Hancocks — 28
        Introduction — 28
        Methodology — 28
        Chronology — 29
        Taphonomy — 30
        Fabrics — 30
        Surface finish — 31
        Sooting — 31
        Forms — 31
        Vessel size and function — 31
        Catalogue of illustrated pottery by phase and fabric (Figs 17–18) — 31
        Mortaria by Kay Hartley — 36
        Samian pottery by Steven Willis — 36
        Pottery discussion by Annette Hancocks — 38

Chapter 3: Area B: the Livestock Herding Structures (Field 1) — 41

Results by Alex Jones and Josh Williams — 41
    Phasing — 41
    Phase 1: Early enclosure (B1), the first livestock 'funnel', early 2nd century (Figs 21–23, Plate 7) — 41
        Description of Phase 1 features — 41

FIGURES

Chapter 1, Introduction

1 Roman west midlands and the road network; dashed lines show hypothetical tribal boundaries (after White 2007, fig. 12). Inset: location of Birmingham
2 Location of Longdales Road excavations, Metchley fort and Ryknild Street
3 Longdales Road, relief and draft geology and plan of all investigations
4 Longdales Road, detailed plan of Area A–D investigations and main features identified
5 Longdales Road, line of Ryknild Street and surrounding sites investigated (x5 vertical exaggeration of topography: Areas A, B and C–D shown)
6 Longdales Road and surrounds, Ordnance Survey map of 1890 showing projected line of Ryknild Street and Areas A–D, and suggested boundary of *Hellerelege* after Demidowicz 2003. Area excavations are blacked in

Chapter 2, Area A, the double-ditched enclosures

7 Area A, simplified plan, features of all phases (scale 1:450)
8 Area A, Phase 1 plan (scale 1:400)
9 Area A, Phase 1 sections (scales 1:25 and 1:10)
10 Area A, Phase 2 plan (scale 1:450)
11 Area A, Phase 2 sections (scale 1:25)
12 Area A, Phase 3 plan (scale 1:450)
13 Area A, Phase 3 sections and Phase 1–3 sections (scales 1:10 and 1:25)
14 Area A, Phase 1–3 plan (scale 1:450)
15 Area A, detailed plan of eaves-drip gully F318 (scale 1:50)
16 Area A, small finds (scale 1:4)
17 Area A, pottery, Nos 1–26 (scale 1:4)
18 Area A, pottery, Nos 27–50 (scale 1:4)
19 Area A, pottery, fabric groups by percentage weight
20 Area A, pottery, vessel classes by percentage rim EVE

Chapter 3, Area B, the livestock herding structures

21 Area B, simplified plan, features of all phases (scale 1:400)
22 Area B, phase plans (scale 1:500)
23 Area B, sections (scale 1:25)
24 Area B, fabric groups by percentage weight
25 Area B, pottery, Nos 1–11 and 13–21 (scale 1:4)
26 Area B, vessel classes by percentage rim EVE

Chapter 4, Area C–D, the roadside area

27 Area C–D, simplified plan, Phase 1–2 features north (overlaps with Fig. 28; scale 1:500)
28 Area C–D, simplified plan, Phase 1–2 features south (overlaps with Fig. 27; scale 1:500)
29 Area C–D Phase 1 sections (scale 1:25)
30 Area C–D detailed ring-gully R1–R2 plans (scale 1:100)
31 Area C–D Phase 1–2 sections (scale 1:25)
32 Area C–D pottery, fabric groups by percentage weight
33 Area C–D pottery, Nos 1–13 (scale 1:4)
34 Area C–D pottery, vessel classes (percentage rim EVE)

Chapter 5, the watching brief

35 Watching brief, plan (scale 1:1000)
36 Watching brief, plan and sections (scales 1:200 and 1:20)

Chapter 6, discussion and conclusion

37 Areas A and B, simplified plan of phasing
38 First Edition Ordance Survey map, the evidence for the first and second stages of plot layouts
39 Simplified comparative plans of Romano-British livestock complexes, (A) Site 29, M6 Toll, (B) Birdlip quarry, (C) Orton Hall Farm, Cambridgeshire, (D) Metchley Roman fort, Birmingham, Area 9

TABLES

Chapter 2

1 Area A, Phase 3 dating evidence
2 Area A, Romano-British coarse ware pottery, fabrics, sources and quantities
3 Area A, samian, summary of chronology
4 Area A, samian, composition by fabric, form and functional type

Chapter 3

5 Area B, Romano-British coarse ware pottery, summary of the assemblage by phase
6 Area B, Romano-British coarse ware pottery, fabrics, sources and quantities
7 Area B, Romano-British coarse ware pottery, summary of the assemblage by feature type
8 Area B, samian, composition of assemblage by date
9 Area B, samian, composition of assemblage, number of examples represented
10 Area B, charred plant remains

Chapter 4

11 Area C–D, Romano-British coarse ware pottery, summary of the assemblage by phase
12 Area C–D, Romano-British coarse ware pottery, summary of the assemblage by feature type
13 Area C–D, Romano-British coarse ware pottery, summary of the assemblage by ditch (D), or ring-gully (R)
14 Area C–D, Romano-British coarse ware pottery, fabrics, sources and quantities

Chapter 5

15 Watching brief, summary of the Romano-British coarse ware pottery

Chapter 6

16 Suggested physical evidence for animal husbandry at Longdales Road
17 Composition of the pottery assemblages, Longdales Road and other Romano-British rural sites

APPENDIX

Appendix A: Chapter 2

- A1   Pottery, list of fabrics
- A2   Pottery, vessel classes within assemblage
- A3   Pottery, occurrence of vessel forms by fabric and phase
- A4   Pottery, occurrence of fabrics by phase (by count)

Appendix B: Chapter 3

- B1   Pottery, list of fabrics represented
- B2   Pottery, vessel classes within assemblage
- B3   Pottery, occurrence of vessel forms by fabric and phase
- B4   Pottery, occurrence of fabrics by phase

Appendix C: Chapter 4

- C1   Pottery, list of fabrics represented
- C2   Pottery, vessel classes within assemblage
- C3   Pottery, occurrence of vessel forms by phase
- C4   Pottery, occurrence of forms by fabric
- C5   Pottery, occurrence of fabrics by phase

PLATES

Cover Ryknild Street and surrounds in 2007, aerial view: north (copyright Peter Leather)

1. Aerial view of roadside area and Area C–D excavation, view: southeast
2. Ryknild Street and surrounds in 2007, aerial view: north (copyright Peter Leather)
3. Field 1, Trial-trench 10, stone surface 6147A
4. Area A, excavation in progress, view: northeast
5. Area A, excavation in progress within Enclosure A1–A2, view: southeast
6. Area A, Enclosure A1 sub-enclosure, view: south
7. Area B, general view of excavation, view: west
8. Area B, Phase 3B stone surface F442, view: south
9. Area C–D, road Plot A/B boundary, view: east
10. Area C–D, Plot B, ring-gully R1 R2, view: northeast
11. Area C–D, detail of gully D2, view: south

Chapter 1

Summary and Introduction

SUMMARY

Areas adjoining Ryknild Street, King's Norton, Birmingham (centred on NGR SP 05337761) were investigated between 2002 and 2007. The fieldwork was undertaken by Birmingham Archaeology on instruction from Birmingham City Council in advance of a new cemetery development. It comprised geophysical survey, trial-trenching, area excavation, watching brief and salvage recording.

Adjoining the western Roman roadside frontage were revealed a series of plots, defined by ditches and adjoining metalled roads, in use from the 2nd century and into the 3rd century AD. The plots contained a ditched enclosure, two roundhouses, and other contemporary features. A double-ditched enclosure (A1) was laid out further to the west, set within a ditched compound. Both the enclosure and the compound contained elaborate, 'funnel-like' entrance arrangements, which suggest use by livestock. The interior of the first enclosure was also subdivided, creating a series of livestock pens. The enclosure and compound were in use from around AD 120, and into the 3rd century, during which time the enclosure was redefined (Enclosure A2), reducing the spacing between the ditches. The enclosures contained a roundhouse, an area of stone surfacing, pits and post-holes. The enclosures and associated compound formed part of an elaborate livestock management system, possibly functioning as a collecting point for livestock from the surrounding countryside.

Following abandonment of the second enclosure in the later 3rd century further features, including a ditch and circular gullies associated with further roundhouses, were laid out. At approximately the same time the roadside plots were abandoned, and a small enclosure was laid out to the rear of the western roadside plots. This later Romano-British occupation is suggested to be small scale, or temporary in nature. The site was abandoned in the mid–late-4th century.

Based on the excavated and historic map evidence two layouts are apparent on the western Ryknild Street frontage, separated by 10 degrees in alignment. The earliest layout comprises Enclosures A1–A2, the integral livestock compound, and other possible roadside plots in the south of the settlement. A later re-alignment of the roadside plot boundaries saw further plots laid out to the north, during the continued use of the enclosure and presumably of the earlier plot boundary series.

The Longdales Road site lies within the bounds of the *Hellerelege* Anglo-Saxon estate described in a charter dated AD 699 (Sawyer 1968, S 64). The adjoining Lilycroft Farm is first recorded in a deed dated 1314. More widely, traces of medieval cultivation sealing evidence of industrial activity have been recorded to the east of Ryknild Street.

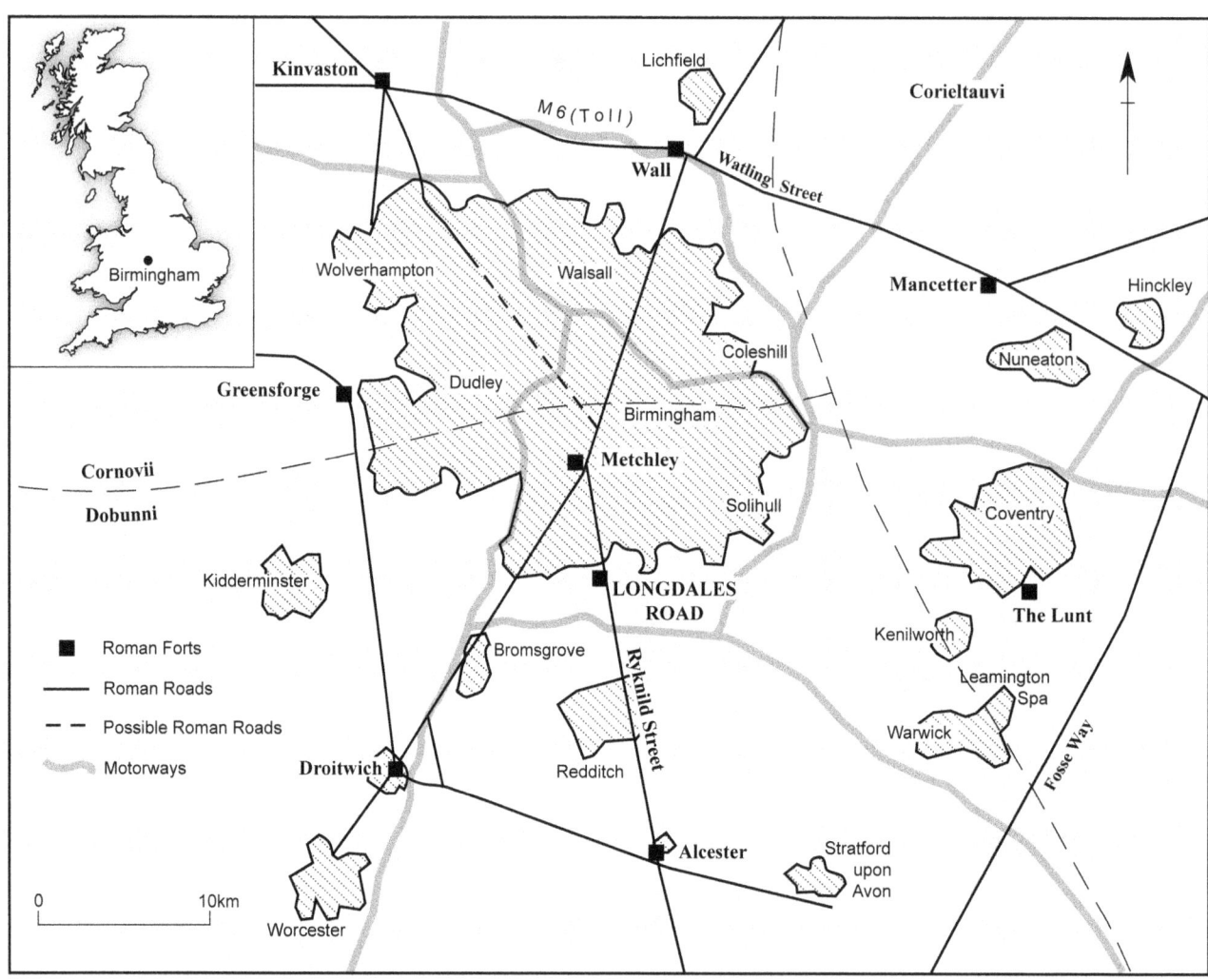

Figure 1. Roman west midlands and the road network; dashed lines show hypothetical tribal boundaries (after White 2007, fig. 12). Inset: location of Birmingham

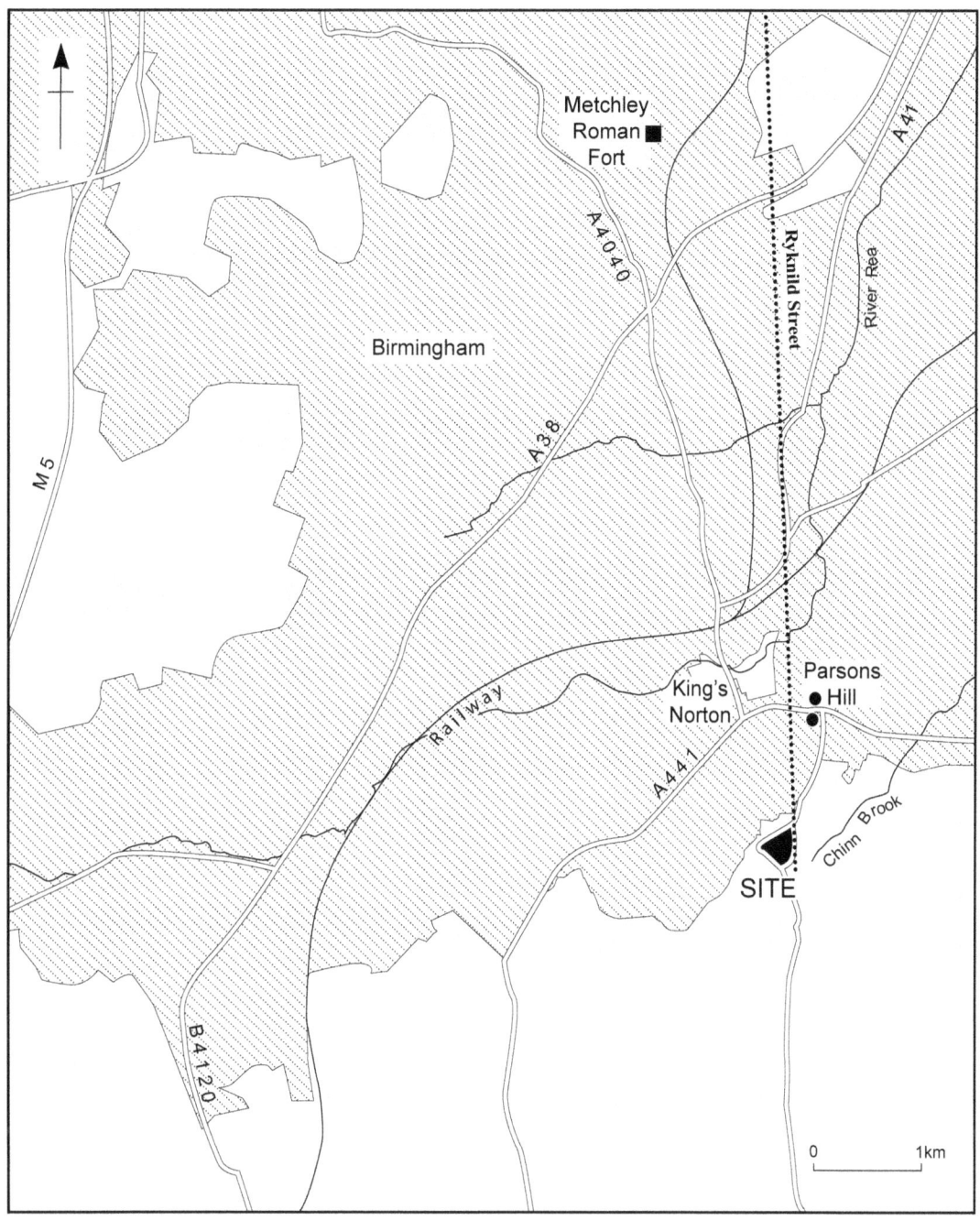

Figure 2. Location of Longdales Road excavations, Metchley fort and Ryknild Street

INTRODUCTION

by Alex Jones and John Halsted

The fieldwork described in this report was undertaken by Birmingham Archaeology (formerly Birmingham University Field Archaeology Unit), on instruction from Birmingham City Council, in advance of the construction of a new cemetery at Longdales Road, King's Norton, Birmingham (centred on NGR SP 05337761, Figs 1–2, Fields 1–4). The new cemetery (Fig. 2) is bounded by Longdales Road, Icknield Street, which follows the line of the Roman road Ryknild Street (Plates 1–2, Margary 1967, road 18b, 284–5), and Primrose Hill.

A series of archaeological investigations were undertaken in advance of the layout of the new cemetery (Figs 3–4). Briefly, these comprised a desk-based assessment and trial-trenching (by Worcestershire County Council), followed by further trial-trenching, excavations (Areas A and B), excavation and salvage recording (Area C–D), and an extensive watching brief undertaken by Birmingham Archaeology. Further trial-trenching has also tested areas to the east and south of the proposed cemetery.

The Longdales Road site overlies a natural ridge (Figs 4–5). The solid and drift geology is shown on Fig. 3. The site is located on soils of the Brocklehurst 3 association (Soil Survey of England and Wales sheet 3, Midlands and Western England) and stagnogleyic soils in fine loamy drift which are usually wet and heavy to work (Ragg *et al.* 1984). At the time of the fieldwork the land was overgrown pasture.

Background

There is no clear late prehistoric context for the King's Norton area, and comparatively little information from the whole of the Birmingham area as a whole for the immediate pre-Roman period. A glass bead from Bromford, and Iron Age pottery from King's Norton and Selly Park, evidence Iron Age activity (Hodder 2004, 47). A ditched enclosure of Mid–Late Iron Age date has been excavated at Site 29 of the M6 Toll (Langley Mill Farm), to the north of Birmingham (Powell and Ritchie 2006). Booth (1996, 32) has suggested a local government function for Alcester within the northern part of the territory of the *Dobunni*. The Iron Age political geography of the western midlands has been reconstructed with reference to the Coleshill temple complex (Magilton 2006) and, in particular, the placement of temples elsewhere along tribal boundaries. Coleshill (Fig. 1) may have been sited close to the junction of the territories of the *Dobunni*, the *Cornovii*, and the *Corieltauvi*.

It is difficult to establish the precise chronology of the Roman military advance in the west midlands because of the undoubted limitations in dating the archaeological and historical evidence (*contra* Webster 1981). The earliest Romano-British feature at Longdales Road will have been Ryknild Street (Margary 1967, route 18b), laid out between Bourton-on-the-Water and Derby in the mid–late-1st century to serve the needs of military communication. The Roman army probably reached Warwickshire in AD 47 (Booth and Evans 2001, 303). The excavated sequence of activity at Metchley and Alcester, located respectively approximately 6km and 16km from Longdales Road, in particular, helps to place the results from Longdales Road into their early Roman context. The earliest military activity at Metchley (Jones 2001, 10) and at Lower Alvesley Lodge, Alcester (Booth and Evans 2001, 301), is likely to be of Claudian date. Other Claudian military occupation is suggested at The Lunt (Hobley 1969), Greensforge (Welfare and Swann 1995), Mancetter (Scott 1984) and Droitwich, northeast of Dodderhill (Hurst ed. 2006).

Wall was probably a Neronian military foundation (Lyons and Gould 1964; Round 1983), established at the Ryknild Street/ Watling Street crossroads. The garrison at Metchley was probably replaced in the early Neronian period by a military stores depot (Jones 2001). This included ditched enclosures for livestock, livestock 'funnels' (Jones 2002, Jones forthcoming), and stables/ grooms' quarters. The second fort at Alcester, in the Baromix area, is also dated to the AD 60s (Booth and Evans 2001, 301). Mancetter and Baginton were abandoned by the military in the AD 70s (Booth 1996, 30). In the later Neronian/ early Flavian period a small garrison of around 500 men was re-established at Metchley (Jones 2001, 118). Similarly, the military occupation of Wall was also extended into the Flavian period (Round 1983; Gould 1964). Continued military occupation into the 2nd century is recorded at Alcester (Booth and Evans 2001, 303) and Dodderhill, Droitwich, where the military presence was associated with the exploitation of salt (Hurst ed. 2006). By contrast, the early 2nd-century occupation of Wall is suggested to be purely civilian in character (Gould 1968; Round 1983, 14).

In parts of Alcester there is evidence for a hiatus in activity up to 70 years in duration between the end of military occupation and the first civilian activity (Booth 1994, 165). The 2nd-century expansion of Alcester is represented, first, by the layout of a network of irregular streets and, later, by earthwork defences (*ibid.*, 164). As might be anticipated, the extra-mural area contained a large number of timber and stone-built structures, and a large metalled area, interpreted as a market place, underlining the function of the town as a market centre for the surrounding countryside. The possible *mansio* (*ibid.*, 164), will have provided accommodation for travellers on official business (Black 1995).

A contrast with Alcester is provided by the later sequence of activity at Metchley, where the latest garrison fort was given up no later than the AD 80s (Jones 2001, 119). Later Roman military activity at Metchley, until final abandonment around AD 200, was probably small scale in nature and is likely to have fulfilled a specialist

Summary and Introduction

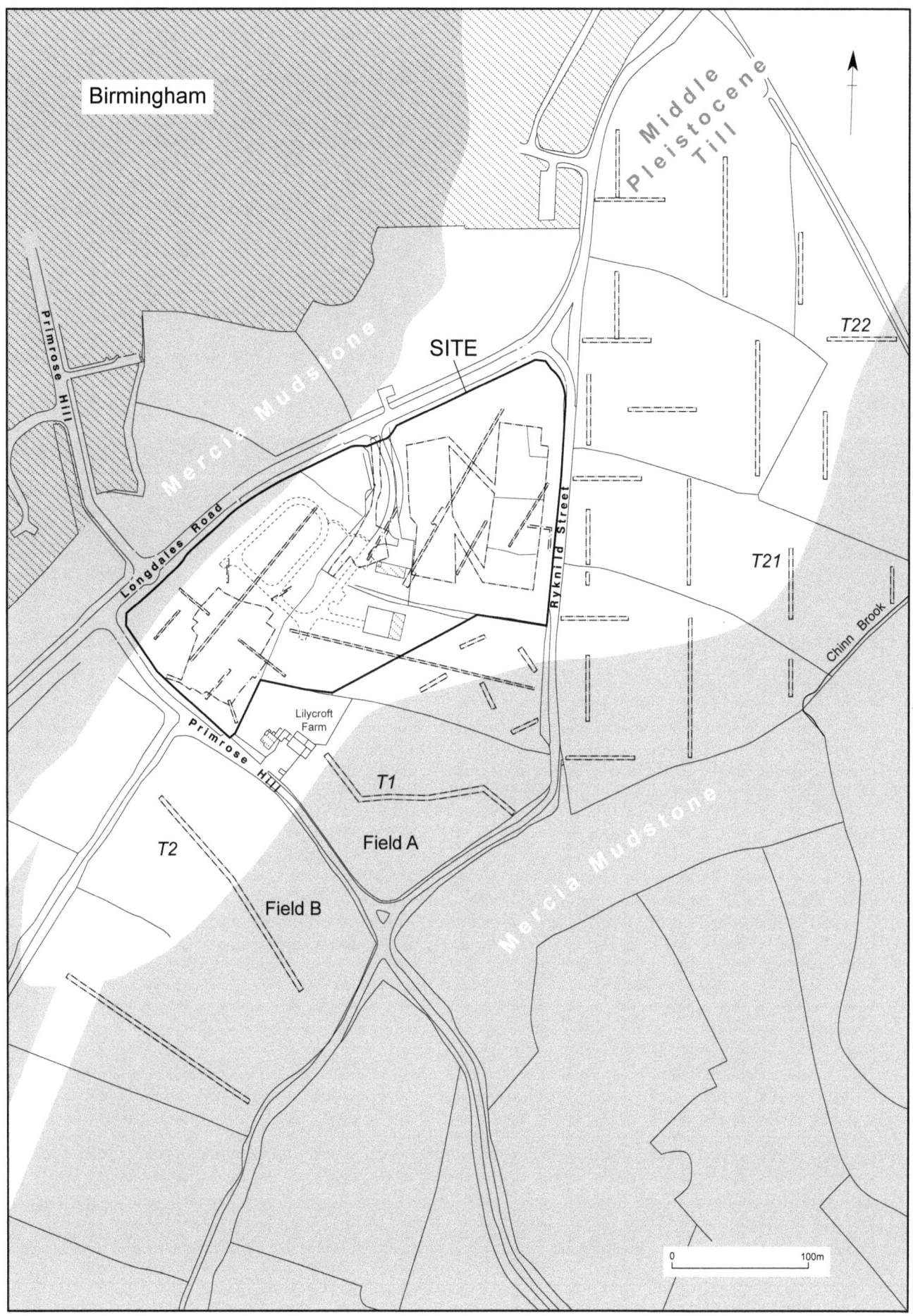

Figure 3. Longdales Road, relief and draft geology and plan of all investigations

function. This could have been associated with the *cursus publicus*, or a police post staffed by a small group of the military (Rankov 1999) providing supervision at the road junction (Jones 2005), or another small-scale military function. In contrast, a civilian settlement extended for a distance of approximately 1.5km along Watling Street at Wall (Burnham and Wacher 1990, 276), close to the junction with Ryknild Street. A bath house and possible *mansio* (Round 1992) highlight the evidence for the mid-Romano-British prosperity of this site. The latest Romano-British activity at Wall comprised a defended enclosure, one of series of five laid out at intervals north of Towcester, possibly forming a chain of *burgi* (Jones 1998; Burnham and Wacher 1990, 276; Gould 1999).

There is growing evidence for Romano-British activity within the King's Norton area. Mike Nixon identified gravel floors, sealed by burnt deposits containing late 1st–3rd-century pottery and daub, at Parsons Hill (Birmingham SMR 02939, Fig. 2). More recently, a Romano-British ditch was excavated further to the north of the former site, also at Parsons Hill (Birmingham SMR 20768, Fig. 2). The ditch re-cut contained charcoal and weed seeds. Both sites adjoined the suggested line of Ryknild Street to the north of Longdales Road. Romano-British pottery has also been found during excavations at the Saracen's Head, King's Norton Green (Charles *et al.* 2007), and a complete pot, possibly a cremation vessel, was recently found at Westhill Road.

Overall, there is comparatively little information about Anglo-Saxon settlement in the Birmingham area. By contrast, an Anglo-Saxon charter, describing the estate of *Hellerelege* (Fig. 6), including the Longdales Road site towards its centre, provides evidence of settlement in the surrounding area (Demidowicz 2003). Demidowicz's reinterpretation (2003, 117–19) of the *Hellerelege* boundary (*ibid.*) identifies the estate as occupying a raised spur of ground (see Fig. 5) aligned approximately southwest-northeast, its southeastern side defined by the Chinn Brook, and its northwestern limit by the *Leontan/ Liontan* (River Rea). The estate extended to Lindsworth Farm to the northeast, and near Redhill Road to the southwest (*ibid.*, 112, fig. 4). The proximity of the Longdales Road Romano-British settlement to Lilycroft Farm could suggest continuity in settlement into the Anglo-Saxon period, as is suggested elsewhere in Birmingham – for example at Over Green and Wiggins Hill (Hodder 2004, 83). It has been noted above that the Romano-British occupation of the Longdales Road site may have ended in the mid-4th century. The woodland adjoining Longdales Road may have been cleared in the later Anglo-Saxon period, with remaining areas falling to clearances in the 12th and early 13th centuries (Demidowicz 2003; Edwards and Jackson 1998). Detailed analysis of post-Roman pollen spectra from Metchley suggest a wood dominated by oak, with evidence for clearings and traces of rye (Greig 2005, 78).

Parts of the nearby medieval village centre of King's Norton have been investigated by excavation (Jones *et al.* 2001; Charles *et al.* 2007). Its medieval focus was The Green, adjoining St Nicholas's Church, mainly 14–15th century in fabric but incorporating earlier stonework (Hodder 2004, 98). To the south of The Green, timber-framed buildings of 13–14th-century date have been recorded by excavation. The Saracen's Head is 15th century in date, with traces of earlier structural phases. Hodder (2004, 99) suggested that reorganisation and rebuilding of the village may have been associated with an increase in the importance of the wool trade. Primrose Hill Farm, King's Norton, is another relict of the 15th-century landscape (Hodder 2004, 101). Most relevant to the Longdales Road site, the adjoining Lilycroft Farm site was first mentioned in a document of 1314 when John le Harpere de Horsebrook granted land near Walker's Heath to Walter Lilie and his wife Felicia (Demidowicz 2003, 112). The same farm was later known as Lilycroft Farm (Fig. 4).

Longdales Road fieldwork 2002–2007

Early stages of work comprised desk-based assessment, walkover survey, and trial-trenching carried out by Worcestershire County Council (Vaughan 2002; Fig. 4) in March 2002. The trial-trenching involved machine-cut trenches in Fields 1–2 and 4 which revealed ditches, shallow gullies and some pits/ post-holes. The features were interpreted as a forming a Romano-British settlement focus, consisting of a ditched enclosure complex to the west of Lilycroft Farm, with an associated ditched field system to the north.

The next stage of fieldwork was undertaken by Birmingham Archaeology later in 2002 (Williams 2003a). This included further trial-trenching in Field 1, close to Ryknild Street, to identify any activity in this roadside zone, revealing ditches, pits and cobbled surfaces (Plate 3). Following further trial-trenching in Field 2, an excavation (Area A) investigated a Romano-British enclosure complex and later activity. The sequence of Romano-British activity was divided into three phases: the first two represented by successive double-ditched enclosures occupied from AD 120. The enclosures were set within a compound, the eastern and northeastern sides of which were respected by the modern Field 2 boundaries. Later, unenclosed activity may have continued into the earlier 4th century.

The area excavated in 2003 (Area B, Field 1), was also first examined by trial-trenching in 2002. Excavation revealed a sequence of re-cut enclosure ditches, interpreted as forming successive 'funnel-type' arrangements dated from AD 120, used for the sorting of livestock (Williams 2003b) entering or leaving Field 2, a livestock compound probably laid out at the same time as the first Area A enclosure. The latest occupation in Area B was represented by finds accumulated over a pebble surface after its disuse. This produced pottery of later 3rd- and early 4th-century date.

A watching brief was maintained in 2004 during groundworks associated with the construction of the main

SUMMARY AND INTRODUCTION

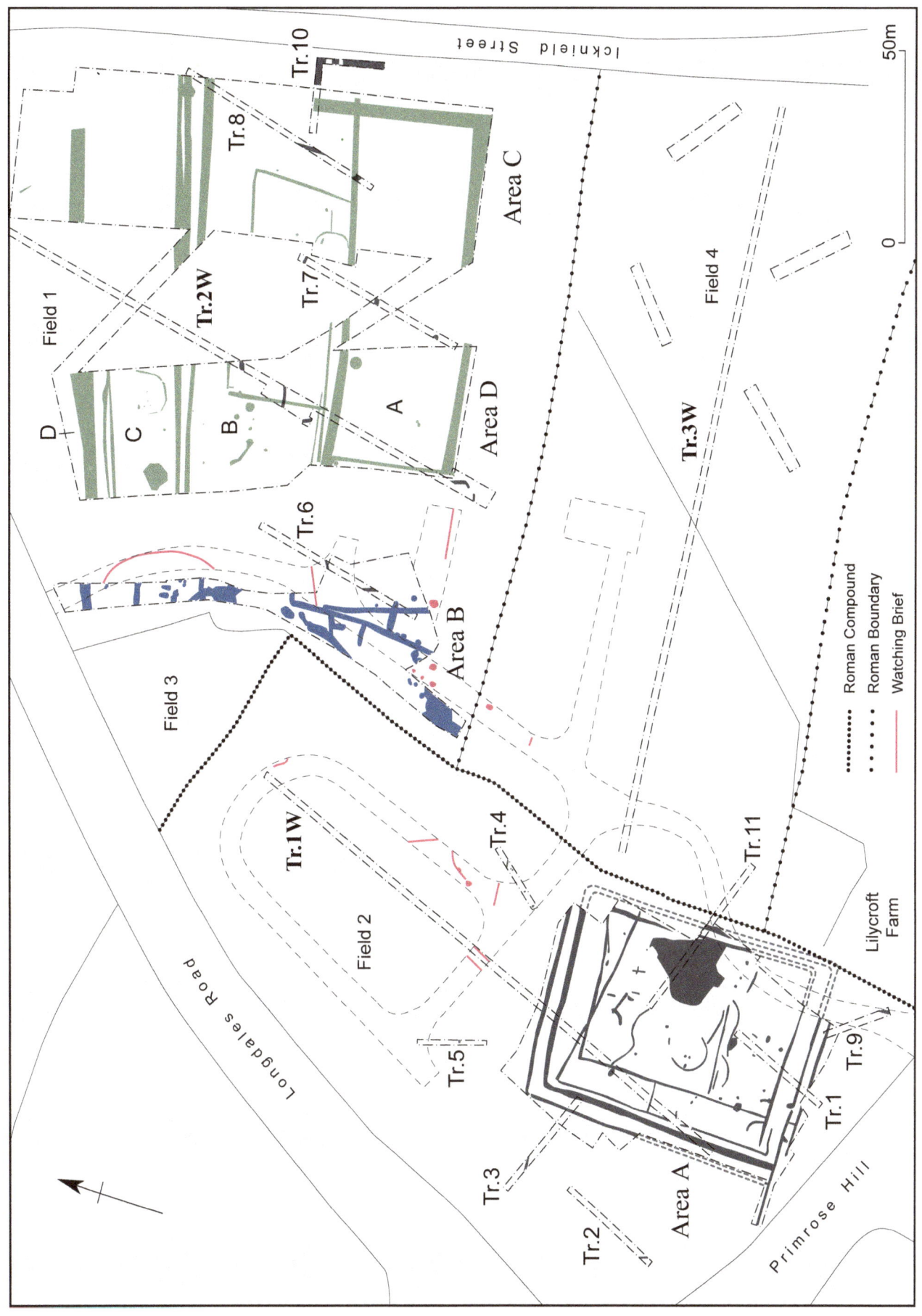

Figure 4. Longdales Road, detailed plan of Area A–D investigations and main features identified

cemetery roads, and associated drainage works (Mason 2004) within Fields 1, 2 and 4. A number of ditched plot boundaries and other features were identified (*ibid.*, fig. 3).

Two areas were excavated in 2006, one (C) immediately adjoining the Ryknild Street road frontage, another (D) slightly to the rear (Burrows 2006). The earliest activity probably comprised the layout of ditched plot boundaries at approximately right-angles to the Roman road. The full width of three plots, and part of a fourth, were recorded. The plot boundaries were further defined by metalled roads adjoining the ditched boundaries. A pebble surface was recorded along part of the immediate road frontage. One plot contained a rectangular ditched enclosure within which was sited a ring-gully. A further ring-gully was also recorded to the north. The plots were in use in the mid–late 2nd and 3rd century. Later activity, continuing into the earlier part of the 4th century, was more limited. It comprised the northeastern angle of a ditched enclosure, cut through an earlier road surface. It may be significant that the more lowlying area adjoining the Ryknild Street frontage was probably the first to be given up.

Further trial-trenching was undertaken to the east and south of the main areas investigated 2002–2006. To the south was revealed an east-west aligned pebble road, pits and post-holes of 2nd–4th-century date (Patrick and Darch 2002). Trenching to the east of Ryknild Street (Edwards and Jackson 1998) provided evidence of medieval agriculture, settlement and industrial activity (Hodder 2004, 124).

Aims

The general aims of the excavations (Areas A–D) were to identify archaeological remains, and to preserve those remains by record. The specific aims were to reveal, excavate and interpret any features associated with the occupation of the western frontage of Icknield Street and the area to the rear of the road frontage, where evidence of ditched enclosures, plot or field boundaries might be anticipated.

Methodology (Fig. 4)

Excavation within Area A was undertaken in two stages, the second stage providing an opportunity to examine most of the enclosure ditch circuit and interior not recorded within the preceding open area investigation. The fieldwork methodology in Areas A and B was the same. The overburden was removed by a mechanical excavator working under archaeological supervision. Following selective hand-cleaning of the machined surface, a plan of the main features was prepared, which provided the basis for the initial definition of the excavation strategy.

The 2006 fieldwork was undertaken in two stages. In Stage 1, two trenches, each measuring 50m by 2m were excavated, positioned at an oblique angle to the main areas for excavation and between them. Stage 2 comprised the investigation of the two main areas (C and D) selected for investigation, following completion of work in the two trenches. A base plan was prepared, from

Figure 5. Longdales Road, line of Ryknild Street and surrounding sites investigated (x5 vertical exaggeration of topography: Areas A, B and C–D shown)

which the detailed strategy for sampling by hand-excavation was devised. Within 60% of the excavated area sampling by hand-excavation tested half of each discrete feature, and 20–50% of the linear features associated with settlement. This sampling strategy was applied to the westernmost of the two areas investigated (Area D). Within the roadside area (Area C), where the feature density was less intense, a single excavated slot was dug through each feature identified, and discrete features were half-sectioned. As an exception, the eaves-drip gully was sampled by means of several hand-dug segments. Further investigation of the eaves-drip gully area was also undertaken in 2007.

Recording was by means of pre-printed pro formas for contexts and features. Within the Area A and B excavations and the 2004 watching brief, recording employed feature numbers (three digit numbers prefixed 'F') and contexts (four digit numbers). Recording in Area C–D employed a continuously numbered sequence of cut and context numbers, both using four-digit numbers. During all fieldwork, pre-printed pro formas were completed, together with digitally surveyed plans (1:50) and hand-drawn sections (1:20 and 1:10). Monochrome and colour slide photographs were also taken.

The finds and paper archive will be deposited with Birmingham Museum and Art Gallery.

Arrangement of report

The following chapters describe the results of the main investigations. The Area A excavation, and other investigations in Field 2 are described in Chapter 2. Chapter 3 describes the results from the Area B excavation in Field 1. The 2006 investigations closer to the Ryknild Street frontage (Area C–D) are described in Chapter 4. Chapter 5 summarises the results of the 2004 watching brief and the other investigations undertaken in the area adjoining the present cemetery. Finally, Chapter 6 provides an integrated discussion and synthesis of the evidence from all the fieldwork stages reported in this volume. Chapter 7 contains the acknowledgements and references.

The report is based on the information available on 1 February 2008.

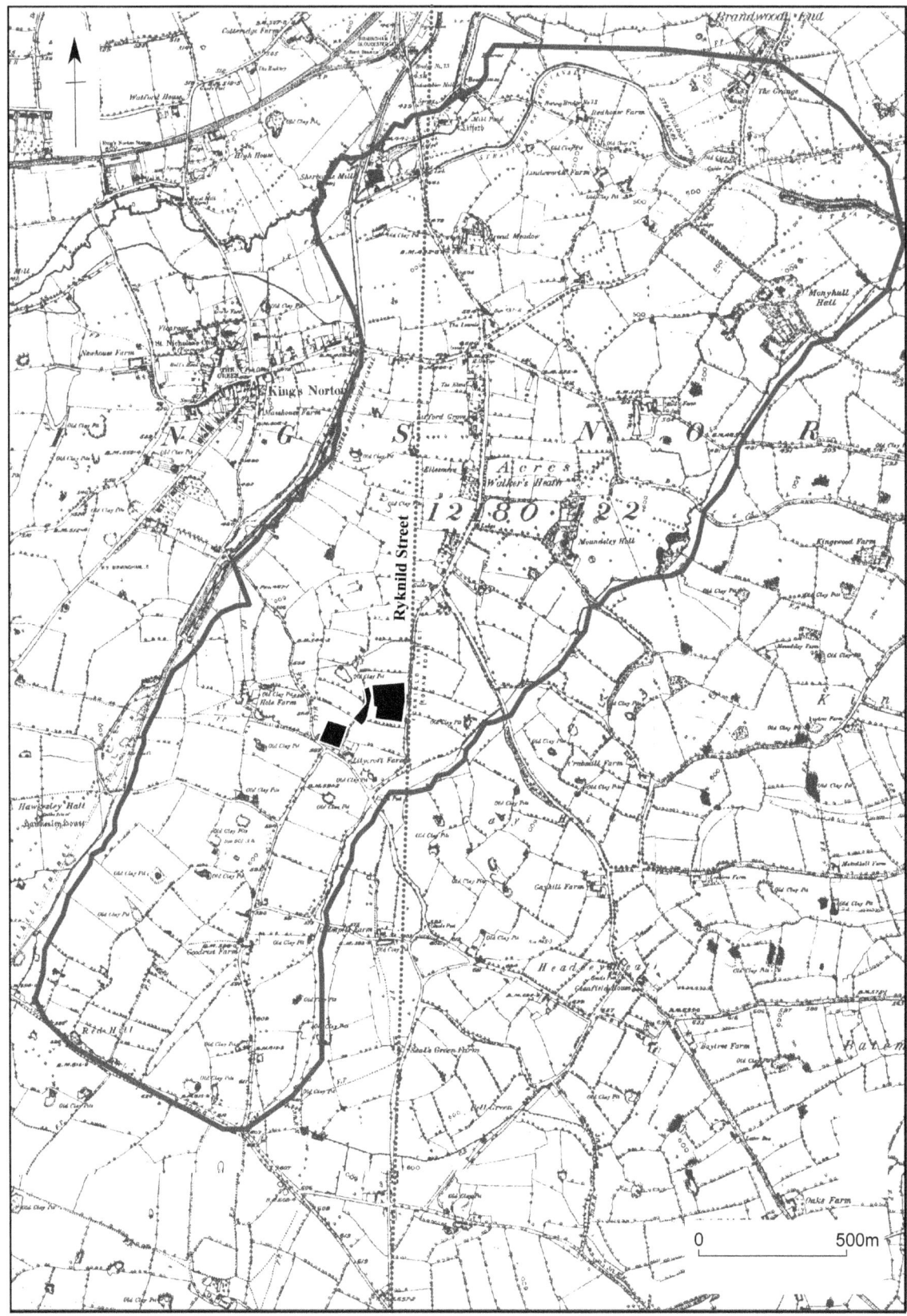

Figure 6. Longdales Road and surrounds, Ordnance Survey map of 1890 showing projected line of Ryknild Street and Areas A–D, and suggested boundary of *Hellerelege* after Demidowicz 2003. Area excavations are blacked in

Plate 1. Aerial view of roadside area and Area C–D excavation, view: southeast

Plate 2. Ryknild Street in 2007, aerial view: north (copyright Peter Leather)

Plate 3. Field 1, Trial-trench 10, stone surface 6147A

Chapter 2

Area A   The Double-Ditched Enclosures (Field 2)

RESULTS

by Alex Jones and Josh Williams

Phasing

The results from Area A trial-trenching and excavation (Fig. 4) have been conflated and divided into four phases, as follows:

Phase 1   First double-ditched enclosure (A1), AD 120–mid-2nd century
Phase 2   Second double-ditched enclosure (A2), late 2nd–3rd century
Phase 3   Later Romano-British activity, 3rd–early 4th century
Phase 4   All post-Roman activity

The phasing is based on the recorded stratigraphy and spot-dating of the finds. It is further refined in Chapter 6 (below) with reference to the wider historic field boundaries. Only a few feature intersections were recorded, and much of the pottery was undiagnostic Severn Valley ware. For these reasons it has not been possible to phase many of the features identified within the enclosure interiors, which have been therefore ascribed to Phase 1–3.

The natural subsoil comprised a red-brown clay (1002) with patches of yellow sand.

Phase 1: First double-ditched enclosure (Enclosure A1), AD 120–mid-2nd century (Figs 7–9, Plates 4–6)

This phase represents the earliest Romano-British activity at Longdales Road, with the exception of Ryknild Street, which was not excavated. The main Phase 1 feature was a rectangular double-ditched enclosure (Enclosure A1) laid out approximately 220m to the west of the Roman road on a gently west-sloping plateau. Of particular interest was the complex treatment of the southwestern enclosure entrance.

Description of Phase 1 Features

The main axis of Phase 1 double-ditched Enclosure A1 was north-south. It measured 74m by 58m (from the outer edges of the outermost ditches). The outermost ditch contained an area of 0.43ha, and the innermost ditch an area of 0.23ha. The full circuit of both ditches was not defined at excavation. Where both ditches were recorded along the same side, the separation recorded was approximately 9m (measured centre to centre). Lengths of the northern, western and southern ditches were identified by excavation; the course of the outermost eastern enclosure ditch was probably partly respected by a modern field boundary (see below). Only the extreme western end of the outermost northern ditch (A2, Fig. 9.S.1) survived Phase 2 re-cutting (see below). The southern half of the outermost western ditch (A6, A12 and A14, Fig. 9.S.2) only was recorded – the remainder of this ditch was dug away by a Phase 3 re-cut (see below). The outermost southern Phase 1 ditch was wholly dug away by a Phase 2 re-cut (see below). The innermost enclosure ditch was fully defined on its northern (A4, Fig. 9.S.3), western (A10/A10a, Fig. 9.S.4–S.5) and southern (A26, Fig. 9.S.6) sides. The course of the Phase 1 innermost eastern ditch was defined by a Phase 2 re-cut (see below).

The northwestern angle of the enclosure was probably irregular in plan, possibly because of difficulties in surveying over irregular ground. Post-hole F322, recorded at the exact centre of the innermost enclosure circuit, could possibly have formed a surveying point. The outer northern ditch of the Phase 1 enclosure was irregular in plan, particularly towards its western terminal, possibly because of Phase 2 re-cutting.

The northern outer ditch (A2, Fig. 9.S.1) was cut to a V-shaped profile, although its full size could not be identified because of a Phase 2 re-cut. The surviving lengths of the western outer Phase 1 ditch (A6, A12 and A14, Fig. 9.S.2) were interrupted by two possible entry-gaps measuring 5m and 2.2m in width. This ditch was cut to a U-shaped profile, measuring an average of 0.45m in width and 0.04m in depth. The innermost northern ditch of the enclosure (A4, Fig. 9.S.3) was dug to a U-shaped profile and measured an average of 0.6m in depth and 0.3m in depth. Its excavated eastern end was cut by the northern terminal of a tangential ditch (A24, Fig. 9.S.3) which could not be related to any other excavated feature. The primary ditch defining the innermost western side of the enclosure (A10, Fig. 9.S.4–S.5) was cut to a U-shaped profile and measured an average of 0.5m in width and 0.16m in depth. Its re-cut (A10a) was of similar profile. The re-cut extended from the northern terminal of ditch A10 to its junction with ditch A9 to the south (see below). The change in size along ditch A10 may have been caused by differential plough truncation. The Phase 1 re-cut (A10a, S.4) recorded along the northern part of ditch A10 was presumably not continued southwards along the eastern side of the sub-enclosure, unless the re-cut had entirely dug away the earlier ditch profile. The innermost southern ditch of the enclosure (A26, Fig. 9.S.6) was cut to a U-shaped profile and measured an average of 0.75m in width and 0.25m in depth. This ditch was notably smaller towards the two terminals.

A Romano-British Livestock Complex in Birmingham

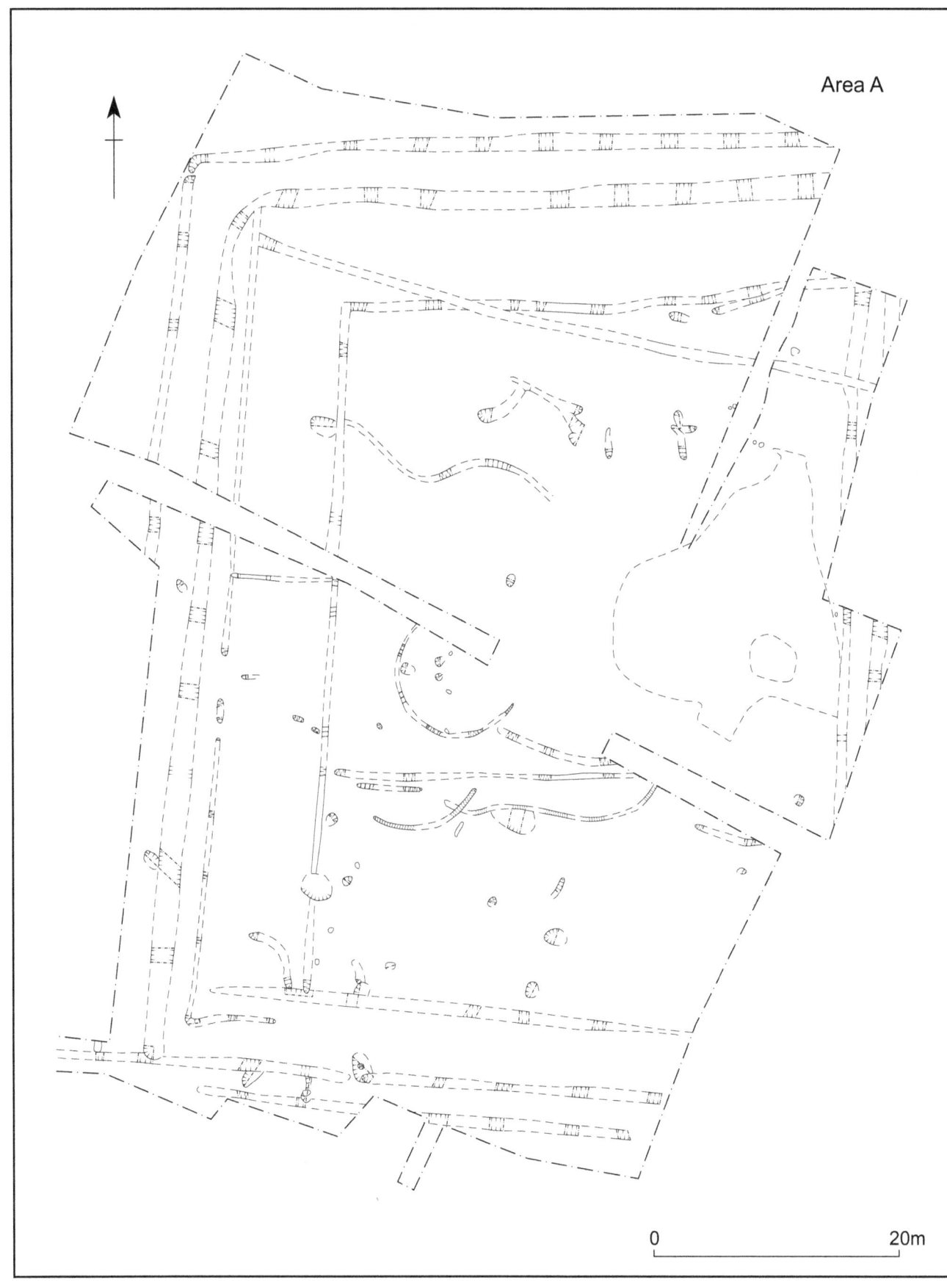

Figure 7. Area A, simplified plan, features of all phases (scale 1:450)

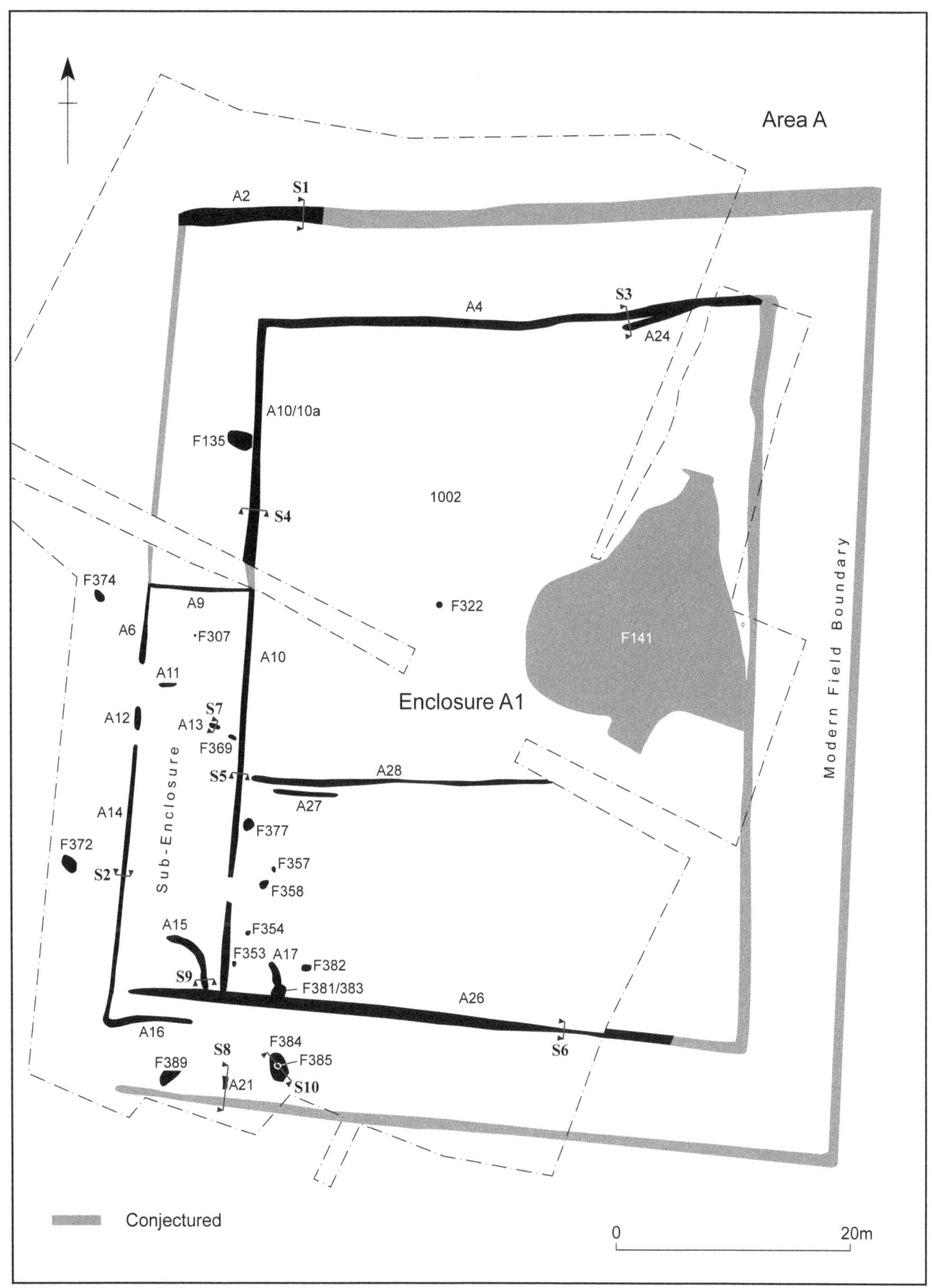

Figure 8. Area A, Phase 1 plan (scale 1:450)

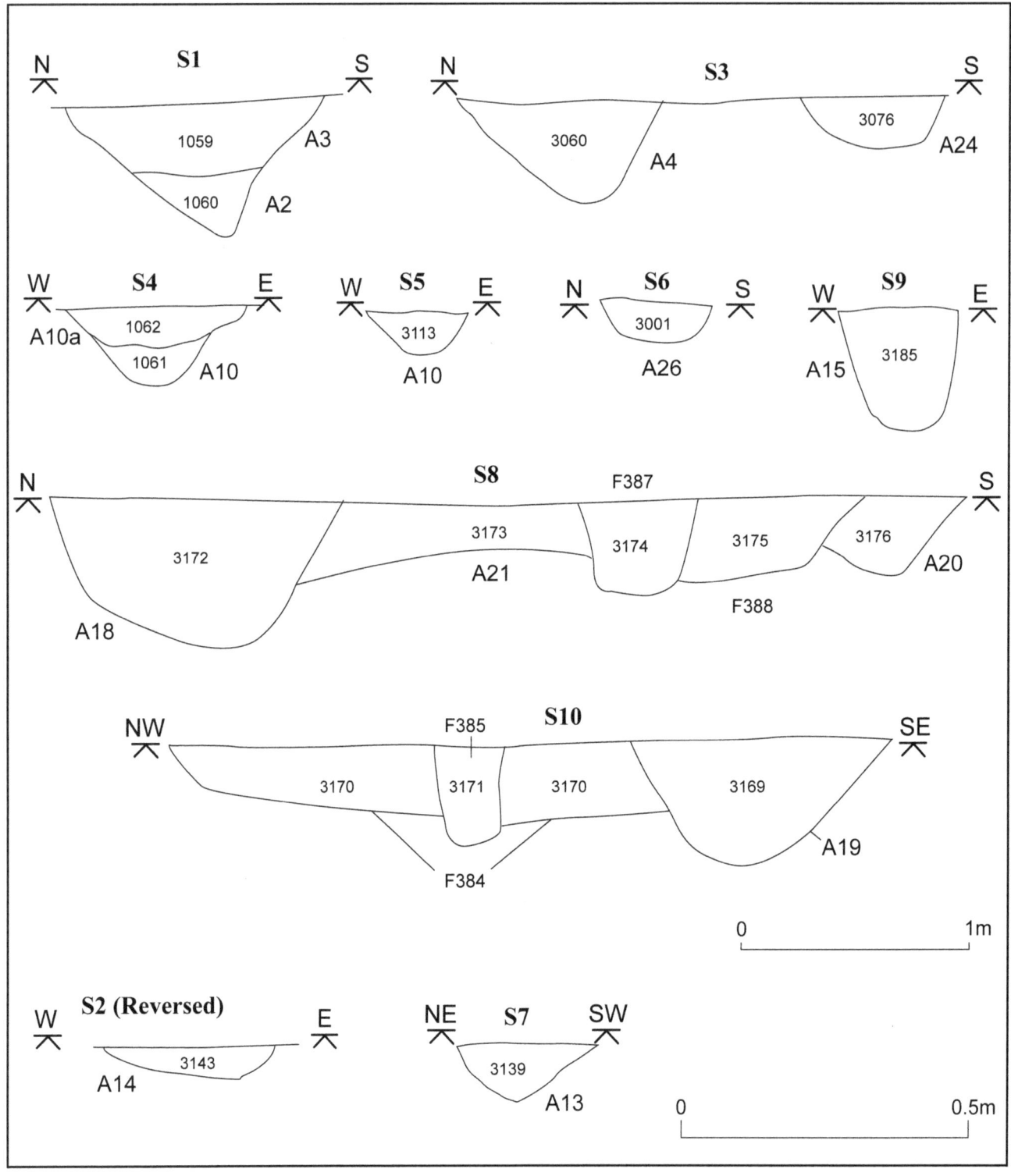

Figure 9. Area A, Phase 1 sections (scales 1:25 and 1:10)

The 'gap' between the outermost (A6, A12 and A14) and innermost (A10) ditches on the western side of the enclosure was bisected by a dividing, east-west aligned ditch (A9), positioned off-centre along this side of the enclosure. The relationship between ditches A6 and A9 could not be established because of a Phase 3 re-cut (see below). Ditch A9 formed the northern side of a sub-enclosure, measuring 8m (east-west) by 31m (north-south), enclosing an area of 0.024ha (Plate 6). A gap measuring 2m in width along the innermost western ditch of the enclosure (A10) may have been provided for access into the sub-enclosure from the enclosure interior. This sub-enclosure contained a number of features. A short length of an east-west aligned ditch (A11) may have been associated with the entrance defined by the adjoining terminals of ditches A6 and A12. Other internal features comprised a short length of a further east-west aligned ditch (A13, Fig. 9.S.7), a pit (F369) and a post-hole (F307). In contrast, with the exception of features associated with the southwestern entrance to the enclosure (see below), only one contemporary feature, a pit (F135), was recorded between the outermost and innermost enclosure ditches along the remainder of the enclosure circuit. It should be noted that the eastern side of the enclosure was not investigated in detail.

The main enclosure entrance was located at the southwestern angle of the enclosure and measured 4.2m in width. The entrance was framed on its northern side by a slightly irregular, east-west aligned ditch (A16), recorded for a length of 7.6m, and on its southern side by the line of the southern outer ditch of the enclosure. A pit (F389), positioned flush with the eastern terminal of ditch A16, and a short length of a north-south aligned ditch (A21, Fig. 9.S.8), located further to the east, probably also formed part of this outer entrance arrangement. Ditch A21 was also positioned flush with the projected southward continuation of ditch A10. An entry-gap measuring 1.6m wide was retained between ditches A16 and A26. A further entry-gap of similar size was recorded in the extreme southwest of the sub-enclosure. A curvilinear ditch (A15, Fig. 9.S.9) may have defined the southwestern side of a further entrance arrangement in the extreme southeastern angle of the sub-enclosure.

Traces of a further entry-gap arrangement were recorded in the extreme southwestern angle of the inner enclosure, which measured 5m in width. The eastern side of this entrance was framed by a curving gully (A17), which cut ditch A26. In turn, gully A17 was cut by two post-pits (F381, F383). Since the segment of ditch A26 crossing the entry-gap was uninterrupted, it may be assumed that the ditch may have been backfilled when the entrance was laid out, unless it was originally crossed by a bridging structure leaving no trace at excavation. A northeast-southwest aligned fenceline, 8.5m long, defined by irregularly spaced pits (F353, F354, F358 and F357), may have also formed the western side of this entrance arrangement, along with nearby pit F377. To the east of this entrance was a further pit (F382) which may have been contemporary with this arrangement. A post-pit (F384), containing a post-pipe (F385, Fig. 9.S.10) positioned flush with gully A17 and between the two southern enclosure ditches, may have further defined the eastern side of this entry-gap.

Within the Phase 1 enclosure interior were two parallel, east-west aligned ditches (A27 and A28), measuring respectively 5m and 26m in length, which may have extended across most of the width of the enclosure, dividing it off-centre. The two ditches were separated by a gap measuring 0.3m wide. An entry-gap measuring 0.7m in width was retained between the western terminal of ditch A28 and the innermost western ditch (A10). These dividing ditches measured an average of 0.39m in width and 0.06m in depth.

Other excavated internal features may have been contemporary with the Phase 1 enclosure, but can only be attributed to Phase 1–3 (see below). The truncated and irregularly shaped pebble surface (F141, see Phase 1–Phase 3 below) in the east of the enclosure could have originated in Phase 1.

The only Phase 1 features external to the enclosure were two oval pits (F374, F372), the latter cut by a Phase 2 ditch (see below). The pits measured 1.2–0.8m in diameter and 0.36m in depth.

The majority of the Phase 1 ditch circuit was backfilled at the end of Phase 1, possibly as a preliminary to the layout of the Phase 2 enclosure (see below). Along the outermost ditch circuit, the northern ditch (A2) was backfilled with blue-grey clay, and the western ditch (A6, A12 and A14) was backfilled with light grey-brown clay-silt. Along the innermost ditch circuit, the northern ditch (A4) was backfilled with light grey-brown sand-clay-silt, and the western ditch (A10/A10a) was backfilled with grey silt-clay. Finally, the innermost southern ditch (A26) was backfilled with red/orange silt-clay.

Finds and dating evidence from Phase 1 features

The pair of northern ditches (A2 and A4), the western ditches (A4, A6 and A14 and A10/A10a) and the innermost southern ditch (A26) all contained 2nd–4th-century pottery. The northern ditch (A9) of the sub-enclosure contained pottery of 2nd–4th-century date. Of the Phase 1 internal features, entrance-pit F389 and post-hole F307 in the sub-enclosure both contained pottery of 2nd–4th-century date. Post-hole F369 contained part of a possible secondary hone stone. This post-hole also contained a spindle-whorl fragment and part of a possible ceramic loom-weight.

Interpretation of Phase 1 features

The double-ditched Enclosure A1 probably represented the earliest excavated occupation of the Longdales Road site. The enclosure was positioned slightly downslope of the higher ridge to the east, possibly for better drainage. The enclosure was defined by ditches, but no surviving evidence of any associated earthwork banks could be identified. Although reduced in size by ploughing, the ditches are unlikely to have been originally substantial in size. It is therefore possible that they were originally complemented by a timber palisade. This could have been dug into an earthen bank – since no trace of the palisade post-holes survived at excavation. A rectangular double-ditched enclosure of late 1st–2nd-century date was found at Shenstone, Staffordshire (Hodgkinson and Chatwin 1944). The outer ditch enclosed an area measuring approximately 100m (north-south) by 93m (east-west), the two ditches being separated by an average distance of 7m. The Shenstone enclosure was larger than the Longdales Road enclosure, although both were defined by concentric ditches. Only limited trenching was possible within the interior of the Shenstone enclosure (*ibid.*) and no evidence of internal structures was found, only deposits of occupation material. The toilet instruments, and fragments of flue tiles, tesserae and window glass from the Shenstone site (*ibid.*, 29), suggest high-status occupation.

Double ditches separated by a distance of 9m were recorded along parts of the western and northern sides of the original Enclosure A1 layout at Longdales Road. The same separation was recorded between the innermost southern

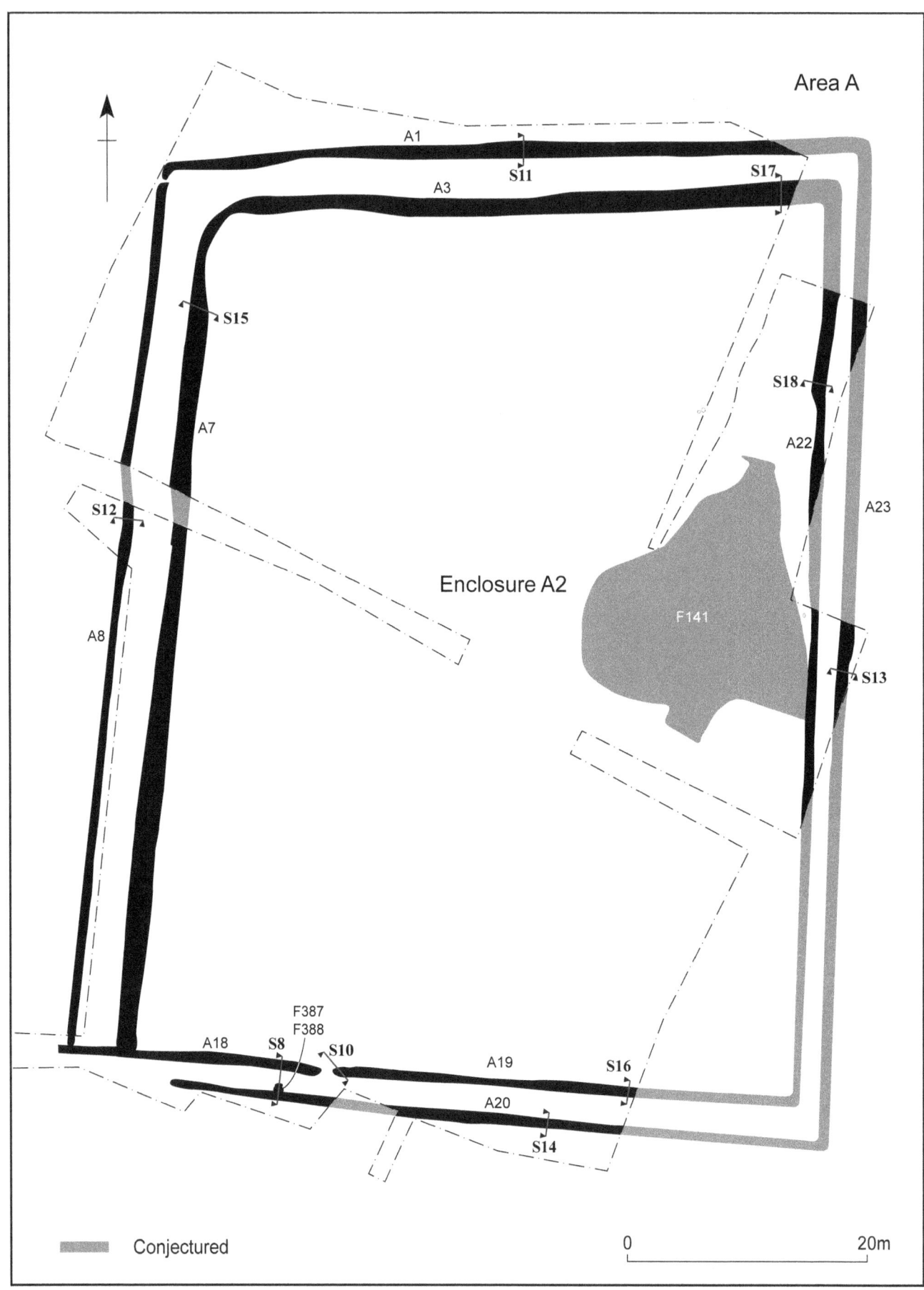

Figure 10. Area A, Phase 2 plan (scale 1:450)

ditch (A26) and Phase 2 ditch A20 (Fig. 10), which is therefore interpreted as a re-cut of the outermost Phase 1 southern ditch. A similar separation was also recorded between the modern eastern Field 2 boundary and Phase 2 ditch A22 (Fig. 10). Phase 2 ditch A22 and the modern field boundary may therefore be interpreted as together representing the original eastern pair of ditches of Enclosure A1. This enclosure was located within a Romano-British compound. The eastern, and part of the northern, compound boundaries are respected by modern field boundaries (shown on Fig. 4). The evidence for this interpretation is considered in Chapter 3 (below).

The Enclosure A1 interior was subdivided by two east-west aligned ditches (A27 and A28). Other features identified within the interior of the innermost ditch cannot be identified to phase. The most substantial of this group was an area of pebble surfacing (F141) in the east of the enclosure, which could have formed a yard surface. Ditch A9 divided the space between the innermost and outermost western ditches on the western side of the enclosure. To the south of this division were identified a number of internal features.

A number of entrance features were located in the southwestern angle of the enclosure. These entrance features, in particular their positioning at one of the enclosure corners, suggest that the enclosure may have been used for the herding of livestock (Pryor 1998). It is not clear if this was the sole function of the enclosure or whether, alternatively, roundhouses belonging to herdsman (see Phase 1–Phase 3 below) might also have been sited within it. The broad gap retained between the inner and outer enclosure ditches could have facilitated the movement of livestock around the enclosure perimeter, which was notably kept clear of features.

Post-hole F322, located in the centre of the enclosure, could have formed a surveying point. Alternatively, it could have contained a post, which could have been imbued with symbolic or religious significance, as is suggested by Booth (1994, 174) for the single free-standing post excavated in the possible market place in Alcester.

With the exception of pits F372 and F374, no contemporary external features could be identified.

Phase 2: Second double-ditched enclosure (Enclosure A2), late 2nd–3rd century (Figs 7, 10–11)

The main Phase 2 feature was a double-ditched enclosure (Enclosure A2), its position and alignment broadly respecting Phase 1 Enclosure A1. Another element of continuity between the enclosures of the two phases was the maintenance of an entrance within the southwestern angle of Enclosure A2. The Phase 2 enclosure interior may have contained a stone surface and, possibly, other internal features.

Description of Phase 2 features

The main axis of the Phase 2 double-ditched enclosure (Enclosure A2) was north-south. From the outer ditch edges of the outermost ditches it measured 78m by 62m, enclosing an area of 0.48ha. The innermost Phase 2 ditch enclosed an area measuring 68m by 52m, enclosing 0.35ha. Parts of all four sides of the enclosure were identified at excavation, although examination of the eastern ditches was comparatively limited. The positioning of the Phase 2 enclosure approximately followed that of the Phase 1 enclosure. The Phase 2 enclosure was sited approximately 7m to the west, and 4m to the north, of the Phase 1 enclosure. The Phase 2 Enclosure A2 ditches were also positioned at an average separation of 4m.

The outermost northern (A1, Fig. 11.S.11), western (A8, Fig. 11.S.12) and eastern (A23, Fig. 11.S.13) ditches of the Phase 2 enclosure were cut into the subsoil. The outermost southern (A20, Fig. 11.S.14) ditch of the Phase 2 enclosure was cut along the projected line of the outermost southern Phase 1 enclosure ditch. The innermost western (A7, Fig. 11.S.15) and southern (A18, Fig. 9.S.8; and A19, Fig. 9.S.10, Fig. 11.S.16) sides of the Phase 2 enclosure were cut into the subsoil. The innermost northern (A3, Fig. 11.S.17) and eastern (A22, Fig. 11.S.18) ditches of Enclosure A2 were cut along the outer northern ditch of the Phase 1 enclosure (A2, Fig. 8) and the line of the projected innermost eastern ditch of the Phase 1 enclosure, respectively.

The innermost southern ditch (A18) was continued to the west of Enclosure A2, presumably forming a field boundary. In plan, Enclosure A2 was mostly rectangular. The northwestern angle of the enclosure, like its predecessor, was irregular. In particular, the northwestern angle of the internal ditch was defined by a curvilinear ditch. At the southwestern angle of the enclosure, the southern terminals of the two western ditches (A7 and A8) were approximately flush – and presumably contemporary with – the innermost southern ditch (A18).

The outermost northern ditch (A1, Fig. 11.S.11) was cut to a V-shaped profile and measured an average of 1m in width and 0.5m in depth. The outermost western ditch (A8) was similar in size and profile to ditch A1, but become smaller approaching the southern terminal of the northwestern entrance to the enclosure. The southern outermost ditch (A20, Fig. 9.S.8; Fig. 11.S.14) was cut to a V-shaped profile and measured an average of 0.55m in width and 0.25m in depth. The outermost eastern enclosure ditch (A23) was cut to a U-shaped profile and measured an average of 0.4m in width and 0.28m in depth.

The innermost ditch was usually the larger of the two ditches around the enclosure perimeter, particularly along the western side, topographically the lowest side of the enclosure. The innermost northern ditch (A3) was cut to a V-shaped profile and measured between 0.96–1.9m in width and between 0.52–0.7m in depth. Its western continuation (A7) was also cut to a V-shaped profile and measured between 2m–1m in width and between 0.68–

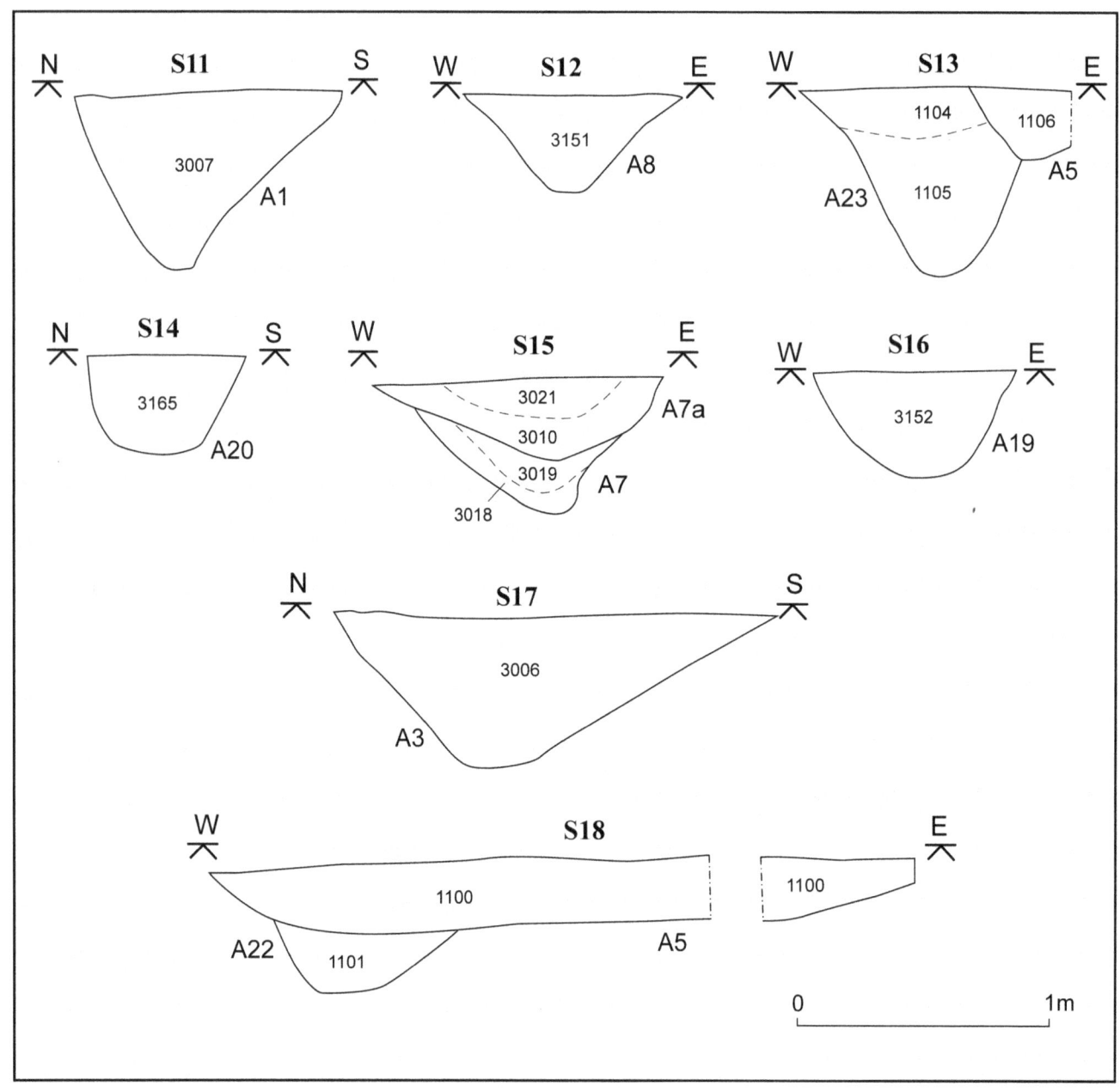

Figure 11. Area A, Phase 2 sections (scale 1:25)

0.35m in depth. A re-cut was recorded towards the northern end of this side (Fig. 11.S.15). The southern innermost ditch of the enclosure (A18 and A19) was cut to a V-shaped profile and measured an average of 0.9m in width and 0.4m in depth. Finally, the eastern innermost enclosure ditch (A22) was cut to a U-shaped profile and measured an average of 1m in width and 0.45m in depth.

Two entry-gaps were recorded along the Phase 2 enclosure perimeter. The first was located along the outer ditch circuit, at the northwestern angle of the enclosure, and measured only 0.5m in width. In plan, the different shape and slight misalignment of the two ditch terminals suggests that the original entry-gap may have been encroached upon by re-cutting. No corresponding entry-gap was recorded along the innermost ditch circuit, although the rounded form of this part of the ditch perimeter could suggest that it was not an original feature, but was formed by cutting across an entrance-gap. The second entry-gap was located towards the western end of the innermost southern ditch (A18 and A19). This entry-gap measured 0.8m in width. It may have been associated with two re-cut possible post-pits (F387; F388, Fig. 9.S.8). This arrangement may have formed an L-shaped funnel, controlling entry between the western ends of the two southern ditches of the enclosure (A18 and A20) and into the enclosure interior.

The internal features belonging to Phase 1, 2, or 3 activity are described below (Phase 1–Phase 3). It is notable that the gap between the two Phase 2 ditches was kept clear of features, and may have been used for circulation between the concentric ditches, although the separation between the enclosure ditches had been reduced in this phase. The pebble surface (F141) may have also been in use during Phase 2.

Most of the Enclosure A2 ditch circuit was backfilled at the end of this phase. The outermost Phase 2 enclosure northern ditch (A1) was backfilled with grey silt-clay. The outermost western ditch (A8) was backfilled with red or grey silt-clay. The outermost southern ditch (A20) was backfilled with brown or grey silt-clay. The outermost eastern ditch (A23) was backfilled with grey silt-clay. The innermost northern ditch (A3) was backfilled with red/brown silt-clay, or sand-clay. The innermost western ditch (A7) was backfilled with grey-brown silt-clay sealed by brown and blue clay. The innermost southern (A19) and eastern (A22) ditches were backfilled with red/ grey-brown silt-clay.

Finds and dating evidence from Phase 2 features

The northern outermost (A1) and innermost (A3) ditches backfills contained pottery dating to the 2nd–4th centuries. The western inner ditch (A7) was the best dated of all Phase 2 features. It contained pottery of 2nd–4th-century, AD 120–200, 165–200, late 2nd- to 3rd-century date, and samian dating AD 120–200, 160–200 and 165–200. The southern inner ditch (A19) contained pottery of 2nd–3rd-century date. The eastern inner ditch (A22) contained pottery of 2nd–3rd-century and 2nd–4th-century date. The eastern outer ditch (A23) contained pottery of only 2nd–4th-century date.

Ditch A7 notably contained an unusually large portion of a Ludowici Th plain dish, noted by Willis (below) to be a rare form. Often rare samian forms occurring at rural sites are associated with burials, watery deposits or structured deposition. There was no evidence of human (or animal) bone from Longdales Road because of the acid subsoil.

Interpretation of Phase 2 features

Phase 2 activity, like that of Phase 1, was concentrated within a double-ditched enclosure (Enclosure A2). The similarity in alignment and positioning of the two enclosures may suggest an element of continuity, although the dating evidence from both phases is limited. This continuity in layout is most clearly marked by the presumed re-cutting of the southern outermost and northern innermost ditches of the Phase 1 enclosure in Phase 2 (re-cuts A20 and A3). The innermost eastern ditch of Enclosure A1 was also probably re-cut in Phase 2 (A23). Enclosure A2 was re-positioned to the west of Enclosure 1, possibly to create space for a droveway between the eastern side of the enclosure and the eastern boundary of the Romano-British compound (respected by the eastern boundary of Field 2, Fig. 4). Despite this slight relocation, the enclosure was maintained at roughly the same size as its predecessor by re-cutting the entire ditch perimeter. This suggests that it was functionally important to maintain a similarly sized enclosure. The southern side of the enclosure (A18) was continued to its west, presumably forming a field boundary following the enclosure's alignment. The southern terminals of western enclosure ditches (A7 and A8) respected the field boundary, which was contemporary.

In contrast to the Phase 1 enclosure, the Enclosure A2 ditches were cut at a separation of only 4m. Around the ditch perimeter, the outermost ditch was the shallower of the pair and may have been no more than a palisade trench. Once again, there was no evidence for timber uprights in the form of post-holes along such a palisade.

Another element of continuity between the Phase 1 and 2 enclosures was in the location of their southwestern entrances. The entry-gap retained between ditches A18 and A19 respected the position of the eastern side of the Phase 1 entrance, defined on its eastern side by feature A17, further emphasising continuity between the two enclosures. The entry-gap between Phase 2 ditches A18 and A20 was further defined by two post-pits (F387 and F388), cutting through ditch A20 and into Phase 1 ditch A21 (Fig. 9.S.8). A new feature of the Phase 2 enclosure was the entry-gap retained at its northwestern angle, probably much reduced in size as a result of re-cutting. The alignment of the adjoining innermost ditch suggests that it was not an original feature.

The treatment of the Phase 2 enclosure entrances and the evidence for continuity with Enclosure A1 suggest that the enclosure continued to be used for animal husbandry, at least in part. Pebble surface F141 could have continued in use.

Phase 1–2 features (not illustrated in detail)

Description and interpretation

The features attributed to Phase 1–2 were located within trial-trenches and cannot be related to the main sequence of activity (see Fig. 4 for a simplified plan; note that features are not individually numbered).

Three east-west aligned gullies (F107, F108 and F111), a pit (F109, cutting feature F108), a northeast-southwest aligned gully (F110), and an east-west aligned gully (F118) were recorded in Trench 3. Two pits (F123, F127) and a post-hole (F124), containing a post burnt *in situ*, were recorded in Trench 4. These features represent an unenclosed focus of Romano-British activity outside Enclosures A1–A2 within the Field 2 Roman compound. Other Romano-British features were found in the same field outside the enclosures during the watching brief (see Chapter 5 below). The east-west alignment recorded in Trenches 3 and 4 is the same as that of the Phase 1–2 enclosures, and of Phase 2 ditch/ field boundary A118 in particular. Ditch F128 (not illustrated, Trench 9, Fig. 4) could have followed the alignment of Phase 2 ditch A22.

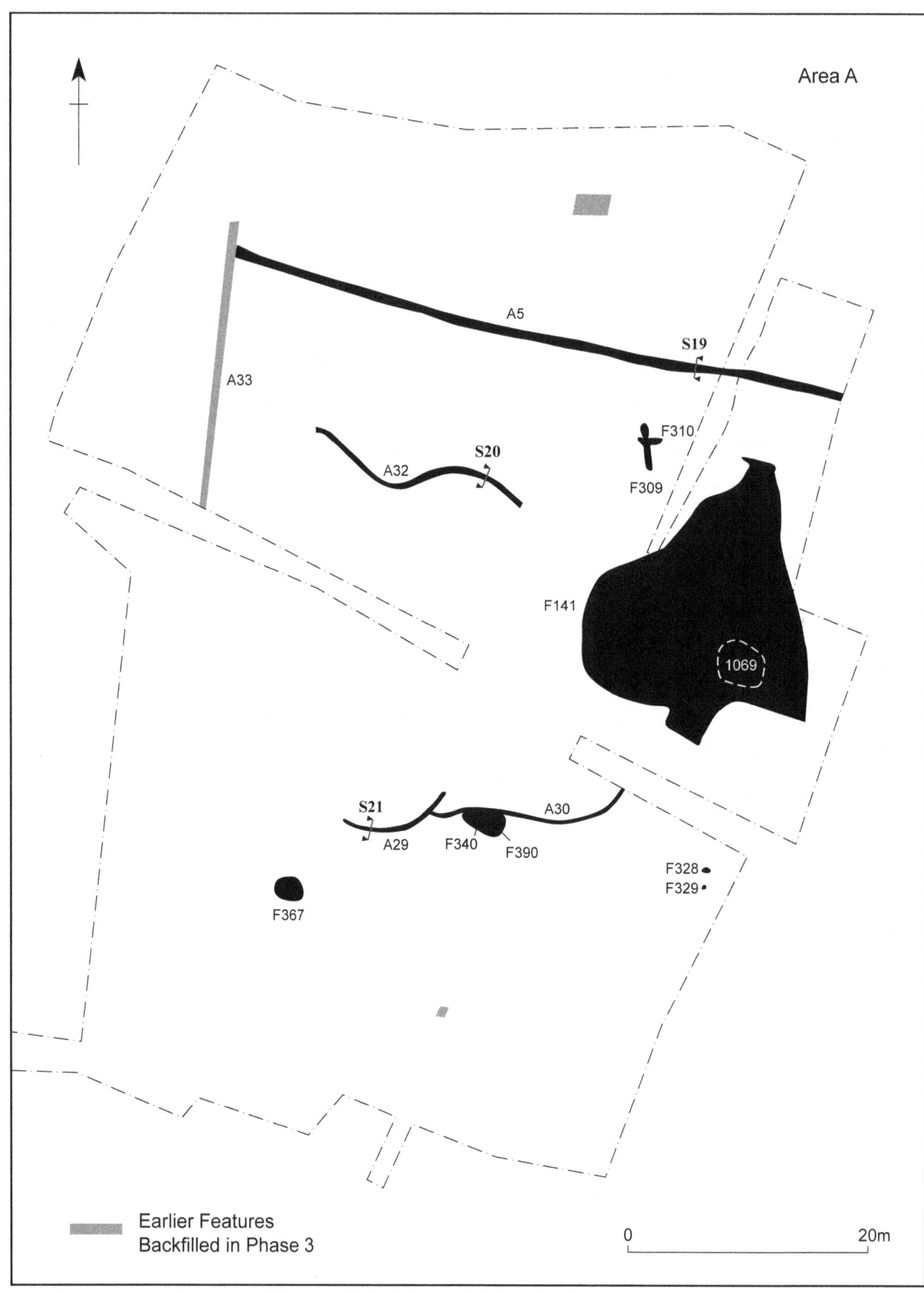

Figure 12. Area A, Phase 3 plan (scale 1:450)

AREA A THE DOUBLE-DITCHED ENCLOSURES (FIELD 2)

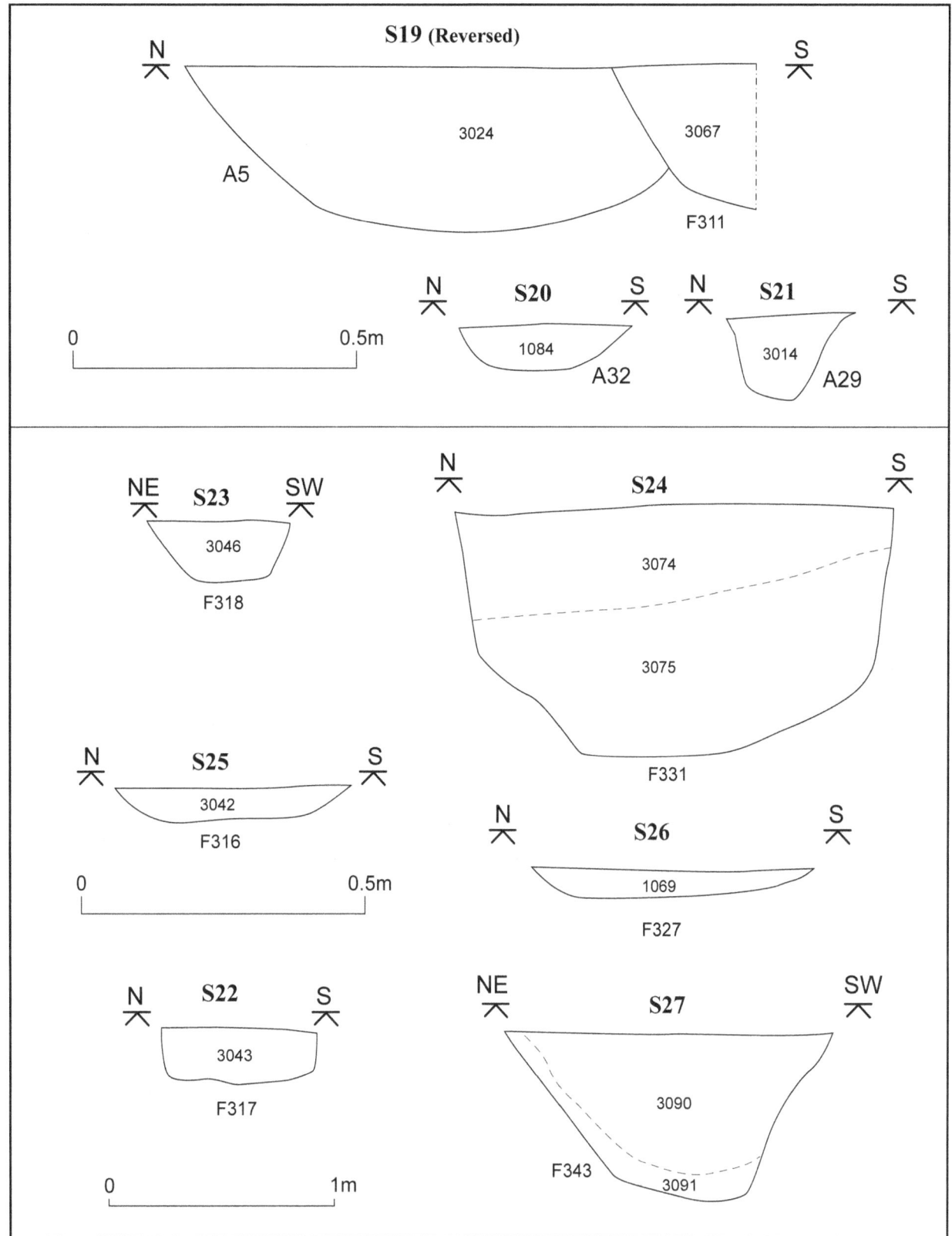

Figure 13. Area A, Phase 3 sections and Phase 1–3 sections (scales 1:10 and 1:25)

Phase 3: Later Romano-British activity, 3rd–early 4th century (Figs 7, 12–13)

Description of Phase 3 features

The features attributed to Phase 3 are limited in number, and more difficult to interpret. In contrast to preceding Phase 1–2 occupation, Phase 3 activity could have been partly unenclosed, although possibly including limited re-cutting or backfilling of earlier ditches.

The main Phase 3 feature was a northwest-southeast aligned ditch (A5, Fig. 11.S.18; Fig. 13.S.19), recorded for a length of 52m. The ditch was cut tangential to the alignment of the Phase 1–2 enclosures. It was cut across backfilled Phase 1 enclosure ditch A4, and Phase 2 enclosure ditch A22. The Phase 3 ditch was cut to a U-shaped profile and measured an average of 0.7m in width and 0.15m in depth. It was backfilled with brown silt-clay. A length of Phase 2 ditch A7 (Fig. 10) was also re-cut (A33) in this phase. Together with ditch A5, with which it may have been associated, the re-cut formed an L-shape in plan.

Further, possibly contemporary features were recorded to the south of ditch A5. A mainly northwest-southeast aligned curvilinear gully (A32, Fig. 13.S.20), followed the approximate alignment of ditch A5. The western terminal of ditch A32 was cut into the backfilled Phase 1 enclosure ditch A10 and Phase 1 pit F135. Gully A32, which was recorded for a length of 22m, was cut to a U-shaped profile, measuring an average of 0.3m in width and 0.08m in depth. It was backfilled with grey-brown clay-silt. To the east of ditch A5 were two intercutting gullies (F309 and F310); the latter cut the former.

Further to the south, two intercutting curvilinear gullies were recorded (A29, Fig. 13.S.21; and A30). Feature A29 cut A30. Gully A30 was cut into Phase 3 stone surface F390, itself cut by a single post-hole (F340). Gullies A29 and A30 were recorded for lengths of 12m and 11m respectively. These features were cut to a U-shaped profile and measured an average of 0.4m in width and 0.1m in depth. They were backfilled with red-brown silt-clay.

An oval pit (F367) to the southwest may also belong to this phase. It was cut through the backfilled Phase 1 ditch A10, and into the subsoil. The pit measured a maximum of 2.5m in diameter and 1m in depth. It was backfilled with grey clay, separated by a lens of charcoal-rich soil.

One of the largest Phase 3 features was the pebble surface (F141) which may have originated in Phase 1 or Phase 2. The irregularly shaped surface (1068) measured a maximum of 23m north-south and 19m east-west. A Phase 3 layer of grey silt (1069) sealed the surface. Also sealing the surface was a dump of charcoal-rich soil (1108, not illustrated), also attributed to Phase 3. No relationship could be recorded between layers 1069 and 1108. To the south of this feature were a pair of adjoining post-holes (F328 and F329) which may have represented the uprights of a loom. Similar pairs of Phase 1–Phase 3 features were also recorded (see below). The internal features belonging to the Phase 1, 2, or 3 activity are described below.

Lengths of Phase 1 ditch A26 and Phase 2 ditch A3 were finally infilled during Phase 3. It is not clear if these ditch lengths were deliberately backfilled or, alternatively, if the remaining hollows of these ditches were backfilled deliberately to counteract sinkage.

Table 1 details the Phase 3 dating evidence. Over 55% of the pottery recovered from Area A was attributed to this phase, of which 43.71% comprised Severn Valley ware. A fragment of a child's lathe-turned shale bracelet was recovered from surface F141.

Table 1. Area A, Phase 3 dating evidence

Feature (fill)	Dating Range
Pebble surface F141 (1068)	2nd–4th century, 3rd–4th, late 3rd, 4th (residual material dated AD 120–200, 140–200, 160–200 and 2nd–3rd)
Pebble surface F141 (overlying silt 1069)	Mortaria, 2nd half of 2nd century, late 3rd–4th, AD 240–400, AD 100–400; coarse wares 2nd–4th (residual coarse wares)
Ditch A5	2nd–3rd century, 2nd–4th
Curvilinear gully A32	2nd–4th century
Features F308 and F367	2nd–4th century, latter also 3rd–4th (both residual 3rd)
Features F309 and F310	2nd–4th and 3rd–4th, respectively
Feature F340	2nd–3rd century, later 3rd–4th
Feature F390	4th century
Phase 3 re-cut (A33) of Phase 1 ditch A7	AD 280–370, late 3rd–4th century, post AD 250 (residual Samian dated AD 160–240 and 120–160)
Segment of Phase 1 ditch backfilled in Phase 3	Post-dating AD 250
Segment of Phase 2 ditch A3 backfilled in Phase 3	Post-dating AD 250, late 3rd century

Interpretation of Phase 3 features

Phase 3 represents the first unenclosed phase of settlement in Field 2, as well as the latest Romano-British activity here. Ditches A5 and A33 may have defined part of the northern and western limits of this latest Romano-British settlement, but the other sides could have been open, or marked by slight fences leaving no surviving trace at excavation. Curvilinear gullies A32, A29 and A30 probably provided drainage around shallow ring-gullies of which no trace survived at excavation. Intercutting gullies A29 and A30 indicate more than one phase of occupation. Domestic occupation is also indicated by the quantities of pottery deposited in Phase 3 over Phase 1–Phase 3 hardstanding F141. This hardstanding could have formed a yard area or even the base for one or more timber-framed buildings constructed on earth-fast foundations. The surface could originally have been more extensive, as is suggested by the quantities of small pebbles present in the topsoil within

Area A The Double-Ditched Enclosures (Field 2)

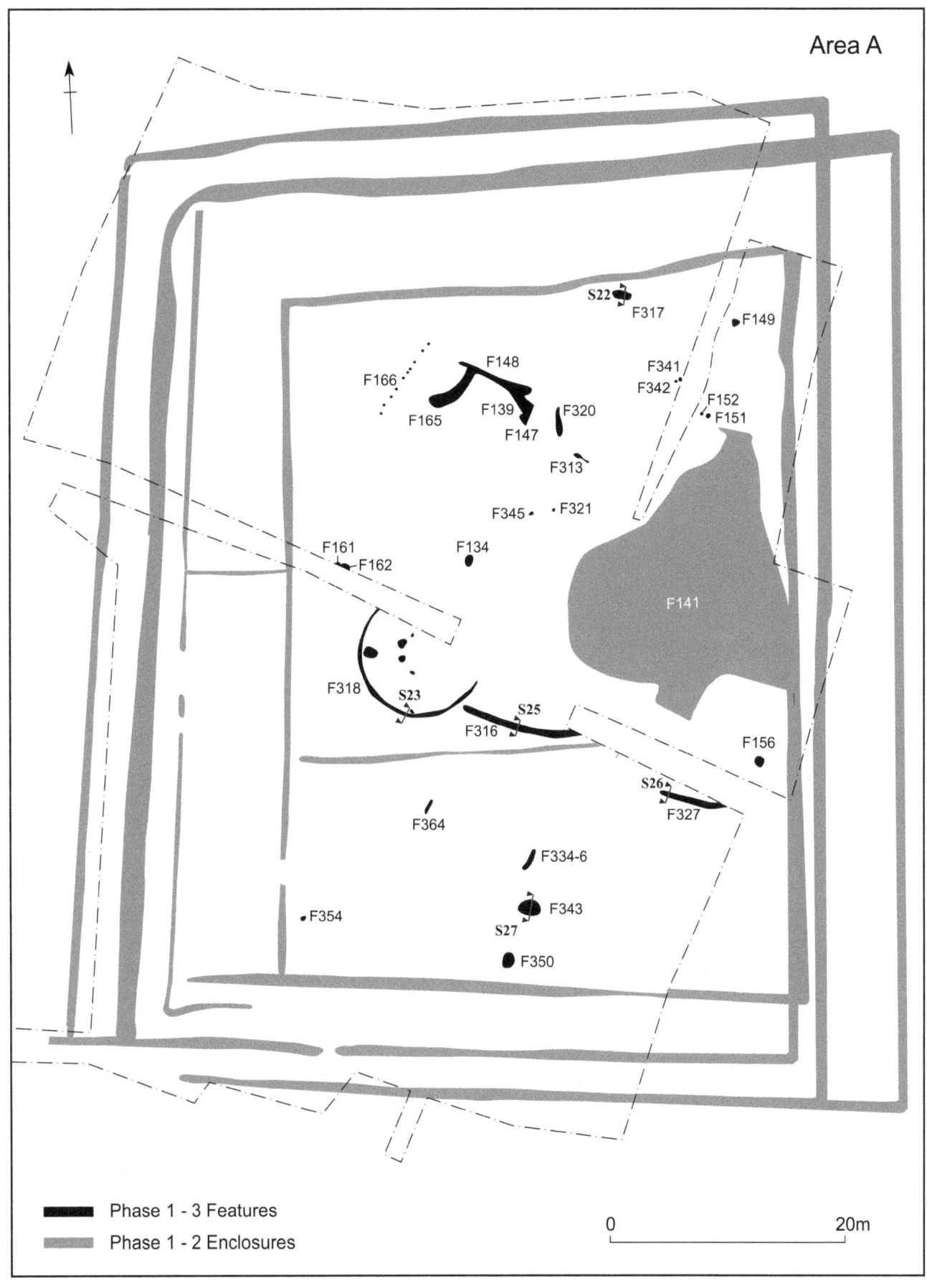

Figure 14. Area A, Phase 1–3 plan (scale 1:450)

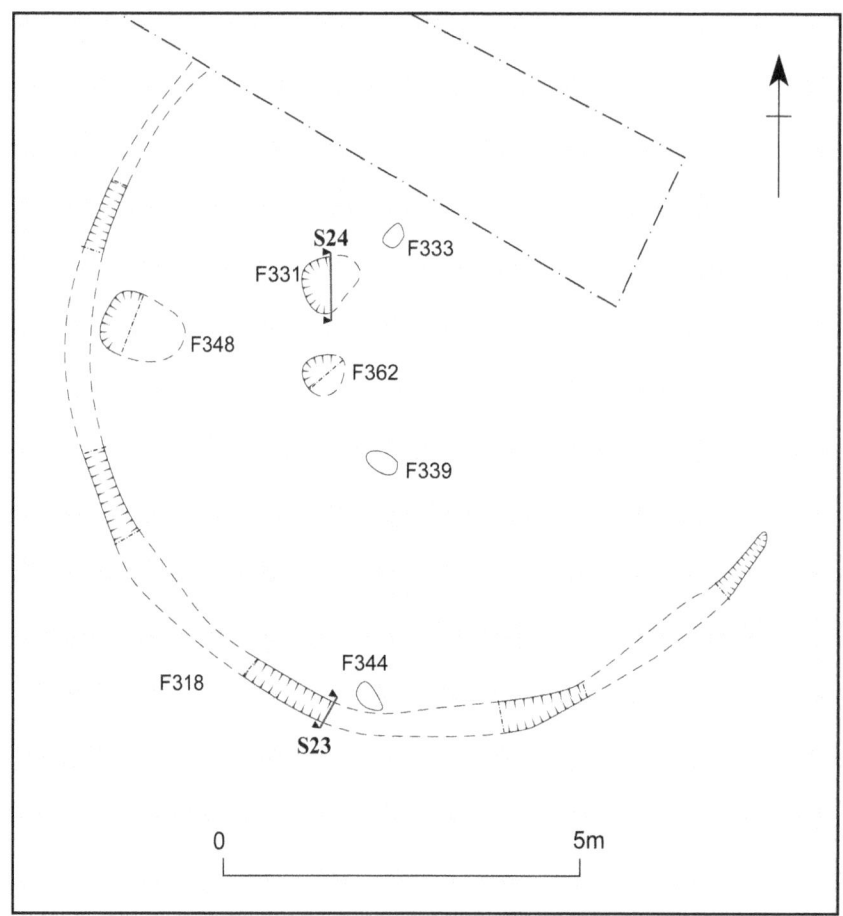

Figure 15. Area A, detailed plan of eaves-drip gully F318 (scale 1:50)

Area A. The pottery evidence also indicates that short lengths of both Phase 1 and Phase 2 enclosure ditches remained open into this phase, before being finally backfilled. It is possible that some of the features attributed to Phase 1–3 (see below) may have been contemporary with Phase 3 occupation, but this cannot be proved in the absence of more precise dating evidence.

Phase 1–Phase 3 features (Figs 7, 13–15)

Description of Phase 1–Phase 3 features

The features attributed to Phase 1–Phase 3 are those which are located in the interior of the Phase 1 or Phase 2 enclosures, or which could be attributable to later Romano-British activity (Phase 3). The internal features comprised stake-holes, post-holes, pits and gullies. None of these features could be attributed securely to a single phase. Of particular interest was an incomplete circular ring-gully (F318, Fig. 15), measuring 10m in diameter, associated with a group of internal post-holes and pits. The internal features are described in order roughly from north to south.

In the north of the enclosure interior were located a number of post-holes (F149, F341, F342, F151, F152, F321, F345). The paired arrangement of adjoining post-holes (F341–F342 and F151 and F152, F321 and F345) may have represented the uprights of a loom. These post-holes were backfilled with grey silt-clay-sand. Also identified in this part of the enclosure were scattered lengths of gullies (F317, Fig. 13.S.22; F320). The gullies followed mainly east-west or north-south aligned orientations, apparently respecting the Enclosure A1–A2 ditch alignments. To the west was a group of intersecting curvilinear gullies (F165, F148, F147, F139). Gully F147 cut feature F139; features F148 and F165 may have been contemporary. The gullies were backfilled with grey or orange silt-sand. Further to the west was a northeast-southwest aligned fenceline (F166), defined by a line comprising a total of ten irregularly spaced stake-holes. Further to the south were three pits (F134, F161, F162). Pit F162 cut feature F161. Feature F313 was an oval oven, backfilled with charcoal-rich soil.

The main feature recorded towards the centre of the enclosure was part of a circular ring-gully (F318, Fig. 15; Fig. 13.S.23), measuring 10m in diameter and 22m in circumference. The northeastern half of the feature had presumably been scoured out by truncation. The ring-gully was cut to a U-shaped profile and measured an average of 0.3m in width and 0.12m in depth. It was backfilled with grey silt-clay. A number of associated features were recorded within the ring-gully interior. Three post-holes (F333, F339 and F344) and three oval pits (F331, Fig. 13.S.24; F362 and F348), one a hearth, were located within the ring-gully interior. These internal features were backfilled with grey-orange silt-sand, mottled with charcoal. The post-holes may have divided the interior of the ring-gully into two halves. The pits were backfilled with grey sand with charcoal flecks. To the east of the ring-gully was a contemporary slightly curvilinear gully (F316, Fig. 13.S.25), mainly aligned east-west. Further to the east was a second curvilinear gully (F327, Fig. 13.S.26). Other adjoining post-holes (F156 and F330) were also recorded.

Finally, in the south of the enclosure interior were recorded a number of other features. These comprised a short length of two northeast-southwest aligned gullies (F364, F334–F336) and two pits (F343, Fig. 13.S.27; and F350). This feature group was backfilled with grey-brown silt-sand.

Finds and dating evidence from Phase 1–Phase 3 features

Only broadly dated coarse ware pottery was recovered from the backfills of features attributed to Phase 1–3. Features F139 and F321 contained pottery of 2nd–3rd-century date. Features F333, F317 and F156 contained pottery of 2nd–4th-century date. With the exception of feature F149, which contained residual pottery of 1st-century date, no other Phase 1–3 features contained datable pottery.

Interpretation of Phase 1–Phase 3 features

A range of features, including post-holes, ring-gullies and a line of stake-holes, were recorded within the area excavated. These features are unlikely to have all been contemporary. Some may have been associated with the Phase 1 or Phase 2 enclosures, and others with the largely unenclosed Phase 3 settlement.

Many of these features are difficult to interpret. The paired arrangement of post-holes (F341–2; F151–2; F161–2) may be interpreted as the post-holes belonging to upright looms. A loom-weight was found in Phase feature F357. Ring-gully F318 contained a hearth and post-holes supporting the roof of the structure. Circular ring-gullies measuring 12–14m in diameter were recorded at Alcester (Mahany 1994, fig. 109), while the pre-temple ring-gullies at Coleshill measured between 9–12m in diameter (Magilton 2006, fig. 4). The line of stake-holes (F166) formed a fence-line, cut at a tangent to the main axis of the Phase 1–2 enclosures.

Phase 4: All post-Roman activity

The post-Roman features comprise plough furrows and modern field drains, which are not illustrated. An alternative phasing of Phase 1 post-hole F357 is considered in the discussion (Chapter 6 below).

FINDS

Small finds by Erica Macey-Bracken with Rob Ixer (Fig. 16)

Catalogue

1   Spindle-whorl, 36mm in diameter, 9mm thick. A moderate yellowish brown (10YR 4/4 on the G. S.

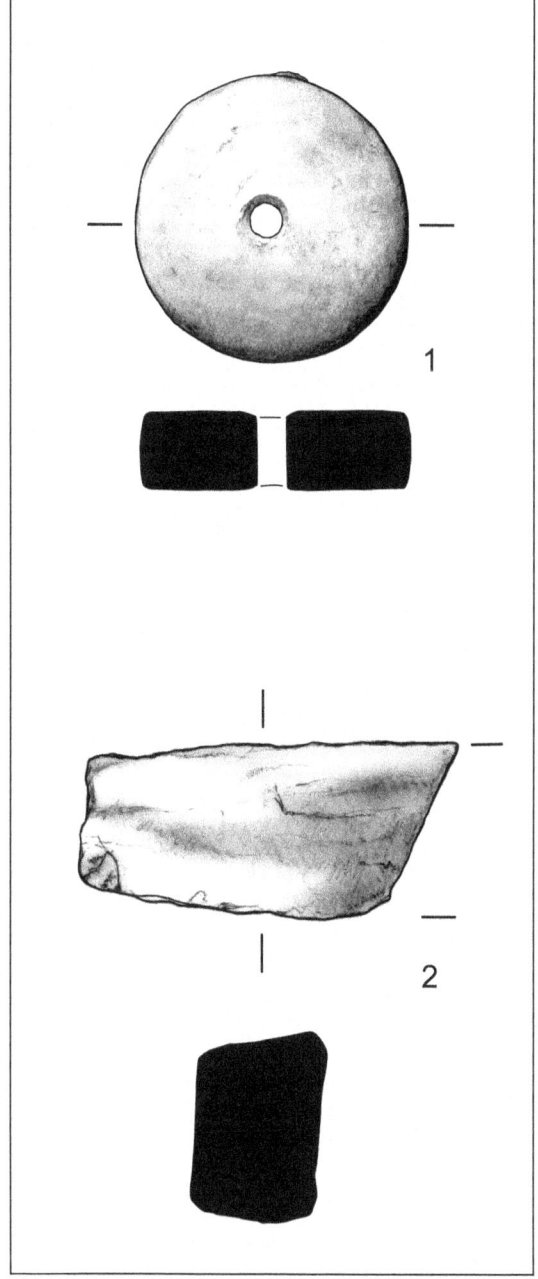

Figure 16. Area A, small finds (scale 1:4)

A. rock-color chart), fine-grained (<187µm grain size), micaceous, Permo-Triassic sandstone. The surfaces have small, black, iron-rich concretions up to 2mm in diameter. A similar-sized spindle-whorl was found at Castleford (Cool and Philo 1998, 258–9). Post-hole F357, 3114, Phase 1, interior of Enclosure A1. Fig. 16.1.

2   Fragment of lathe-turned shale bracelet. 24mm long, 6mm wide. This item is very fragmentary, and only a short section survives. The section is almost D-shaped, and is similar to a fragmentary shale bracelet from Castleford (*ibid.*, 254). No decoration was noted on the item, which has a rounded external surface. The small inner diameter (6mm) of the item suggests that, as with most of

3 the shale bracelets at the Lankhills cemetery (Clarke 1979, 312), this item was a child's bracelet. Surface F141, 1069, Phase 3. Not illustrated.

3   Part of a possible secondary hone, 59mm long, 21mm wide, 18mm thick. One polished thin section was made from the lithic. The polished thin section was described using a x20 hand lens and the G. S. A. rock-color chart and then by transmitted light microscopy using x6 and x12 air lenses and by reflected light microscopy using x8 air, x16 oil and x40 oil immersion lenses. All phases were identified using their optical properties. F369, 3138, Phase 1, sub-enclosure to Enclosure A1. Fig. 16.3.

Lithological identification: A dolomitised, pyritised, fossiliferous, black chert, possibly used as a secondary hone.

Description – Macroscopical description

Artifact. A homogeneous, dark-coloured, hard, chert band is present within an oxidised, silicified ?limestone. Despite the hardness and smoothness of the rock and its suitability as a hone there are no wear traces on the ?artifact, nor any sign that it has been fashioned. In addition, although black jaspers (chert) have been used for precious metal assaying, there is no sign that the ?artifact was used as a touchstone. The top and bottom surfaces are limonite-coated to give a pale yellowish brown (10YR 6/2 Geological Society of America rock-color chart) colour. The cut surface shows up to 1.5cm thick, light bluish grey (5B 6/1), glassy chert within a light olive grey (5Y 6/1) vuggy, silica-rich sediment that carries up to 0.3mm diameter, brassy, cubic sulphides. Small, up to 0.1mm diameter, pale-coloured crystals are present throughout the rock. Thin Section: the core carries rare, 0.1m diameter, pale-coloured rhombs and is a pale yellowish brown (10YR 6/2). The edges are up to 5mm thick and carry 0.1 to 0.3mm in size, euhedral pyrite.

Microscopical description

The majority of the rock comprises fine-grained quartz and banded silica with minor amounts of euhedral, zoned, 60–140μm diameter, rhombic dolomite and trace amounts of 5–50μm diameter, carbonaceous matter, single quartz grains and 20–50μm diameter, pale-coloured TiO_2 minerals. Pyrite is widespread as 2–10 diameter framboids, locally in clusters up to 80μm across, but mainly as discrete, euhedral, pentagonal dodecahedral crystals up to 200μm in diameter. Towards the oxidised edges of the rock, pyrite is extensively replaced by limonite.

The chert is highly fossiliferous with abundant, 25–60μm diameter, sponge spicules showing this to be a sedimentary chert. Trace amounts of calcite are present as laths and spheres and also represent fossil debris; no large fossil material was recognised.

Provenance

Probably the chert is not local unless it is Carboniferous in age from the Carboniferous Limestone, then it could be from the glacial drift. If, however, it is Mesozoic in age then it is an anthropogenic import.

Use. If it is an artifact then it was probably a secondary hone.

4   Part of ceramic object, possibly a loom-weight, made from very coarse pottery. Coarse sandy red fabric with large sub-rounded pebble inclusions. 50mm long, 26mm thick. The circular shape of the item suggests that if it is a loom-weight it is likely to be of Anglo-Saxon date, as circular loom-weights are normally attributed to the Anglo-Saxon period (Bryant 2004, 366). As the context that produced this item is dated to Phase 1, it is possible that this item is intrusive. F357, 3114, Phase 1. Fig. 16.2.

Romano-British pottery
by Annette Hancocks

Introduction

A total of 1,439 sherds of Romano-British pottery from the evaluation and excavation fieldwork stages in Area A was subjected to detailed analysis and reporting. The ceramic dating was such that only a single distinct ceramic phase could be identified and dated to the 2nd–4th century AD.

The pottery was derived from stratified contexts that date from the 2nd–4th century AD which contained c 86% of the total ceramic assemblage. The remaining 14% comprised mainly unstratified and post-Roman ceramics which are not considered further. The ceramics weighed 15.49kg and had an average sherd weight (avsw) of 10.77g. Full quantification of the ceramics by fabric type appears in Table 2. A selection of the pottery has been illustrated (Figs 17–18).

Methodology

The material was recorded using the standard Birmingham Archaeology pottery recording system (Hancocks 1997) and analysed using Access database software. The assemblage was quantified in full by sherd count, weight (g), and estimated vessel equivalent (EVE). Only rim equivalents (EVEs) are published, but percentages for bases are recorded in the archive. The level of abrasion was recorded for individual sherds. The fabrics are listed and

Table 2. Area A, Romano-British coarse ware pottery, fabrics, sources and quantities

Fabric Name	Qty	% Qty	Wt (g)	% Wt (g)	Rim EVE	% Rim EVE
B02	90	6.25%	1,174	7.58%	159	12.59%
C02	1	0.07%	1	0.01%	6	0.48%
G04	5	0.35%	83	0.54%	12	0.95%
G05	47	3.27%	567	3.66%	144	11.40%
G06.5	72	5.00%	638	4.12%	80	6.33%
G06.7	7	0.49%	75	0.48%	-	-
G06.8	1	0.07%	32	0.21%	22	1.74%
G06.9	9	0.63%	34	0.22%	18	1.43%
G06.12	10	0.69%	124	0.80%	-	-
M02	5	0.35%	122	0.79%	-	-
M04c	7	0.49%	104	0.67%	-	-
M04cv	4	0.28%	142	0.92%	-	-
N02.1	17	1.18%	927	5.98%	65	5.15%
N02.2	52	3.60%	269	1.74%	11	0.87%
O02	10	0.69%	86	0.55%	26	2.06%
O02.1	904	62.83%	8,143	52.54%	566	44.82%
O02.12	4	0.28%	64	0.41%	-	-
O02.13	4	0.28%	52	0.34%	16	1.27%
O03.1	72	5.00%	1,082	6.98%	75	5.94%
O03.2	2	0.14%	34	0.22%	-	-
O03.3	3	0.21%	37	0.24%	-	-
O06.01	14	0.97%	149	0.96%	19	1.5%
O06.09	30	2.08%	528	3.41%	16	1.27%
O06.10	3	0.21%	74	0.48%	-	-
O06.11	5	0.35%	102	0.66%	-	-
O06.22	2	0.14%	14	0.09%	-	-
O06.91	29	2.02%	191	1.23%	-	-
S03	23	1.60%	426	2.75%	19	1.5%
S04R	3	0.21%	171	1.10%	-	-
W11	3	0.21%	12	0.08%	9	0.71%
W11.2	1	0.07%	37	0.24%	-	-
Total	**1,439**	**100.0%**	**15,494**	**100.0%**	**1,263**	**100.0%**

described in Appendix A1, where they have not been published before. Other characteristics noted included decoration, evidence for manufacture (wasters) and, if present, repairs (rivets and rivet holes). The form catalogue is presented by fabric group. Form codes are listed in Appendix A2. For ease of reference much of the pottery information is tabulated by phase (Appendices A3–A4).

This report comprises brief discussions arranged by phase, focusing on the chronological dating evidence. The evidence for broader trends in dating, taphonomy, site function and supply is considered in the discussion section. This is followed by a concluding section summarising the contribution of the assemblage to wider studies.

Chronology

One of the key research aims was to establish the site chronology. Overall, the ceramics proved valuable in enhancing the stratigraphic and morphological study. Ceramically, it has not proved possible to identify distinct phases, although it has been possible to determine a series of stratigraphic events, which has led the excavator to determine three distinct phases of Romano-British activity. The ceramics broadly date to the 2nd–4th century AD, with an emphasis on the 3rd–4th century AD.

Phase 1 Double-ditched Enclosure A1, AD 120–mid-2nd century
Phase 2 Double-ditched Enclosure A2, late 2nd–3rd century
Phase 3 Later Romano-British activity, 3rd–early 4th century

Phase 1

A small amount of pottery (6.75%) was assigned to Phase 1, the first double-ditched Enclosure (A1). Three diagnostic sherds were recognised. These comprised a wheelmade cooking pot with moderately splayed, everted rim (Fig. 17.3) from Enclosure A1 ditch A10 (F131, 1076), a Severn Valley Ware flat base angle from a globular jar (Fig 17.4) from post-hole F307 and a wide-mouthed jar with pointed bead rim (Fig. 17.6) from fill 1042, F130, part of enclosure ditch A10.

Phase 2

Some 20.90% of the total ceramic assemblage was assigned to Phase 2 and is associated with double-ditched Enclosure A2. A total of twelve diagnostic rim forms are illustrated from this phase of activity. A Black Burnished Ware cooking pot with moderately splayed, everted rim and all-over burnish (Fig. 17.8) was recovered from fill 3022 of F301, part of Enclosure ditch A3.

The most notable fabric in the Phase 2 assemblage is oxidised Severn Valley ware (13.20%). Six diagnostic rim forms were recognised. These mainly comprised five jar forms and a tankard (see Fig. 17.12–17). All derived from three features: ditch A22 (F158), ditch A7 (F338), and ditch A3 (F301).

Phase 1–2

This phase was represented by only 1.26% of the total ceramic assemblage recovered from Area A. Three diagnostic form sherds were observed, restricted mainly to the Malvernian and Severn Valley Ware traditions such as a handmade cooking pot with simple, plain rim (Fig. 17.20) and a wheelmade upright tankard with simple bead rim with groove (Fig. 17.21). All derive from evaluation Trenches 2 and 3 – which could not be related to the main stratigraphic sequence.

Phase 1–Phase 3

The quantity of pottery recovered from this phase (1.39% of the total recovered ceramic assemblage) and the range of fabrics, was similar to that found in Phase 1–2 contexts. Diagnostic rim forms included a Black Burnished ware straight-sided dish with simple rim and all over burnish (Fig. 17.23), a handmade Malvernian straight-sided dish with all over burnish and external sooting (Fig. 17.24) and a Severn Valley Ware jar and upright tankard (Fig. 17.25 and Fig. 17.26).

Phase 3

Some 55.54% of the overall ceramic assemblage was assigned to this phase, with 43.71% of the pottery from Phase 3 being Severn Valley Ware. Ten diagnostic jar forms in this fabric were present, which include four wide-mouthed jars (Fig. 18.43, 18.44 and 18.45–46). The pottery was mainly recovered from Phase 3 layers overlying Phase 1–3 surface F141 and perhaps reflects the reuse of pottery in making-up the ground surface. Additional ceramic material was recovered from ditch A5 and gully A30. A number of Severn Valley Ware upright tankards (Fig. 18.47-8) were also recovered. Small quantities of Black Burnished Ware were recorded and included a few datable forms such as straight-sided dishes with simple rims and interlocking burnished arcs and external sooting (Fig. 18.27–29) and a cooking pot with moderately splayed, everted rim and all-over burnish (Fig. 18.31 and Fig. 18.32).

Phase 4

Less than 0.5% of the ceramic assemblage derived from this phase. It is likely that this material is residual from Phase 3 activity. Much derives from modern field-drains.

Taphonomy

Most of the pottery came from the stone surfaces, gully and ditch fills. A total of 132 minimum vessels (MV) were observed. The average sherd weight by stratigraphic phase seems to peak within Phase 1 at 14g, with Phase 1–2 at 10.78g; Phase 1–3 at 26.6g; Phase 2 at 14.94g, Phase 3 at 8.16g and Phase 4 at 16.83g. Overall, with the exception of Phase 1, these figures are quite low and compare favourably with the overall average sherd weight of 10.77g.

Levels of fragmentation were deemed to be quite high as a result of the low average sherd weights. This may be a reflection of the depositional processes on stone surfaces, and in gullies and ditches, and their proximity to areas of domestic occupation, and of secondary deposition processes from middens, house floors and yards.

Fabrics

Tweny-nine wheelmade and two handmade fabrics were identified (Fig. 19, Appendix A1). The occurrence of fabrics by phase is detailed in Appendix A4.

One of the defining fabric groups is Black Burnished Ware 1 (6.26%). This fabric is most prominent in Phase 3 (5.21%) and occurs in the assemblage in straight-sided dish forms, including a 'fish dish' (Fig. 17.23, Fig. 18.27–29), flanged bowl/ dish form (Fig. 18.30) and cooking pot forms (Fig. 17.8, Fig. 18.31–32). The fabric group is predominantly Antonine or later in date.

A type of globular/ bulbous colour-coated beaker was recognised throughout the assemblage. This came from stone surface F141 (1069). This sherd, along with the small amount of samian, represents the only fineware pottery recovered from the site. The quantity and quality of the material recovered can give an indication of the status and function of the settlement.

The reduced Severn Valley ware fabrics, G04 and G05, are well represented amongst the assemblage, although they comprise less than 4% of the overall total pottery recovered. Four forms have been illustrated (Fig. 17.1–2, 9, and Fig. 18.34).

Some coarser, sandy variant fabrics, G06.5, G06.7, G06.8, and G06.9 have been recognised at Metchley Roman fort, Birmingham (Green *et al.* 2001). It is interesting to note the continuation of these fabrics into the later Roman period at King's Norton.

This point is emphasised by the occurrence of mortaria within the assemblage, amounting to only 1.12% in Phase 3, from both Mancetter-Hartshill and Oxfordshire. This material confirms the later origins of the Longdales settlement (Hartley below).

Only 4.8% of the overall assemblage comprised handmade Malvernian pottery (fabrics N02.1 and N02.2). These fabrics continued in use into the 2nd century AD and occurred in a common form, the tubby cooking pot (Fig. 17.20 and Fig. 18.37). It would appear that in most instances, the occurrence of this fabric type on site is residual, but it is most prominent in the Phase 2 assemblage (0.62%). It confirms the reliance on regionally traded pottery within the assemblage. This has wider economic implications, which are discussed below.

The greatest range and variety of fabrics occur in Phase 3, when activity is most intense. The oxidised Severn Valley ware fabric group dominates this phase as well as the overall assemblage (44%.) This is not surprising given the proximity of the Longdales settlement to the production centre in Malvern, which is the central production area for pottery of this type.

Surface finish

A range and variety of surface finishes were recorded on all pottery fabrics in the assemblage. The Malvernian tempered wares are characteristically burnished all over and in some instances show vertical burnishing (Fig. 18.37), a cordon at the base of the neck (CA), rustication (MA), black slip (SC), roller stamped rouletting (LA) and incised horizontal lines (GA).

Sooting

A total of 51 sherds, representing four vessels and four different fabric types showed external sooting. Two of the forms include a Black Burnished Ware cooking pot (not illustrated) and a straight-sided dish (Fig. 18.28). A Malvernian, straight-sided dish form also had external sooting (Fig. 17.24).

Forms

The occurrence of form by phase is listed in Appendix A3 and the catalogue of illustrated forms below.

Vessel size and function

The most common diameter range is 20cm for flanged bowls, straight-sided dishes and jars. The most popular vessel size range is 13cm–20cm. The functional diversity of the site is relatively restricted. There is a direct relationship between vessel size and its function or use. There does not appear to be a direct relationship between fabric, form, decoration and colour. Fig. 20 provides an analysis of vessel classes by percentage rim EVE.

Catalogue of illustrated pottery by phase and fabric (Figs 17–18)

The percentage of rim surviving appears in brackets (%)

Fig. 17.1–26

Unphased

G05

1   JN7.01 Wheelmade, narrow-mouthed jar with plain, everted rim with cordon at the base of neck. Diam. 14cm (25%), Trench 2W, E205, gully, unphased.

Phase 1

G04

2   NA1.12. Wheelmade, upright tankard with bead rim with slight groove with horizontal lines at girth. Diam. 14cm (12%), Trench 1W, ditch A6, E106, fill E105.

G06.5

3   JK 7.3. Wheelmade, cooking pot with moderately splayed, everted rim. Diam. 13cm (30%), ditch A10, F131, 1076.

O02.1

4   Base angle 10.04. Wheelmade, flat base angle form a globular jar. Diam. 6cm (100%), post-hole F307, 3029.

5   JG7.12. Wheelmade, globular jar with simple, everted, neckless rim. Diam. 13cm (26%), Trench 1W, ditch A9, E108, fill E107.

O06.01

6   JW 1.04. Wheelmade, wide-mouthed jar with pointed bead rim. Diam. 24cm (16%), ditch A10, F130, 1042.

W11.2

7   Handle type 3. Handmade, two ribbed handle from a flagon. Trench 1W, ditch A6, E105, fill 105.

8   JK 7.3. Wheelmade, cooking pot with moderately splayed, everted rim and all over burnish. Diam. 19cm (23%), ditch A3, F301, 3022.

G04

9   JE 1.01. Wheelmade, necked jar with simple, plain rim with incised horizontal lines at girth. Diam. 22cm (31%), ditch A1, F300, 3007.

G06.8

10 JG 7.01. Wheelmade, globular jar with plain, everted rim. Diam. 12cm (22%), ditch A22, F158, 1092.

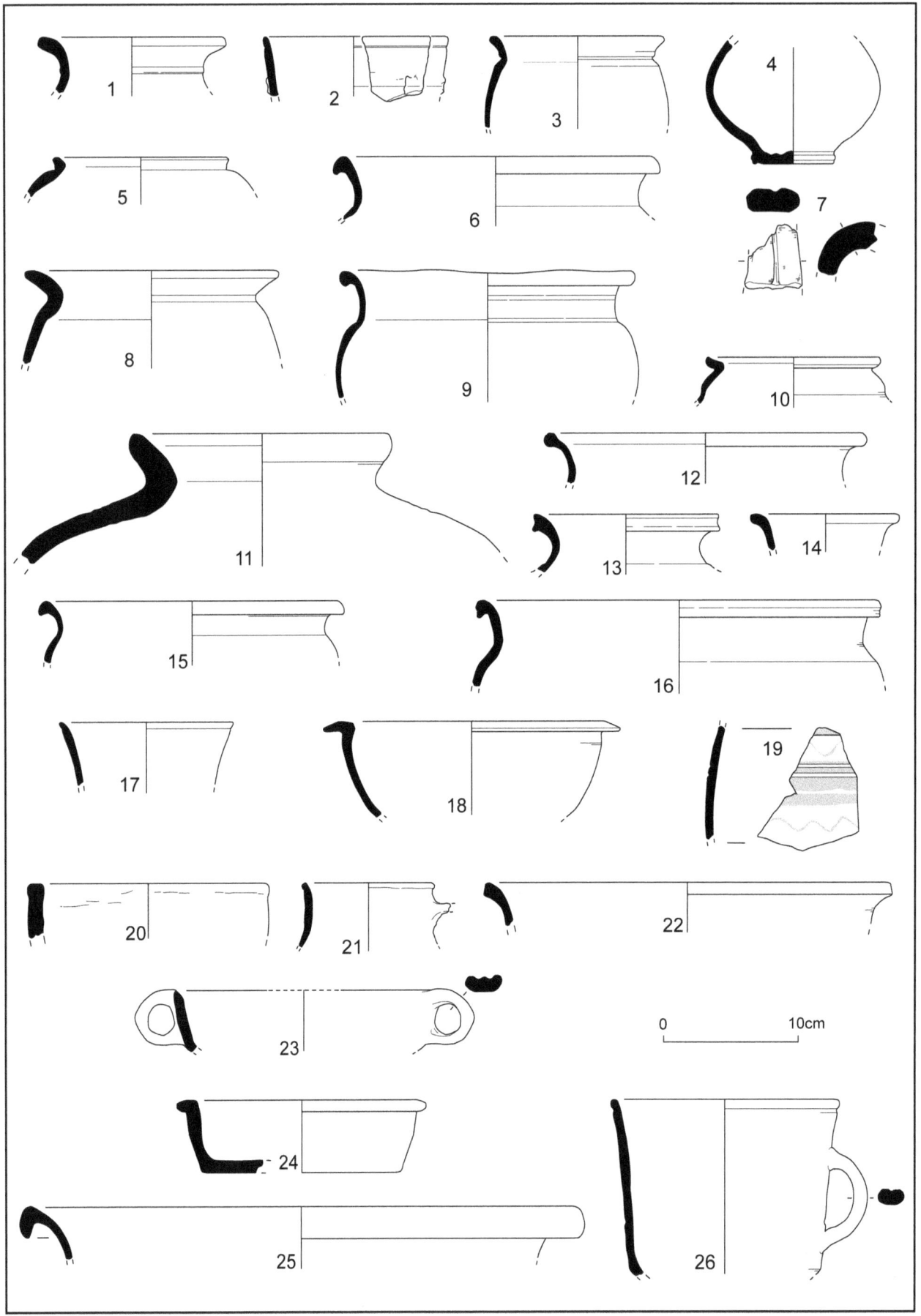

Figure 17. Area A, pottery, nos 1–26 (scale 1:4)

Phase 2

N02.1

11 JL 7.01. Handmade, storage jar with simple, everted rim. Diam. 20cm (23%), ditch A3, F301, 3022.

O02.1

12 JJ 13.02. Wheelmade, lid-seated jar with everted ledge rim. Diam. 24cm (12%), ditch A22, F158, 1101.

13 JL 2.01. Wheelmade, large storage jar with near even, bifid rim. Diam. 14cm (20%), ditch A7, F338, 3127.

14 JN 7.01. Wheelmade, narrow-mouthed jar with simple, everted rim. Diam. 11cm (16%), ditch A22, F158, 1092.

15 JW 1.04. Wheelmade, wide-mouthed jar with pointed-bead rim. Diam. 23cm (11%), ditch A3, F301, 3013.

16 JW 1.04. Wheelmade, wide-mouthed jar with pointed-bead rim. Diam. 30cm (23%), ditch A7, F338, 3127.

17 NA 1.12. Wheelmade, upright tankard with simple bead rim with groove. Diam. 13cm (11%), ditch A22, F158, 1107.

O03.1

18 BI 8.31. Wheelmade, bead and flanged rimmed bowl with simple rim. Diam. 22cm (60%), ditch A19, F376, 3154.

O06.10

19 Decorated body sherd. Wheelmade, decorated body sherd with SC. Ditch A23, F144, 1105.

Phase 1–2

N02.1

20 JK 22.05. Handmade, cooking pot with simple, plain rim. Diam. 18cm (7%), Trench 2, pit, F109, 1012.

O02.1

21 NA 1.12. Wheelmade, upright tankard with simple bead rim with groove. Diam. 10cm (37%), Trench 3, gully F118, 1021.

O02.13

22 JE 7.01. Wheelmade, necked jar with plain, everted rim. Diam. 30cm (16%), Trench 2, pit F109, 1012.

Phase 1–Phase 3

B02

23 DA 1.01. Wheelmade, straight-sided dish with simple rim and all-over burnish. Diam. 15cm (10%), Layer 3045.

N02.1

24 DA 8.31. Handmade, straight-sided dish with all-over burnish and external sooting. Diam. 19cm (26%), post-hole F321, 3038.

O02.1

25 JW 1.04. Wheelmade, wide-mouthed jar with pointed bead rim. Diam. 42cm (5%), gully F139, 1066.

26 NA 1.12. Wheelmade, upright tankard with simple bead rim with groove. Diam. 17cm (15%), post-hole F321, 3038.

Fig. 18.27–50

Phase 3

B02

27 DA 1.01. Wheelmade, straight-sided dish with simple rim and interlocking burnished arcs. Diam. 20cm (17%), surface F141, 1069.

28 DA 1.01. Wheelmade, straight-sided dish with simple bead rim and all over burnish with interlocking burnished arcs and external sooting. Diam. 16cm (33%), gully F310, 3032.

29 DA 1.12. Wheelmade, straight-sided dish with bead rim and slight groove. Interlocking burnished arcs. Diam. 20cm (6%), surface F141, 1069.

30 BI 8.25. Wheelmade, bead and flange-rimmed bowl with straight wall and dropped flange. All over burnishing. Diam. 20cm (22%), surface F141, 1069.

31 JK 7.3 Wheelmade, cooking pot with moderately splayed, everted rim. Diam. 15cm (13%), Trench 5W, ditch A33, cut E122, fill E121.

32 JK 7.3. Wheelmade, cooking pot with moderately splayed, everted rim. All-over burnish. Diam. 20cm (10%), surface F141, 1069.

C02

33 BKD 5.01. Wheelmade, globular/ bulbous beaker with plain cornice rim. Diam. 6cm (6%), surface F141, 1069.

G05

34 J1.01. Wheelmade, jar with simple plain rim. Diam. 16cm (6%), surface F141, 1069.

G06.5

35 BI 8.04. Wheelmade, bead and flange bowl with bead higher than flange. Diam. 20cm (8%), surface F141, 1069.

36 BI 8.04. Wheelmade, bead and flange bowl with bead higher than flange and external sooting. Diam. 20cm (6%), surface F141, 1069.

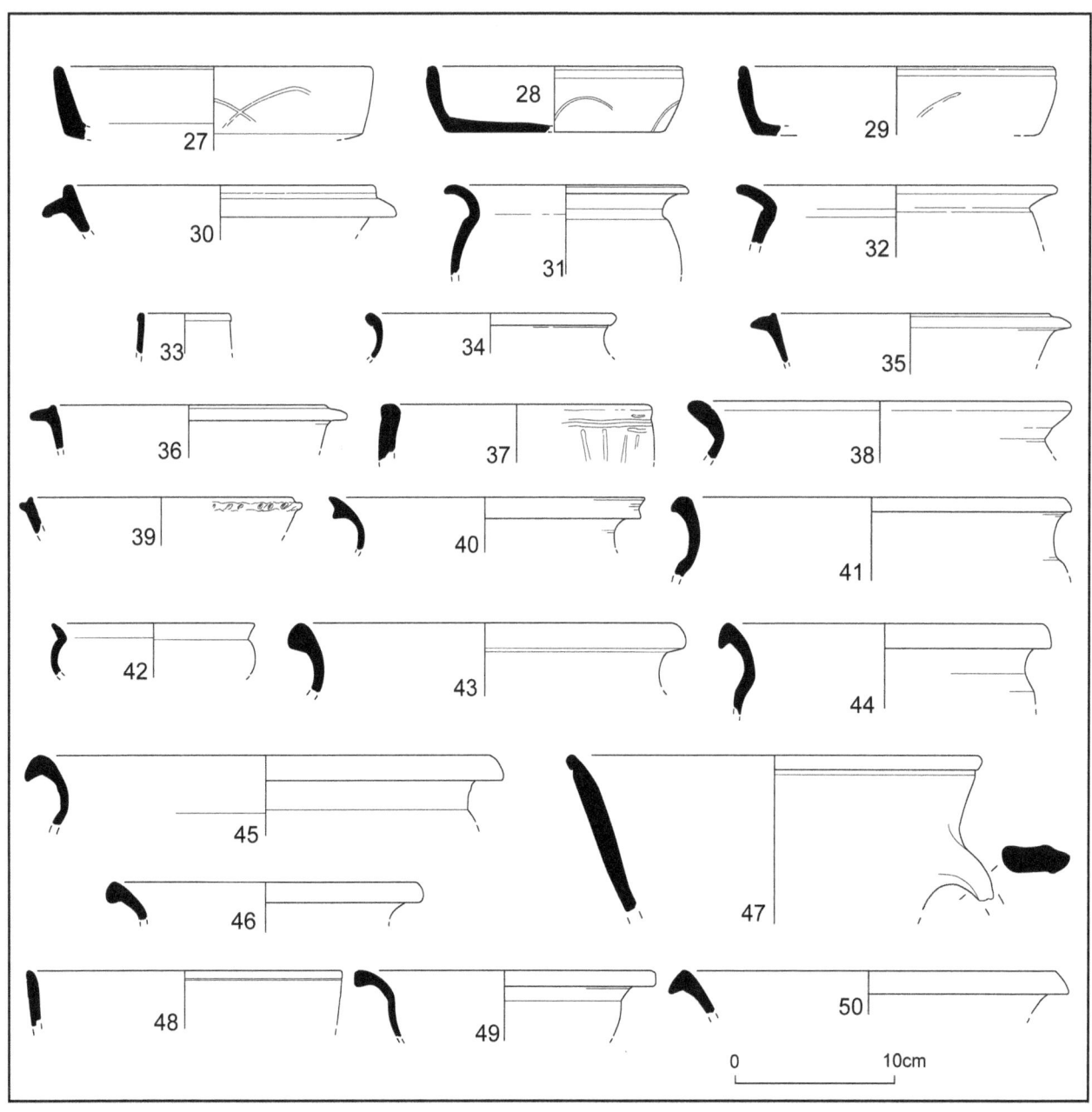

Figure 18. Area A, pottery, nos 27–50 (scale 1:4)

N02.1

37 JK 22.05. Handmade, cooking pot with near upright thickened rim. Burnished all over. Diam. 17cm (9%), post-hole, F328, 3071.

N02.2

38 JK7.01. Handmade, cooking pot with simple, everted rim. Diam. 24cm (11%), Trench 5W, ditch A33, E122, fill E121.

O02.1

39 BI 8.25. Wheelmade, bead and flanged rimmed bowl with straight wall and dropped flange. Incised oblique decorative lines. Diam. 18cm (8%), surface F141, 1069.

40 F 2.11. Wheelmade, flagon with shallow bifurcated rim. Diam. 20cm (5%), surface F141, 1069.

41 JE 1.04. Wheelmade, necked jar with pointed-bead rim. Diam. 25cm (5%), surface F141, 1069.

42 JG 7.01. Wheelmade, globular jar with simple, everted rim. Diam. 13cm (11%), surface F141, 1069.

43 JL 1.04. Wheelmade, large storage jar with pointed-bead rim. Diam. 25cm (16%), surface F141, 1069.

44 JW 1.04. Wheelmade, wide-mouthed jar with pointed-bead rim. Diam. 20cm (6%), gully A30, F319, 3051

45 JW 1.04. Wheelmade, wide-mouthed jar with pointed-bead rim. Diam. 30cm (12%), ditch A5, F153, 1084

Area A The Double-Ditched Enclosures (Field 2)

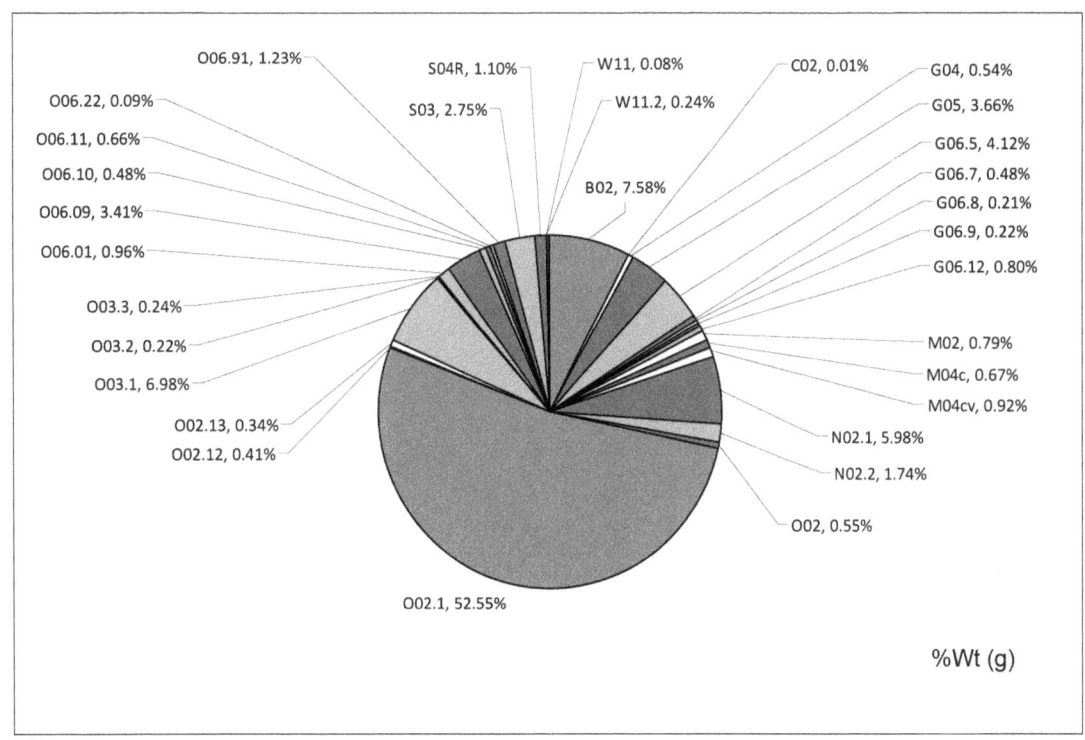

Figure 19. Area A, pottery, fabric groups by percentage weight

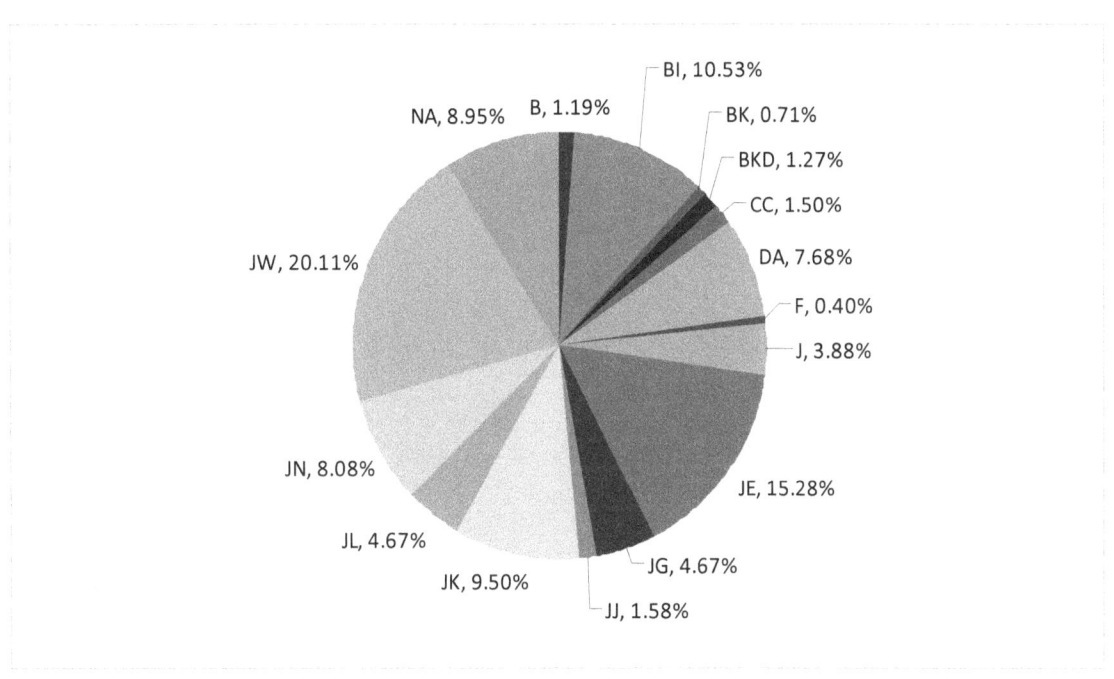

Figure 20. Area A, pottery, vessel classes by percentage rim EVE

46 JW 1.04. Wheelmade, wide-mouthed jar with pointed-bead rim. Diam. 20cm (14%), ditch A5, F153, 1090.

47 NA 1.12. Wheelmade, upright tankard with simple bead rim with groove. Diam. 13cm (15%), surface F141, 1069.

48 NA 1.12. Wheelmade, upright tankard with simple bead rim with groove. Diam. 20cm (8%), surface F141, 1069.

Phase 4

O02.1

49 JW 1.04. Wheelmade, wide-mouthed jar with pointed-bead rim, Diam. 19cm (18%), ploughsoil layer 3001.

O06.09

50 BI 8.31. Wheelmade, bead and flanged rimmed bowl. Diam. 25cm (16%), Trench 5W, ditch E124, fill E123.

Mortaria
by Kay Hartley

A total of 16 sherds were excavated, all from Phase 3 layer 1069 overlying Phase 1–Phase 3 surface F141.

Catalogue (not illustrated)

M02 (Fabric 3)

1 Fragment from a multi-reeded hammerhead mortarium made in the Mancetter-Hartshill potteries. Some burning. Later than AD 230 and, on balance, more likely to be second half of the 3rd century than the 4th. The fabric has been changed to drab shades of orange-brown by the soil conditions and only what may be a deposit on the surfaces bears any resemblance to the original cream colour of the common Mancetter-Hartshill fabric-type to which it belongs.

2 Fragment from a small mortarium with narrow, smooth hammerhead rim, out-tilted at the distal end. This type of small hammerhead, combined with thin wall, was made in the late 3rd or 4th century. Surface badly degraded. Fabric 3 (soft). Mancetter-Hartshill potteries. Probably part of No 12, but does not join.

M04cv (Fabric 2)

3 Footring with hole in the centre, possibly through wear. Oxford potteries. Burnt, discoloured and no slip survives. The fabric is degraded, but the trituration grit indicates an Oxford product. No slip survives, but only the red-slipped forms are recorded with footrings of this type. A date of AD 240–400 is therefore indicated. Joins No 9.

M04c (Fabric 1)

4 Joins No 10. Mortarium rim with right-facing side of spout. Oxford potteries. Form M18 (Young 1977). *c* AD 240–300.

5 Base and side fragment from a mortarium. Oxford potteries AD 100–400. This could be part of No 4, or No 16, but does not join.

M04cv (Fabric 2)

6 A basal fragment from either No 13 or another mortarium identical in fabric, source and date.

M02 (Fabric 3)

7 Fragment from a mortarium with smooth hammerhead rim out-tilted at distal end. Mancetter-Hartshill potteries. AD 250–350. See fabric description of No 1.

8 Bodysherd. Mancetter-Hartshill potteries. Later than AD 130. Probably not from No 1, but No 7 would be a possibility. See fabric description in No 1.

M04cv (Fabric 2)

9 Burnt bodysherd. Oxford potteries. Joins No 3.

M04c (Fabric 1)

10 Joins No 4. Body sherd. See No 4 for comments.

11 Bodysherd. Could well be part of No 4, but does not join. Oxford potteries.

M02 (Fabric 3)

12 Rim fragment probably from No 2, but does not join.

M04cv (Fabric 2)

13 Base fragment. Oxford potteries. The fabric is discoloured, but the trituration grit, red slip and the footring leave no doubt that this is from one of the red-slipped forms made in the Oxford potteries within the period AD 240–400.

14 Tiny bodysherd. Given the other sherds in this context, this can be attributed to Fabric 2 (no slip surviving), Oxford potteries. AD 240–400.

M04c (Fabric 1)

15 Bodysherd. Probably part of No 16 but does not join. Oxford potteries. Burnt black through most of the fabric, outer surface burnt to pink, with original cream colour surviving in centre.

16 Rim sherd from a mortarium of form M18 (Young 1977) made in the Oxford potteries *c* AD 240–300. Heavily burnt to black throughout with pink deposit on part of the surface. Probably part of No 4, but does not join.

Discussion

Sixteen sherds from a minimum of six different vessels were recognised. All the sherds have suffered from burning or environmental conditions in the deposit, or both, to the point that several of the Oxford sherds would not be identifiable without the trituration grit; all this, despite the fact that the fabric produced in both of these potteries survives well in adverse conditions. Three of the mortaria are from the Oxford potteries and three from the Mancetter-Hartshill potteries. As a group they best fit a date in the late 3rd century, but a date in the early 4th would be possible.

Samian pottery
by Steven Willis

Introduction

Some 26 sherds of samian (*terra sigillata*) were recovered during the evaluation and excavation, twelve from the former and 14 from the latter works. Ten vessels are represented. The sherds are, in general, not in a good condition and have clearly been subject to hostile soil environments.

Catalogue

The catalogue lists all the samian sherds submitted for identification and dating. The catalogue adheres to a consistent format. Sherds are listed in order by context number, then the following data are given for each distinct vessel: the number of sherds and their type (i.e. whether a sherd is from the rim, base (footring) or body of a vessel), the source of the item (Central Gaulish is abbreviated to CG and East Gaulish to EG), the vessel form (where identifiable), the weight of the sherds in grams, the percentage of any extant rim (i.e. the RE figure, where 1.00 would represent a complete circumference) or base (i.e. the BE figure) and the rim and base diameters, and an estimate of the date of the sherd in terms of calendar years (this being the date range of deposits with which like pieces are normally associated). None warrants illustration.

Evaluation, Trench 5W, ditch A33, W122, fill W121, Phase 3

1–2 One base sherd and a conjoining body sherd, EG Rheinzabern, Walters 79, 152g, BE: 0.46. Diam. 96mm, *c* AD 160–240. The sherds are somewhat abraded.

3 Ten sherds from the same vessel, CG Lezoux, probably Drag. 27, 3g, *c* AD 120–160. Virtually excoriated.

Area A excavation

Ditch A7, F121.01, 1040, Phase 2

4 Body sherd, CG Lezoux, possibly Drag. 37, 1g, *c* AD 120–200. Virtually excoriated.

Ditch A7, F338.02, 3096, Phase 2

5–11 Four rim sherds, 1 base sherd and 2 body sherds, CG Lezoux, Ludowici Th, 352g, RE: 0.19. Diam. 270mm, BE: 1.00, Diam. 100mm, *c* AD 165–200. Virtually excoriated; heavily weathered; no stamp.

12 Body sherd, CG Lezoux, Drag. 31R (different vessel from item represented by sherd No 6 in F141), 17g, *c* AD 160–200. Virtually excoriated.

Surface F141, 1069, Phase 3

13 Base sherd, CG Lezoux, Drag. 37, 25g, BE: 0.12. Diam. *c* 110m, *c* AD 140–200. Heavily weathered and virtually excoriated. No decoration is represented.

14 Base sherd, CG Lezoux, Drag. 31R, 20g, BE: 0.12. Diam. 120mm, *c* AD 160–200. Excoriated.

15 Base sherd (fragment from footring), CG Lezoux, form not identifiable, 3g, BE: 0.06. Diam. *c* 110mm, *c* AD 120–200. Excoriated.

16 Body sherd, CG Lezoux, probably Drag. 37, 5g, *c* AD 120–200. Excoriated. No decoration is extant.

Post-hole F337, 3084, Phase 3

17 Body sherd, EG Rheinzabern, Drag. 31R, 19g, *c* AD 160–240.

Discussion of the samian pottery

Ten samian vessels are represented amongst the pottery from the excavations (including the evaluation). The chronology of these items is summarised in Table 3. There is no South Gaulish samian and nothing of 1st-century AD date. Typologically the earliest item is the likely Drag. 27 cup, dating to the Hadrianic–early Antonine period, from the evaluation; otherwise the earliest items were all Antonine in date. Although the sample is small the emphasis is clearly Antonine, and there are three vessels at least dating to the period *c* AD 160–200. The Antonine era was the period in which samian importation into Britain, principally from Lezoux, was at its greatest (cf. Willis 1998; 2005; contra Marsh 1981) and the period *c* AD 160–190 is often a peak in any graph plotting numbers of samian vessels at a British site over time. Potentially all the items here may be Antonine arrivals, from *c* AD 140 onwards, though not necessarily so. The two samian vessels represented by sherds recovered during the evaluation (see catalogue) have date ranges consistent with the sherds from the excavation. There are two East Gaulish vessels amongst the total of ten vessels; as their date ranges suggest, they could have arrived on the site in the 3rd century. Often at sites it seems that some proportion of 2nd-century Lezoux vessels will have been in use into the 3rd century.

Table 3. Area A, samian, summary of chronology

Period	No of Vessels Represented
Hadrianic – early Antonine	1
Hadrianic – Antonine	3
Antonine	1
Mid Antonine – late Antonine	3
Mid Antonine – mid-3rd century	1
Total	9

Table 4. Area A, samian, composition by fabric, form and functional type

Form Type	CG Lezoux	EG Rheinzabern
Cups		
Drag. 27	1	-
Decorated Bowls		
Drag. 37	3	-
Plain Bowls		
Drag. 31R	2	1
Dishes		
Drag. 18/31R	1	-
Ludowici Th	1	-
Platters		
Walters 79	-	1
Totals	8	2
(Form not identifiable)	1	-
Aggregate Totals	9	2

Note: number of vessels represented attributable to specific form classes; includes all items.

Table 4 summarises the forms/ functional types present. Since this is such a small sample (from an amalgam of contexts) nothing substantive can be concluded regarding the composition of the group by form. The presence of perhaps three decorated bowls of form Drag. 37 is potentially noteworthy and might be an indicator of some comparative wealth at this site. The occurrence of the plain dish, Ludowici Th, is of intrinsic interest since this is a rare form. This vessel approximates to the examples illustrated by Oswald and Pryce (1920, pl. LVIII, nos 3 and 4). An unusually large portion of this vessel was recovered, coming from ditch A7 (F338.02, fill 3096); this may not be significant, although one may note that at rural sites in Britain there is a strong trend for rare samian forms, when present, to occur whole or in large part, and potentially to be associated with burials, watery contexts, or structured deposits.

It is often instructive when considering the character of a site to examine the proportion that samian forms within any phased pottery groups, as it is clear that the proportions generally correlate with site type (cf. Willis 1998; 2005). Amongst the present assemblage, the pottery assigned to the main site phases represents a sizeable sample and in principle should provide a reasonably reliable indicator of the frequency of samian consumption at this site during its most intensive period. The percentages formed by samian amongst these phases are minimal. Although the samian is a very small proportion in absolute terms, comparison with similar data from other rural sites of 2nd- and 3rd-century date reveals these percentage frequency figures to be consistent with the general pattern at rural sites in Britain where, in the majority of cases, samian proportions by weight are around 2% or less (Willis 2005). Contrastingly, military sites and major civil centres have much higher proportions of samian present.

In so far as samian is a fine table ware its presence at sites is conventionally taken to be an index of affluence and status, being for social display and even a statement of cultural alignment. That rural sites, such as this particular example, have only very low levels of samian present during the 2nd to 3rd centuries demonstrates that they were not normally using samian to advertise wealth. The Longdales Road site seems typical: as at numerous other rural sites of the Roman era, samian ware is, predictably, present, but occurs with a frequency that implies that it was either not employed in everyday use or, if in fact it was in very regular use, formed a small, if conspicuous, part in the procedures of eating and drinking.

Pottery discussion
by Annette Hancocks

The assemblage, although of medium size, is significant at both local and regional level. Very few ceramic assemblages of this type have been recorded to date from within the West Midlands conurbation. The assemblage is of broadly 2nd–4th-century AD date and is indicative of low-status, small-scale, rural Romano-British domestic occupation. Previously, ceramic assemblages have been recovered from military sites, such as Metchley Roman Fort (Green et al. 2001; Hancocks et al. 2005; Evans and Hancocks 2005) and it is only recently that ceramics of the later Romano-British period have begun to be uncovered within the Birmingham locality.

The low level of occurrence may be socially and economically significant. The principal importance of rural assemblages, particularly where they are relatively small, is through comparative study, as representative of a class or classes of site and assemblage which may be situated within a region with considerable diversity of site/ assemblage types. This links to topics such as status (Willis 1997, 55).

The artifact assemblage is comparable with other similar small assemblages from Worcestershire, such as Norton and Lenchwick (Jackson et al. 1996a), Hoarstone Farm (Jackson et al. 1996b) and Frankley (Jackson and Hancocks 1996). All these reflect the dominance of locally and regionally produced Severn Valley and Malvernian wares. There is a distinct lack of finewares in this assemblage, with the exception of a small amount of samian.

Plate 4. Area A, excavation in progress, view: northeast

Plate 5. Area A, excavation in progress within Enclosure A1–A2, view: southeast

Plate 6. Area A, Enclosure A1 sub-enclosure, view: south

Chapter 3

Area B   The Livestock Herding Structures (Field 1)

RESULTS
by Alex Jones and Josh Williams

Phasing

A scheme of four phases, specific to Area B (Fig. 4), has been defined, as follows:

Phase 1	Early enclosure (B1), the first livestock 'funnel', early 2nd century
Phase 2	Later occupation, later 2nd–early 3rd century
Phase 3A–B	Latest Romano-British activity, including livestock 'funnel', early 3rd–mid-4th century; subdivided, as follows: Phase 3A Latest livestock 'funnel' Phase 3B Disuse of road surface F442
Phase 4	Post-Roman activity

Phasing Area B is difficult, because much of the identifiable pottery is dated to the 2nd century AD. The results of the Area C–D investigations which examined the Ryknild Street frontage in Field 1 are described in Chapter 4 (below).

The features were cut into the natural subsoil, a red-brown clay (4002) with patches of white-yellow sand.

Phase 1: Early enclosure (B1), the first livestock 'funnel', early 2nd century (Figs 21–23, Plate 7)

The main feature of this phase was the northwestern angle of a ditched enclosure (Enclosure B1). Further short ditch lengths cut to the west of the enclosure ditch were probably associated.

Description of Phase 1 features

Enclosure B1 was represented by the northern end of its western side (B6, Fig. 23.S.1–S.2) and the extreme western terminal of its northern side (B5). The remaining sides of the enclosure lay outside Area B – and were not recorded as continuing within other nearby investigations (see Chapters 4 and 5, below). Within Area B, the excavated length of the western side of the enclosure comprised two ditch sections with a slight change of angle, both cut to a U-shaped profile and measuring a total of 37m in length. This ditch was both wider (c 1.15m) and deeper (c 0.5m) to the north of the change of angle than to the south (c 0.6m and c 0.3m respectively). The change of angle was further defined by an east-west aligned ditch (B7), measuring a maximum of 0.6m in width and between 0.1–0.3m in depth. It was recorded for a length of 6m to the west of the enclosure. Ditch B7 was cut by ditch B6. The northern enclosure ditch (B5) was recorded for a length of only 3m. It was cut to a U-shaped profile and measured 1.03m in width and 0.32m in depth. A single post-hole (F415, Fig. 21) further defined the angle of the enclosure and a second post-hole (F436, Fig. 21) was cut along ditch B6. No contemporary features could be identified within the small part of the enclosure interior that was excavated.

Other Phase 1 features were located to the west of Enclosure B1. An L-shaped ditch (B8, Fig. 23.S.3) outside Enclosure B1 was probably contemporary, although misaligned with its western side. Ditch B8 measured 0.6m in width, and 0.3m in depth. Further to the north was the northern terminal of a further ditch (B10, Fig. 23.S.4) cut parallel with, and 3m to the west of, the western side of Enclosure B1 and approximately flush with the northeastern angle of Field 2. Ditch B10 measured a maximum of 1m in width and 0.2m in depth. Only the northernmost 5m of ditch B10 survived later Romano-British disturbance (see below).

Enclosure B1 ditches B5 and B6 were backfilled with grey-orange silt-clay. Ditch B7 was backfilled with grey silt-clay. Ditch B8 was backfilled with mixed yellow-grey silt-clay. Ditch B10 was backfilled with grey clay-silt.

Finds and dating evidence from Phase 1 features

Overall, the Phase 1 features only produced small quantities of pottery, including organic Severn Valley wares and sandy wares. Ditch B6 (Enclosure B1) contained sherds of samian dated AD 120–160).

Interpretation of Phase 1 features

From the partial evidence provided by the Area B excavation alone, the layout or function of Enclosure B1 cannot be interpreted. The positioning of external ditches B7 and B8, and in particular that of north-south aligned ditch B10, suggests an arrangement for the running of stock, notably between ditches B10 and B6. Ditches B8 and B10 may therefore have formed a 'funnel' for livestock, similar to that recorded in a banjo enclosure (e.g. Fasham 1987).

The discoveries in Area A may help to provide a broader context for Enclosure B1. In particular, the eastern boundary of modern Field 2 is interpreted as defining one side of a Romano-British livestock compound, forming part of the Enclosure A1–A2 layout (Chapter 2 above; see Fig. 4 for modern field boundaries respecting the line of the Romano-British compound ditches). Returning to the Phase 1 arrangement in Area B, it is notable that the northwestern angle of Enclosure B1 and the northern terminal of ditch B10 are positioned approximately flush with the

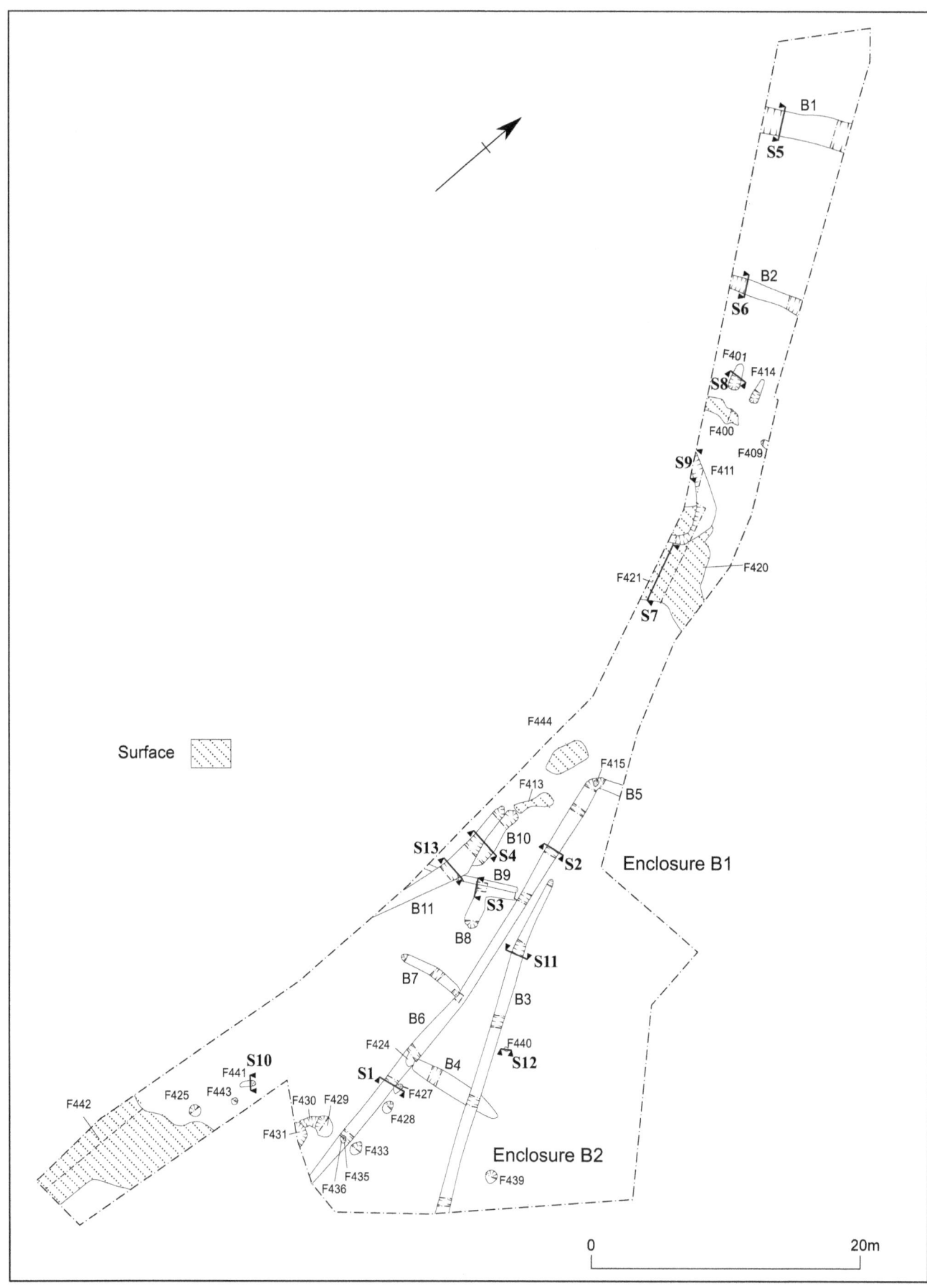

Figure 21. Area B, simplified plan, features of all phases (scale 1:400)

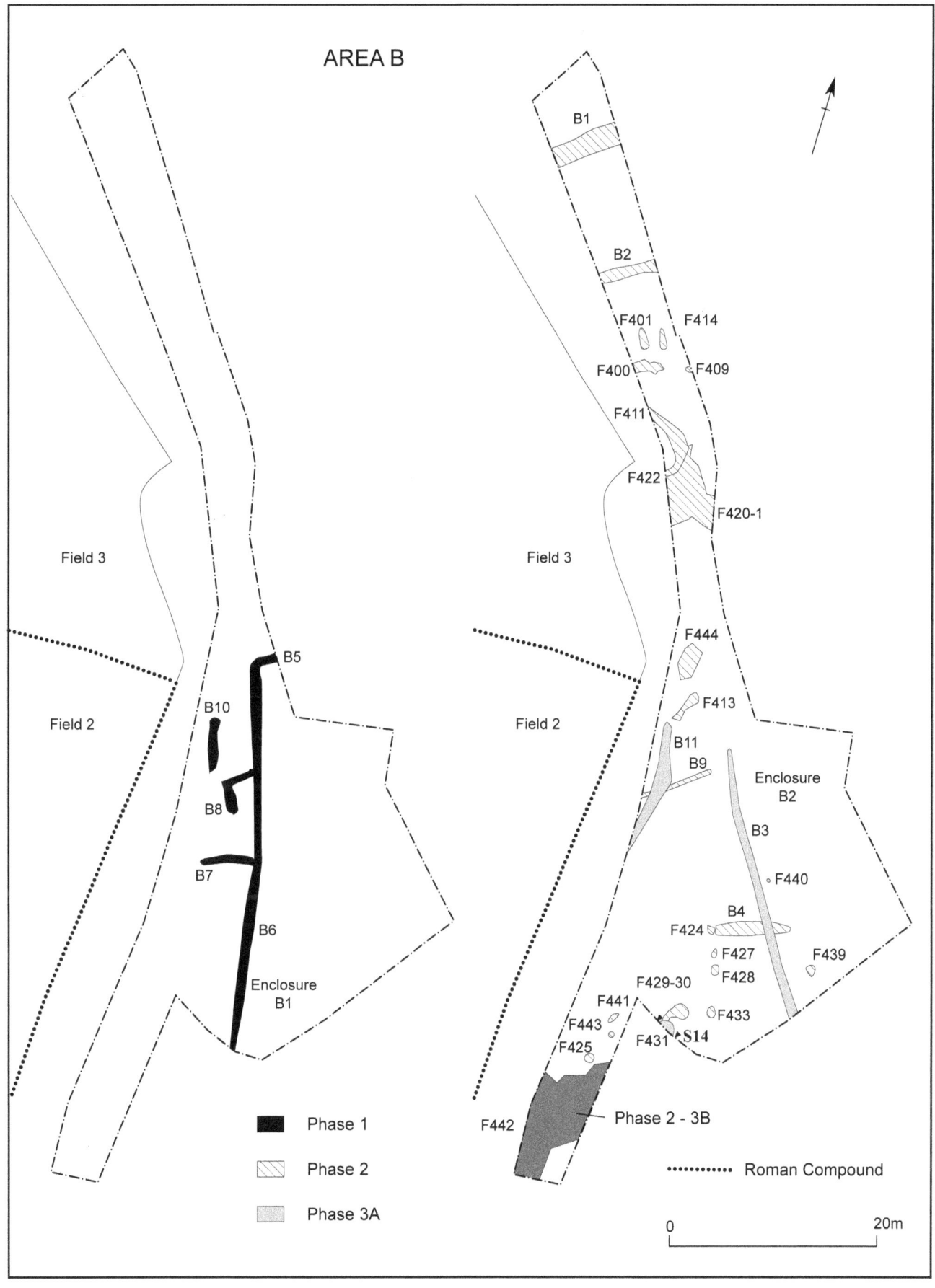

Figure 22. Area B, phase plans (scale 1:500)

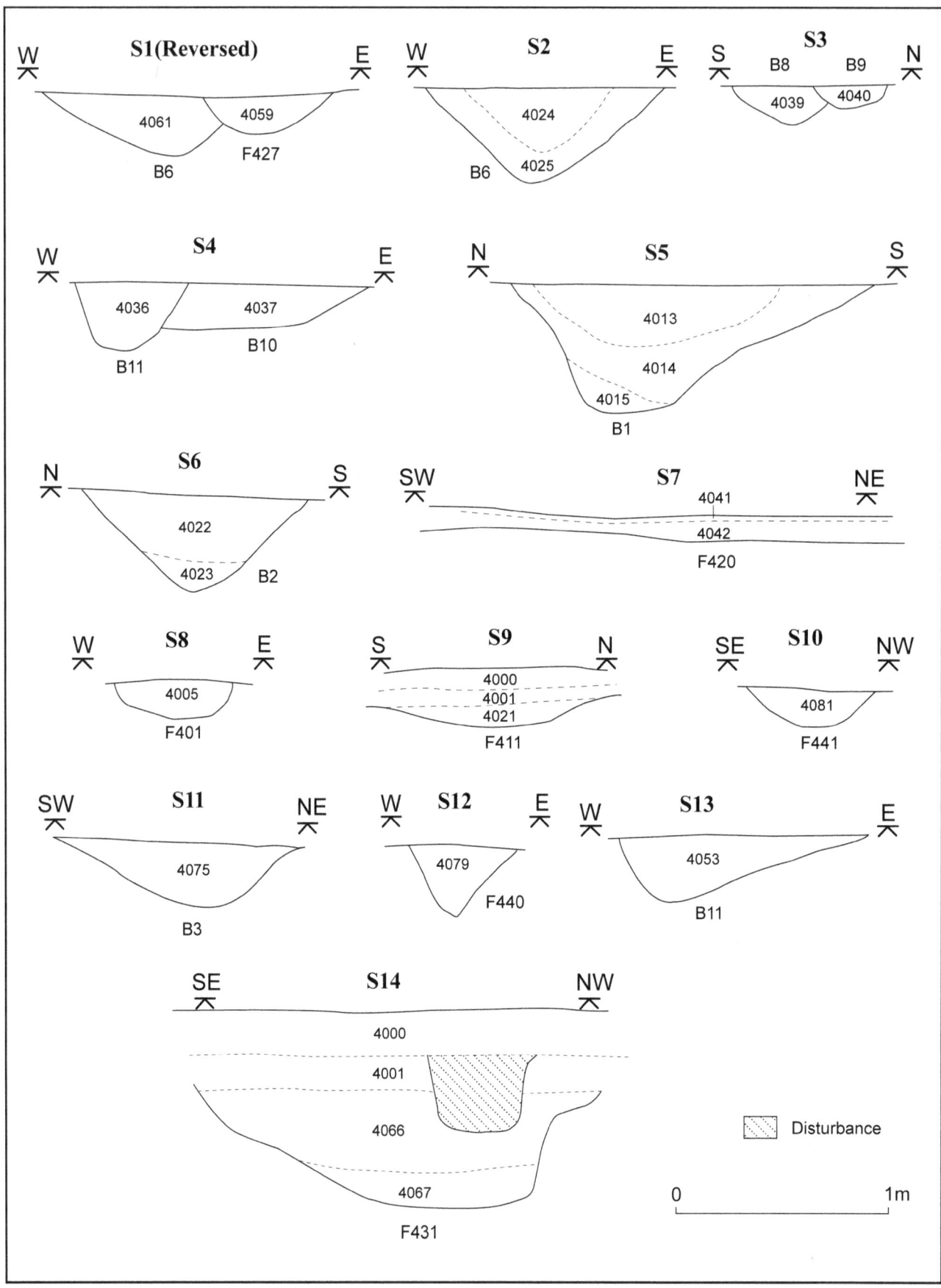

Figure 23. Area B, sections (scale 1:25)

northeastern corner of this Romano-British compound. This combined layout may suggest an arrangement for the control, or sorting, of livestock corralled within that field, further considered in Chapter 6. The limited dating evidence suggests that Phase 1 was broadly contemporary in Areas A and B, as would be suggested by the apparently complimentary layouts.

The apparent discontinuities between the ditched layouts recorded in Area B and in Area C–D closer to the road frontage (Chapter 4 below) may suggest that the roadside plots recorded in Area C–D terminated between that area and the Area B excavation. An exception is the road surface (6147), recorded in the south of Plot A, which continued into Area B (as F442, see below).

Phase 2: Later occupation, later 2nd century–early 3rd century

The majority of the features identified were cut in Phase 2, and they were also more extensive than those of the previous phase. These comprised ditches, pits, post-holes, an eaves-drip gully and areas of stone surfacing, one of the latter continuing in use into Phase 3B (see below).

Description of Phase 2 features

In the north of the area investigated were two ditches (B1 and B2), cut on a roughly east-west alignment. Both ditches were dug to a stepped, U-shaped profile. Ditch B1 (Fig. 23.S.5) was 1.6m wide and 0.55m deep, and ditch B2 (Fig. 23.S.6) was 1m wide and 0.44m in depth. The ditches were not recorded as continuing to the east within areas examined by the watching brief and Area D excavation (Fig. 4). In particular, the arrangement of ditches B1 and B2 did not clearly conform with the layout of plot boundaries recorded in Area D to the east (Chapter 4 below).

A shallow, east-west aligned gully (B9, Fig. 23.S.3) was recorded further to the south. It cut Phase 1 ditch B8 and was truncated by Phase 3 ditch B11 (see below). The eastern terminal of a curvilinear gully (F430), joining a pit (F429), was located just inside the southeastern limit of the excavated area. The pit measured 1.6m in diameter and 0.4m in depth. Gully F430 was truncated by a Phase 3 pit (see below).

Other Phase 2 features belonged to structures and pebble surfaces (F400, F420, Fig. 23.S.7; F421, F413, F442 and F444). These may have been remnants of formerly more extensive pebble surfaces, as is suggested by the quantity of pebbles noted in the excavation baulks. Similar pebble surfaces were recorded within Area A (Chapter 2 above). Surface F442 was aligned approximately northeast-southwest and measured approximately 5m in width. Surface F444 contained larger river pebbles than those recorded elsewhere in Area B and also included numerous heat-shattered pebbles within its matrix.

The northernmost group of Phase 2 structural features comprised two parallel, roughly north-south aligned beam-slots (F401, Fig. 23.S.8; and F414) and the eastern part of a ring-gully (F411, Fig. 23.S.9). The beam-slots measured 2m in length, 0.3m in width and 0.05m in depth. The eaves-drip gully was irregular in plan, probably measuring 7m in diameter. It was cut to a width of 0.5m and a depth of 0.1m. This eaves-drip gully was the only feature in Area B to contain a large number of unabraded sherds of Romano-British pottery.

Three pebble-filled post-pads (F428, F433 and F439) were located further to the south. These features may possibly have defined the extreme northwestern angle of a timber-framed building. The post-pads measured an average of 0.8m in diameter and were 0.55m in depth. Two post-holes (F424 and F427) were located to the northwest of the building. Post-hole F427 was cut into backfilled Phase 1 ditch B6. An east-west band of cobbles (B4, 5m in length), possibly infilling a beam-slot, could have defined the northern external wall of the same building. To the north of surface F442 were two small pits (F443 and F425) and a short length of a beam-slot (F441, Fig. 23.S.10).

Ditch B1 was backfilled with blue-grey clay-silt. Ditch B2 was backfilled with blue-grey silt-clay sealed by dark grey silt-clay. Ring-gully F411 was backfilled with grey sand-silt. Pit F429 and gully F430 were both backfilled with light grey clay-silt. The post-pads comprised pebbles set within a matrix of grey silt. Pit F425 was backfilled with grey silt-clay and adjoining post-hole F443 was backfilled with grey silt-sand.

Finds and dating evidence from Phase 2 features

The coarse pottery from the Phase 2 feature backfills was dated to the mid–late 2nd century, possibly extending into the early 3rd century. The Severn Valley ware was characterised by jars of mid–late 2nd-century date, and jars or bowls of 2nd or 3rd century date, or late 2nd- to 3rd-century date. Also found was a Black Burnished ware jar BB1 dating to the 2nd or 3rd century. Ditches B2 and B4 contained mortaria dating to the 2nd century, and to the 2nd–4th century, respectively.

Structure B1 ring-gully F411 and pit F429 contained samian dating AD 120–200. Post-hole F424 within Structure B2 contained samian sherds dating AD 150–200 (x4), 120–150 and 120–200 (x2). Quantities of samian and mortaria were recovered from surface F420, the samian dating to AD 120–200, 160–200 and 150–200, and the mortaria dating to AD 170–190, 180–240, the 3rd century, and the 2nd–4th century, including products in Oxfordshire ware and from Mancetter-Hartshill.

Interpretation of Phase 2 features

Ditch B1 may perhaps represent part of the boundary between Plots C and D, as recorded in Area D (Chapter 4 below), although not exactly coincident with that boundary. Ditch B2 was not recognised closer to the Ryknild Street frontage or in the adjoining watching brief. Ditches B1 and B2 were cut approximately 15m apart (measured centre to centre). They may have formed the flanking ditches to an east-west aligned metalled road or droveway. Surface F421 to the south may have formed part of the east-west aligned roadway separating Plots C and D in Area D (Chapter 4 below). Ring-gully F411 was probably cut into the surface after it had gone out of use.

The other Phase 2 features are more difficult to interpret. The arrangement of the post-pad group, in particular features F424, F427–8 and F433, may suggest that they defined one side of a building or possibly a fence. Finally, surface F442 in the extreme south of the area investigated formed part of the metalled road forming the southern limit of Plot A in Area D (Chapter 4 below). The excavated part of this surface in Area B (F442) may have been located near a change in alignment, which may explain the greater width of the surface at this point. A possibility is that the surface turned to the south, respecting the eastern edge of Field 2, which itself respected the eastern side of the Romano-British compound (Fig. 4).

Phase 3A–Phase 3B: Latest Romano-British activity, including livestock 'funnel', early 3rd–mid-4th century

Phase 3A: Latest livestock 'funnel'

Description and interpretation of Phase 3A features

Phase 3A was represented by the abandonment of the Phase 2 buildings and by the cutting of two parallel ditches which possibly formed part of a 'funnel' associated with livestock herding.

The main feature of this phase was a mainly northwest-southeast aligned ditch (B3, Fig. 23.S.11), recorded for a distance of 25m. The ditch was cut through Phase 2 feature B4 and into the subsoil. The ditch was cut in two contiguous sections, with a slight change of angle. It was shallower towards its northern terminal. The ditch was cut with a U-shaped profile and measured a maximum of 1m in width and 0.27m in depth. A small post-hole (F440, Fig. 22.S.12), cut just to the east of the ditch, may also have belonged to this phase.

Few other features were assigned to this phase. A mainly north-south aligned ditch (B11, Enclosure B2, Fig. 23.S.13) was recorded for a length of 13m to the west of ditch B3. Ditch B11 was cut into Phase 1 ditch B10, Phase 2 gully B9, and the subsoil. Like ditch B3, ditch B11 was cut in two contiguous sections. The change in angle recorded along both ditches was approximately flush, suggesting that both were contemporary. The entrance gap recorded between the northern terminals of ditches B3 and B11 measured approximately 6m. Ditch B11 measured a maximum of 1.2m in width and 0.35m in depth. A large pit (F431, Fig. 23.S.14) was recorded, cutting Phase 2 gully F430 on the southern edge of the area excavated. The pit was roughly circular (*c* 1.5m in diameter) and 0.45m deep. The lower fills of the pit appeared to be very charcoal-rich and organic although no charred plant remains were recovered.

Ditch B3 was backfilled with grey-brown silt-sand, and associated ditch B11 was backfilled with grey clay-silt. Pit F431 was backfilled with grey silt-clay.

Contemporary Phase 3 ditches B3 and B11 together may have formed a 'funnel' arrangement, used for the sorting of stock, as suggested in particular by their parallel, slightly outward change of angle towards the point of junction which formed the entrance. The 'entrance' between the two Phase 3 ditches was approximately flush with the extreme northeastern corner of Field 2, which may have been originally laid out as a compound in the Romano-British period. This Phase 3A ditch arrangement suggests a return to animal husbandry, as suggested by the evidence from Phase 1 in Area B, although the small size of the area investigated should be noted.

Finds and dating evidence from Phase 3A–B features

The coarse wares from Phase 3A feature backfills all pre-dated the latest Phase 2 activity; this dating and the low average sherd weight recorded suggests that the Phase 3 pottery, including late 2nd–3rd century Severn Valley wares, was redeposited. Phase 3B surface F442 was associated with samian pottery dating AD 120–200, and mortaria dating AD 140+, 150–170+, and AD 250–350+. A quantity of pottery was dropped or discarded onto surface F442.

Phase 3B: Disuse of road surface F442

Description and interpretation of Phase 3B features

The southernmost Phase 2 surface F442 (Plate 8) probably continued in use into Phase 3B (see below). Part of this surface was sealed by an ashy silt layer (4083, not illustrated) which contained charred plant remains. This represented the latest datable deposit within this area that had accumulated after the disuse of this surface. As such, layer 4083 may be contemporary with the cutting of the ditched Enclosure E2 (Chapter 4 below), across the road surface further to the east – both events marking the abandonment of the road.

Phase 4: Post-Roman activity

The post-Roman deposits comprised the topsoil and modern field drains.

FINDS

Romano-British pottery
by C Jane Evans

Introduction

The Area B fieldwork produced total of 1,372 sherds of Romano-British pottery weighing 10.7kg, 31 sherds coming from trial-trenching in 2002 and 1,341 sherds from the main excavation. The pottery came from 32 stratified

Table 5. Area B, Romano-British coarse ware pottery, summary of the assemblage by phase

Phase	Qty	% Qty	Wt (g)	% Wt	Average Sherd Wt (g)	Rim EVE	% Rim EVE
1	22	1.60%	119	1.11%	5	5.05	43.0%
2	616	44.90%	4,585	42.70%	7	4.55	38.70%
3B	498	36.30%	4,469	41.63%	9	0.53	4.50%
3A	88	6.40%	439	4.09%	5	0.02	0.20%
4	4	0.30%	15	0.14%	4	-	-
Unphased	113	8.20%	685	6.38%	6	1.02	8.70%
Trial-trench	31	2.30%	424	3.95%	14	0.58	4.90%
Total	1,372	100.0%	10,736	100.0%	8	11.75	100.0%

Note that the total average sherd weight is based on calculation of the total number of sherds and the total sherd weight

contexts, 18 of which produced less than 10 sherds. A total of 84% of the pottery by weight came from stratified contexts (Table 5). The assemblage provides an important body of data from an area for which few Romano-British pottery assemblages have been published.

Methodology

The pottery was recorded using the Birmingham Archaeology coding system, used during analysis of the Area A assemblage (Hancocks Chapter 2, above). Fabrics were recorded with reference to the Area A fabric series, cross referenced where possible with the National Roman Fabric Reference Collection (NRFRC, Tomber and Dore 1998) and the Metchley fabric and form series (Green et al. 2001; Hancocks et al. 2005; Evans et al. forthcoming). Precise form types and broad vessel classes (for example bowl, flagon, mortarium) were both recorded, where identifiable. The fabrics and forms are listed and described below (Table 6, Figs 24–26, Appendix B1–B2). Evidence for manufacture (wasters), use (sooting) and repair (rivets and rivet holes) was recorded where evident. However, the assemblage was extremely abraded by the acidic soils on site and little surface evidence survived. Enough diagnostic forms were present to provide dating evidence for activity. Where possible these have been illustrated by fabric (Fig. 25), published parallels being cited for more fragmentary rims. The assemblage was quantified by sherd count, weight and rim EVE. Data for base EVEs are recorded in the archive. The pottery data was analysed in relation to the recorded stratigraphy by means of an access database.

Taphonomy

The vast bulk of the pottery was associated with Phase 2 and Phase 3B activity (Table 5). The smallest phase assemblage (four sherds) came from post-Roman Phase 4.

As well as being abraded, the pottery was very fragmentary; the overall average sherd weight was 8g, and as low as 4–5g in Phases 1, 3 and 4 (Table 5). This may partly reflect the soil conditions, or abrasion. Also significant may be the fact that so much of the pottery (65% by weight) came from layers overlying pebble surfaces (Table 6). These layers would have been subject to trampling. However, even the pottery from these surfaces had higher average sherd weights than the pottery from the ditches and pits (Table 6). This suggests that the pottery in these cut features may have been redeposited. The least fragmentary pottery came from the ring-gully, Structure B1.

Chronology

Detailed lists of forms and fabrics by phase can be found in Appendices B3–B4.

Phase 1

The Phase 1 ditches, gullies and pit produced very small quantities of pottery (Table 5). The only diagnostic form was a Drag 18/31R plate or bowl, dated AD 120–160 (Willis below). Fabrics (Appendix B4) included organic-tempered Severn Valley ware (Fabrics O03.1), associated elsewhere with 1st- and 2nd-century activity, and a narrow range of other oxidised Severn Valley wares and sandy wares.

Phase 2

The largest assemblage came from features associated with Phase 2. This assemblage included a range of forms (Appendix B3) and fabrics (Appendix B4).

The datable forms indicated a mid to late 2nd-century phase of activity, possibly extending into the early 3rd century. Latest amongst these forms were an Oxfordshire white mortarium dated AD 180–240 (Hartley below; Young 1977, fig. 20), and a Mancetter Hartshill mortarium dating to AD 170–190, both from pebble surface F420, 4041 (Hartley below). Further dating evidence was provided by 24 sherds of Central Gaulish samian, most dated broadly AD 120–200. Six sherds came from cobbled surfaces (F420, 4041–4042). One of these, a Drag 31R bowl, was dated to AD 160–200. Post-pad F424 (4052) produced a Drag. 31 bowl of a similar date. No 3rd-century samian was recovered although, as Willis notes below, vessels may have remained in use into the 3rd century. Coarse wares included a BB1 jar (not illustrated), also dating to the 2nd

Table 6. Area B, Romano-British coarse ware pottery, fabrics, sources and quantities

Common Name, NRFRC Fabric Code	Fabric Code	Qty	% Qty	Wt (g)	% Wt	Rim EVE	% Rim EVE
Grog-tempered wares	F010	20	1.5%	916	8.5%	-	-
	F011	7	0.5%	24	0.2%	0.18	1.5%
Reduced ware, Sandy	G06.05	8	0.6%	181	1.7%	-	-
	G06.07	3	0.2%	20	0.2%	-	-
	G06.09	35	2.6%	279	2.6%	0.14	1.2%
Oxidised ware, Sandy	O06.01	14	1.0%	88	0.8%	0.27	2.3%
	O06.05	2	0.1%	5	0.1%	-	-
	O06.09	43	3.1%	388	3.6%	0.5	4.3%
Oxidised ware, Grog	O06.10	2	0.1%	57	0.5%	0.08	0.7%
	O06.22	2	0.1%	17	0.2%	-	-
Severn Valley ware	O02	168	12.2%	214	2.0%	-	-
	O02.1	200	14.6%	1,692	15.8%	1.62	13.8%
	O02.13	170	12.4%	1,344	12.5%	2.8	23.8%
Organic variant	O03.1	482	35.1%	3,181	29.6%	3.24	27.6%
	O03.4	19	1.4%	201	1.9%	0.25	2.1%
Reduced variant	G04	23	1.7%	230	2.1%	0.33	2.8%
	G05	36	2.6%	172	1.6%	0.17	1.4%
Total Severn Valley ware		1,098	80.2%	7,034	65.5%	8.41	71.6%
Total Local / Regional wares		**1,234**	**90.0%**	**9,009**	**83.9%**	**9.58**	**81.5%**
Malvernian metamorphic, MAL RE A	N02.1	15	1.1%	213	2.0%	-	-
Black Burnished ware, DOR BB 1	B02	60	4.4%	573	5.3%	1.07	9.1%
Mancetter-Hartshill mortaria, MAH WH	M02	9	0.7%	420	3.9%	0.29	2.5%
Oxfordshire white mortaria, OXF WH	M04c	3	0.2%	55	0.5%	0.11	0.9%
Total Traded wares		**87**	**6.3%**	**1,261**	**11.7%**	**1.47**	**12.5%**
White ware	W16	19	1.4%	62	0.6%	-	-
Total uncertain source		**19**	**1.4%**	**62**	**0.6%**	**0**	**0.0%**
SG Samian, La Graufesenque, LGF SA	S01	2	0.1%	15	0.1%	-	-
CG Samian, Lezoux 2, LEZ SA 2	S03	30	2.2%	389	3.6%	0.7	6.0%
Total Imported		**32**	**2.3%**	**404**	**3.8%**	**0.7**	**6.0%**
TOTAL POTTERY		**1,372**	**100.0%**	**10,736**	**100.0%**	**11.75**	**100.0%**

See Appendix B1 for details of the fabrics.

or 3rd centuries (Seager Smith and Davies 1993, 231, fig. 122, WA Type 2), and a reduced ware jar (Fig. 25.4) dating to the late 2nd century or later.

Some forms appear to be intrusive from Phase 2–3: a late 3rd- or 4th-century Severn Valley ware tankard (Fig. 25.20), from the upper fill of ditch B2, and a jar (Fig. 25.6), from ring-gully F411 (4021). The assemblage also included some clearly residual material: grog-tempered wares (Fabrics F10, F11), including a 1st-century jar (Fig. 25.2), possibly some of the handmade Malvernian ware (Fabric N02.1), and some organic-tempered Severn Valley ware (Fabrics G05, O03.1) jars dated to the 1st to 2nd centuries (Fig. 25.9, 13).

Phase 3B

Another large assemblage, and the latest dating evidence, came from the Phase 3B pebble surface F442. This produced a number of typically late 3rd- or 4th-century forms: a BB1 bowl (Fig. 25.1); a Mancetter Hartshill, multi-reeded hammerhead mortarium, dated *c* AD 250–350+ (Hartley below); and Severn Valley ware jars (Fig. 25.13, 15). Other well-dated forms indicated the presence of residual material: a Mancetter-Hartshill mortarium (from F442, 4084), dated broadly to AD 150–200 (Hartley below), and a Central Gaulish samian Pudding Pan Rock form 15 bowl, dated to AD 150–200. Other Severn Valley ware forms present included a jar typical of the mid–late 2nd century (Fig. 25.3) and various jars and bowls dating

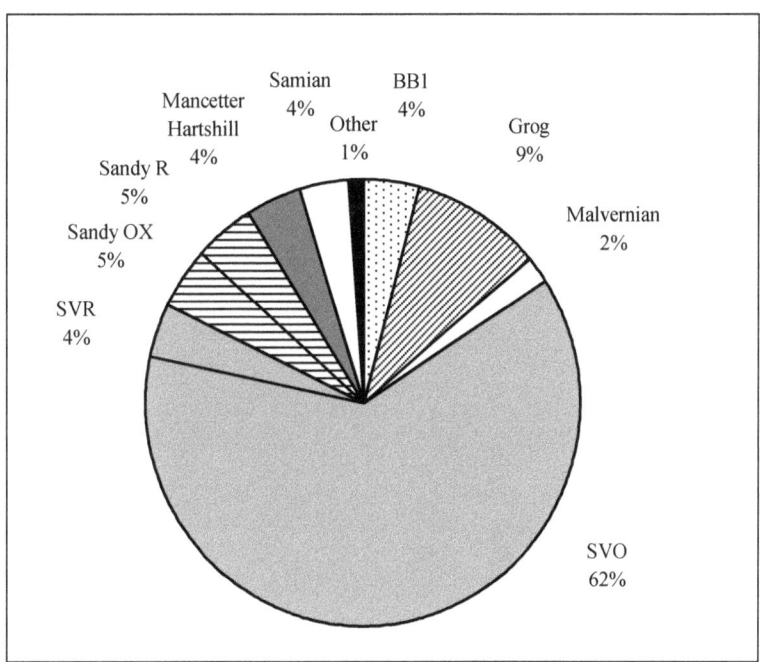

Figure 24. Area B, fabric groups by percentage weight

either to the 2nd to 3rd centuries (Fig. 25.5, 15, 17, 19), or late 2nd to 3rd century (Fig. 25.10–11).

Phase 3

The ditches, pits and post-holes associated with Phase 3 produced another relatively small assemblage (Table 5), with a narrower range of fabrics (Appendix B4). The pottery all pre-dated the latest material from Phase 2. This, and the low average sherd weight (Table 5), suggests that this material may all be redeposited. Severn Valley ware forms included a jar (not illustrated) dating to the late 2nd to 3rd century (Webster 1976, fig. 5, C23, 24), and a tankard, of a similar date (Fig. 25.7). BB1 included a dish with a slightly beaded rim (not illustrated). This type was produced throughout the Roman period, but became increasingly common from the late 2nd century on (Seager Smith and Davies 1993, 233, fig. 123, WA Type 20).

One clearly residual sherd came from a South Gaulish, Drag. 15/17 platter, dated AD 40–100.

Phase 4

The post-Roman features produced the smallest assemblage (Table 5). The only diagnostic form was a Severn Valley ware jar with a hooked rim, broadly dating to the 2nd to 3rd centuries (Webster 1976).

Unstratified

A small proportion of the assemblage came from unstratified deposits (Table 5). This provided further evidence for 1st- to 2nd-century activity on the site, a 'flake' of South Gaulish samian dated to AD 40–100 (Willis below). Sherds of Malvernian ware (Fabric N02.1) and organic-tempered Severn Valley ware (Fabrics G05, O03.1) could also provide evidence for earlier activity. The remainder of the forms (Appendix B3) and fabrics (Appendix B4) fell within the broad date range of the phased material described above.

Fabrics

Nineteen wheelmade and two handmade fabrics were identified (Table 6; Appendix B1). The occurrence of fabrics by phase is detailed in Appendix B4. The divisions between some of the coarse wares may be rather subjective, reflecting varying proportions of a range of inclusions rather than absolute differences.

Severn Valley wares were by far the largest fabric group (Fig. 24), mainly oxidised (O02.1, O02.13, O03.1, O03.4) but including some reduced variants (G04, G05). The most common variant had fine organic inclusions (O03.1). Coarse organic temper is usually indicative of an early Romano-British date (Darlington and Evans 1992, 41). However, similar fine inclusions were noted in predominantly 2nd- to 3rd-century forms at the Malvern, Newland Hopfields production site (Evans *et al.* 2000, 17, fabrics O1 and O5). In Area B, a later date is supported by the range of forms occurring: some dating to the 1st or 2nd century (Fig. 25.13), but most dating to the 2nd to 3rd centuries (Fig. 25.15, 17, 19) or later (Fig. 25.14). This, and the coarser variant (O03.4), had distinctive black inclusions, rather than the burnt-out voids noted in some organic-tempered wares. Petrological analysis of the Newland Hopfield fabrics identified carbonised wood, which does not burn out. The other oxidised variants included plain Severn Valley ware (O02.1; Fig. 25.5–6) and a variant with sand and organic inclusions (O02.13), occurring in forms with various date ranges (Fig. 25.7–12).

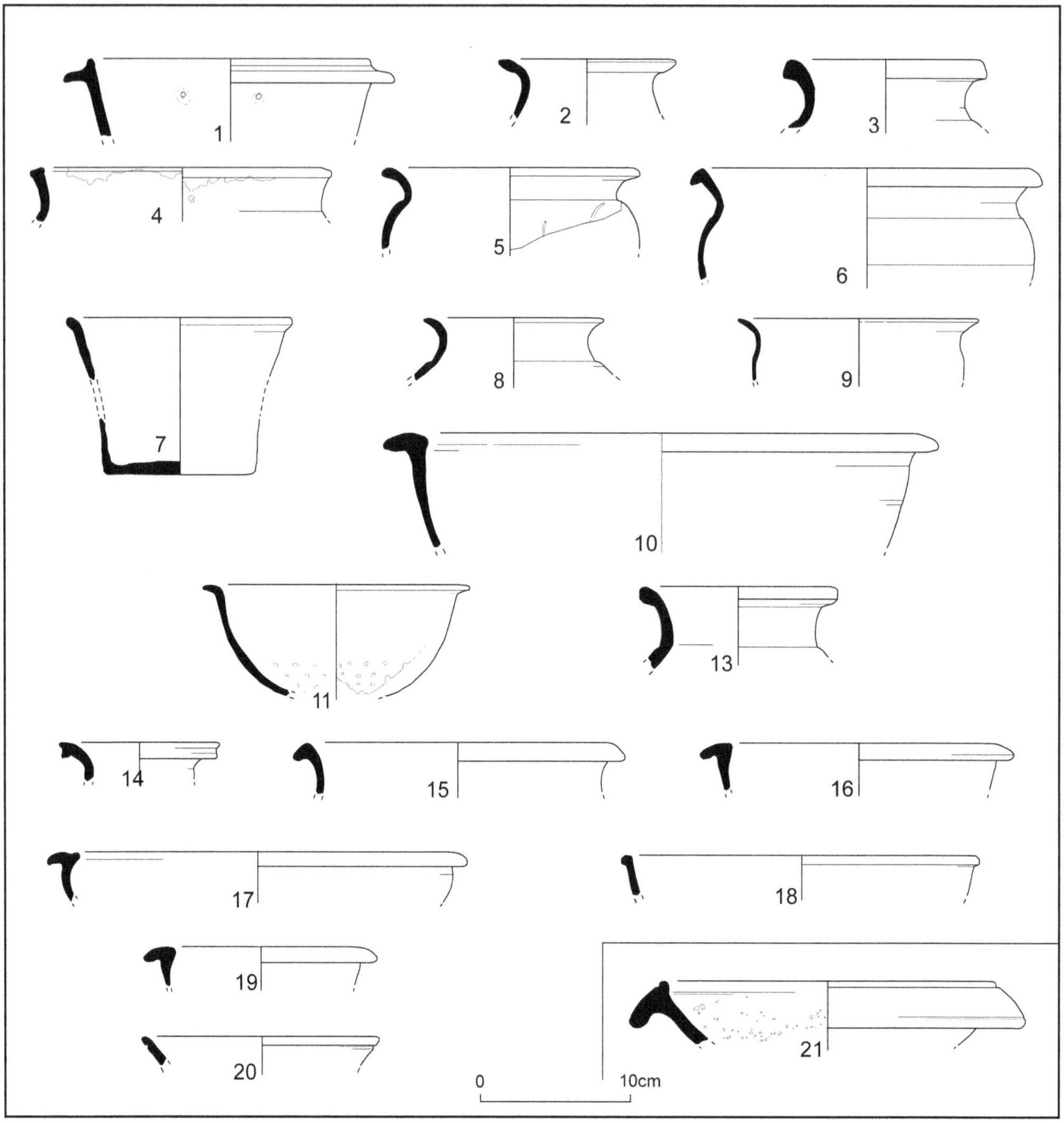

Figure 25. Area B, pottery, nos 1–11 and 13–21 (scale 1:4)

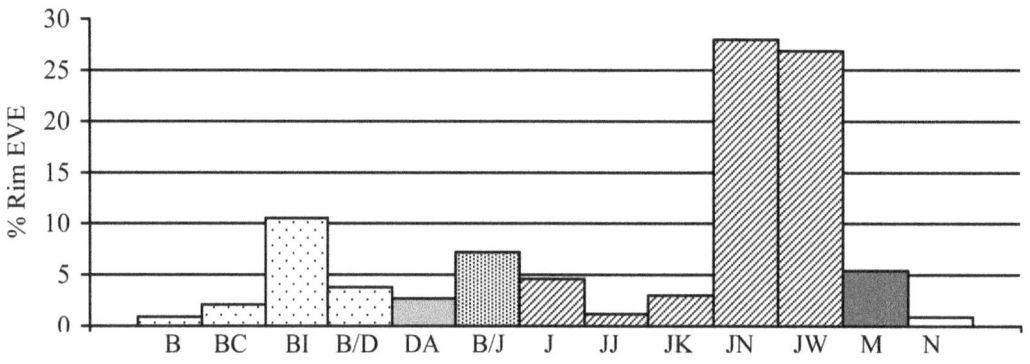

Figure 26. Area B, vessel classes by percentage rim EVE

The source of these wares is uncertain. They may have been produced in the Malvern area. Handmade Malvernian (N02.1) wares were reaching the site (Fig. 24, Table 6) providing evidence of trade contacts. The Area B assemblage includes a warped rim from a 3rd- to 4th-century hooked-mouth jar. While this may be from a 'second' that was used on site, rather than an unusable waster, its presence hints at pottery production somewhere in the vicinity. Severn Valley ware forms were produced in the Birmingham area (for example Sherifoot Lane, Sutton Coldfield; Booth 1987).

The various oxidised sandy wares (O06.01, O06.09, O06.10, O06.22, O06.5) occurred in Severn Valley ware forms: a splayed tankard (Fig. 25.20) and jars with plain, triangular or hooked rims. These could well be local products. The only form noted amongst the reduced sandy wares was a jar (Fig. 25.4) reminiscent of Derbyshire type wares, but possibly an intrusive medieval form. If Romano-British, this was the only vessel to show affinities with pottery traditions to the north and northeast of the Birmingham area rather than to the south and west. Other local or regional wares included the handmade and wheelmade grog-tempered wares (F10 and F11 respectively; Table 6 and Appendix B1), the former including a 1st-century jar type (Fig. 25.2), and the white ware. The latter had distinctive black inclusions, similar to some of the oxidised and reduced ware, and may therefore be from a fairly local source.

Some fabrics represented sources known to have been trading over wider regions. The handmade Malvernian wares referred to above belong to this class. No rims were recovered, but the body sherds indicated that both large storage jars and tubby cooking pots (Peacock 1967) were reaching the site, some time in the 1st or 2nd centuries. From further afield came jars, dishes and bowls in Dorset BB1 (Fabric B02). Most of the mortaria reaching the site came from the nearby Mancetter-Hartshill kilns. These vessels dated mostly to the latter half of the 2nd century (Hartley below), one vessel dating to c AD 250–350+. The Oxfordshire kilns were the only other mortaria source represented, a white ware mortarium being dated broadly to AD 180–240 (Hartley below). No Oxfordshire red colour-coated wares were recovered. These typically date to after c AD 240. There were no amphorae, the only imported ware being Central Gaulish samian.

Catalogue (percentage of rim surviving appears in brackets)

Fig. 25.1–20 (No 12 is not illustrated)

B02

1 BI8.25. Rim from a conical bowl with a dropped flange, WA type 25 (Seager Smith and Davies 1993, 235, fig. 124), broadly dating to the late 3rd or 4th century. The rim is perforated just below the flange, indicating that it was broken and repaired when in use. This sort of repair is normally typical of late Romano-British assemblages. At Wroxeter, for example, it is first noted in assemblages dated c AD 367–450 (Barker *et al.* 1997, 240), becoming more common in contexts dated between c AD 500 and 660. Diam. 17cm (11%). Surface F442, 4083, Phase 3B.

F11

2 JK7.01. Necked jar with a simple, everted rim. Forms in a similar fabric are associated with 1st-century deposits at Metchley Roman fort (Hancocks *et al.* 2005). Diam. 14cm (18%). Ring-gully F411, 4021, Phase 2.

G04

3 JN19.10. Narrow-mouthed jar with a rounded, triangular rim. This is a common Severn Valley ware form, typically dating to the mid–late 2nd century (Webster 1976, fig. 4, C22). Diam. 16cm (30%). Surface F442, 4083, Phase 3B.

G06.9

4 JJ6.08. Cupped-mouth jar. Reminiscent of Derbyshire ware type jars (Tyers 1996, 190–1, fig. 238; Leary 2003), though not in the distinctive Derbyshire fabric. Possibly dating to the later 2nd century or later. Alternatively, this could be an intrusive sherd of medieval pottery. Diam. 19cm (14%). Surface F413, 4028, Phase 2.

O02.1

5 JW7.01. Globular, wide-mouthed jar with a plain, everted rim (Webster 1976, fig. 4.C20). Similar forms were produced at the Malvern, Newland Hopfields kiln (Evans *et al.* 2000, 32, fig. 23, type 2), dating broadly from the mid-2nd to 3rd centuries. At Gloucester similar forms have been dated to the later 2nd century (Rawes 1982, fig. 4.71). Diam. 17cm (17%). Surface F442, layer 4083, Phase 3B.

6 JWS20.01 with graffito. Severn Valley ware hooked-rim, wide-mouthed jar with a short neck. A typically late 3rd- or 4th-century type (Webster 1976, fig. 6, C30, fig. 7, C32). Diam. 22cm (35%). Ring-gully F411, 4021, Phase 2.

O02.13

7 NB1.01. Moderately splayed, Severn valley ware tankard. Broadly dating to the late 2nd to 3rd centuries (Webster 1976, fig. 7, E43). Diam. 15cm (23%). Ditch F423.03, 4069, Phase 3.

8 JN7.01. Narrow-mouthed jar with a simple out-curving rim. This type is very broadly dated by Webster to the mid 1st to 4th centuries (Webster 1976, fig. 1.A1). Diam. 11cm (14%). Ditch B2, F405.01, upper fill 4009, Phase 2.

9 JW7.03. Wide-mouthed jar with a simple, out-curving rim. Dated by Webster to the 1st to 2nd centuries (Webster 1976, fig. 4, C20), and similar to forms from Gloucester dated to the 1st century (Rawes 1982, fig. 4.72, 74). Diam. 15cm (14%). Surface F442, layer 4083, Phase 3B.

10 BI8.41. Large flanged bowl with an internal lip and curving walls. Such bowls are broadly dated by Webster to the late 2nd to 3rd centuries (Webster 1976, fig. 8,

type F). Similar bowls were produced at the Malvern, Newland Hopfields kiln, supporting this dating (Evans *et al.* 2000, fig. 26, type 2). Diam. 28cm (10%). Surface F420, 4041, Phase 2.

11 BI8.31. Small flanged bowl, perforated to form a colander. The form is a broadly late 2nd- to 3rd-century type (cf. Webster 1976, fig. 9, F50, F51). Diam. 17cm (19%). Ditch B2, F405.01, upper fill 4009, Phase 2.

12 JWS20.01 (not illustrated). Severn Valley ware hooked-rim, wide-mouthed jar with a short neck. Similar to 4th-century types produced at the Malvern Hygienic Laundry site (Peacock 1967, 25, fig. 3.36–44) and also found at Malvern, Newland Hopfields (Evans *et al.* 2000, fig. 21, type 50; table 12). Diam. 18cm (5%). Surface F442, 4083, Phase 3B.

O03.1

13 JN1.01. Narrow-mouthed jar with a beaded rim, dating to the late 1st or 2nd century (Webster 1976, fig. 1, A2). Diam. 12cm (41%). Structure B1 ring-gully F411, 4021, Phase 2.

14 JN2.01. Narrow-mouthed jar with a 'pulley' rim, a 3rd- to 4th-century type (Webster 1976, fig. 3.A10, 11, 13; Peacock 1967, fig. 3.30). Diam. 11cm (28%). Surface F442, 4083, Phase 3B.

15 JW20.01. Wide-mouthed jar with a hooked rim, a broadly mid 2nd- to late 3rd-century type (Webster 1976, fig. 5, C23). Diam. 21cm (16%). Surface F442, layer 4083, Phase 3B.

16 BI8.41. Large, flanged bowl with an internal lip and curving walls, similar to No 11 above. Diam. 20cm (18%). Surface F442, layer 4083, Phase 3B.

17 BC8.04. Severn Valley ware flanged bowl with a grooved rim and curving walls, Webster's group G (Webster 1976, cf. fig. 9, G57). Webster dates the form broadly to the 2nd to 3rd centuries. This date is supported by the presence of the form in the Malvern, Newland Hopfields kiln assemblage (Evans *et al.* 2000, 37–8 type 3.11, fig. 28 BT41). Diam. 20cm (10%). Surface F442, 4083, Phase 3B.

18 BC1.01. Bead-rim bowl, Webster type I (cf. Webster 1976, fig. 9.61), broadly dating from the 2nd to 4th centuries., Diam. 17cm (5%). Cleaning layer 4003, unstratified.

19 BC8.33. Curving-sided bowl with a slightly down-turned flange and an internal lip, Webster type F (Webster 1976, fig. 8, F46–48) dated 2nd to 3rd centuries. Similar forms were produced at the Malvern, Newland Hopfields kiln (Evans *et al.* 2000, type 2, 35–6, fig. 26). Diam. 20cm (3%). Surface F442, 4083, Phase 3B.

O06.01

20 NC1.01. Splayed, Severn Valley ware tankard, a 4th-century type (Webster 1976, fig. 7 E44). Diam. 14cm (10%). Ditch B2, F405.02, upper fill 4022, Phase 2.

Function

The narrow range of vessel classes (Fig. 26), and in particular the emphasis on jars (Evans 2001, 28), is typical of a relatively low-status rural site. Jars, representing 67% of the assemblage by rim EVE, would have been used for storage and cooking. Forms used for preparing or serving food included bowls and dishes, in Severn Valley ware and BB1; a colander; mortaria; and tankards. No flagons were noted, though some were found in Area A (Hancocks, Chapter 2 above; Appendix B2). The only fine table wares were in samian: bowls, bowls/dishes and platters, but no cups (Willis below). The platter, a Drag 15/17, was represented by a base and is not therefore included in quantifications by rim EVE.

Discussion (Table 7)

Combined with the assemblage from the Area A excavations, this group provides evidence for pottery use on a rural site in an area where very little material has previously been recorded. The narrow repertoire of utilitarian vessels is typical of a low-status, rural assemblage. The main period of activity appears to date from the late 2nd to perhaps the early 3rd century, though

Table 7. Area B, Romano-British coarse ware pottery, summary of the assemblage by feature type

Feature Type	Qty	% Qty	Wt (g)	% Wt	Average Sherd Wt	Rim EVE	% Rim EVE
Trial-trench	31	2.3%	424	3.9%	14	0.58	4.9%
Ditch	114	8.3%	827	7.7%	7	1.35	11.5%
Layer	87	6.3%	544	5.1%	6	0.76	6.5%
Pit	70	5.1%	408	3.8%	6	0.37	3.2%
Post pad	121	8.8%	700	6.5%	6	0.52	4.4%
Ring gully	75	5.5%	825	7.7%	11	1.74	14.8%
Surface	848	61.8%	6867	64.0%	8	6.17	52.5%
Unassigned	26	1.9%	141	1.3%	5	0.26	2.2%
Total	1,372	100.0%	10,736	100.0%	8	11.75	100.0%

there was some 1st-century pottery, and some firm evidence for late 3rd- to 4th-century activity. The latter compliments the evidence from the watching brief (Chapter 5 below), which produced a late 3rd- to 4th-century BB1 jar (Seagar Smith and Davies 1993, fig. 122, WA type 3), a 4th-century Severn Valley ware jar (cf. Webster 1976, fig. 6.31), and an Oxfordshire mortarium dated AD 240–400+ (Young 1977, fig. 23, M22).

The pattern of pottery use is very much in keeping with the broad Severn Valley region, dominated by oxidised Severn Valley ware fabrics and forms. The nearest known source of Severn Valley ware was the Malvern area (Webster 1976; Evans et al. 2000). However, the range of fabric variants leads this author to suspect that there may have been a more local source. This is supported by the presence of at least one waster in the assemblage, and the fact that kilns producing Severn Valley ware vessels have been located in the Birmingham area (Hughes 1959).

Other regional sources were supplying the site: storage jars from the Malvern area, perhaps traded for their contents, and mortaria from the specialist workshops at Mancetter-Hartshill. The site was also linking in to more distant trade networks, with Black Burnished wares reaching the site from Dorset, and other mortaria coming from workshops in the Oxfordshire region. No amphorae were recovered, perhaps reflecting the date of the site as well as its rural, civilian status. The only imports were samian vessels from Central Gaul.

Mortaria
by Kay Hartley

A total of 13 sherds were recovered from Area B. All sherds are from Phase 2, or Phase 3B (using fabric descriptions provided earlier and repeated below). Only No 13 is illustrated.

Catalogue

1   One bodysherd (5 actual sherds from modern breaks) from the upper part of a mortarium. The fabric is badly discoloured, probably through very heavy burning or some other adverse conditions. The source cannot be regarded as certain, but the trituration grit would fit with production in the Mancetter-Hartshill potteries in Warwickshire (Fabric 3). No rim survives, but the upper part of the sherd suggests a 2nd-century rather than a later date. 75g. Ditch B2, F405, 4009.

2   Diam. c 250mm (8%). The almost complete rim-section of a mortarium in Fabric 3, made in the Mancetter-Hartshill potteries. This is a type characteristic of the transition period immediately after the cessation of stamping in these potteries and before attempts to develop more streamlined rim-profiles. It retains features current in the latest mortaria being stamped (cf. Hartley 1959, 9, fig. 4: mortaria of Maurus and Sennius), but it is stubbier and has a higher bead. Taken together, all of these features point to an optimum date of AD 170–190. 40g. Surface F420, 4041, Phase 2.

3   Diam. 240mm (10%). One sherd (2 with modern break) in Fabric 1, made in the Oxford potteries. This is form M11 which Young (1977) dates to AD 180–240. There is some difficulty with the dating of forms M10 and 11 because they were being produced in the Verulamium region from c AD 150 and appear in the Antonine fire at Verulamium (e.g. Frere 1984, 2675–2680, 2683. There are also some other examples in Frere 1972 and 1983 from contexts of similar date). There is sufficient evidence in the pottery forms to indicate that some of the potters in the Verulamium area were involved in the setting up, if not the further development of, the Oxford potteries. It is difficult to understand why there should have been such a time gap in the production of these forms. 40g. Surface F420, 4041.

4   One bodysherd (2 modern breaks) in Fabric 1 (Oxford potteries) which could be from the above mortarium. 10g. Surface F420, 4041, Phase 2.

5   Incomplete rim sherd from a mortarium in fabric 3 with high, wide bead and downward and outward going flange, made in the Mancetter-Hartshill potteries. Not earlier than the Antonine period and could be 3rd century. 45g. Surface F420, 4041, Phase 2.

6–7   One indeterminate bodysherd and one base/ bodysherd, Fabrics 1 or 3. 10g. Surface F420, 4041, Phase 2.

8   Fragment with folded-up end of flange, possibly from spout area. Fabric 1. Oxford potteries. It could possibly be from the same mortarium as No 3 above, but is more likely to be from another vessel. 2nd–4th century. 5g. Surface F420, 4041, Phase 2.

9   One indeterminate sherd (break modern) with eroded surface, in Fabric 1 or 3. 2nd to 4th century. 10g. Ditch B4, F438, 4076, Phase 2.

10   A badly eroded, multi-reeded hammerhead mortarium in Fabric 3, made in the Mancetter-Hartshill potteries c AD 250–350+. 30g. F442, 4083, Phase 3B.

11–12   Two eroded bodysherds in Fabric 3. Mancetter-Hartshill potteries, later than c AD 140. 60g. F442, 4083, Phase 3B.

13   Diam. 260mm (19%). Well-preserved rimsherd from a mortarium in Fabric 3, made in the Mancetter-Hartshill potteries. This form was used by the latest stamping potters, it can be matched in the work of Ruicocco (AD 150–170+); it probably continued to be produced later. The overall period of production is AD 150–200. Worn. 150g. F442, 4084, Phase 3B. Fig. 25.21.

Discussion

Discounting modern breaks, there are 13 sherds (20 with modern breaks) from a probable minimum of six vessels. As with Area A at Longdales Road, the only two sources represented are the Mancetter-Hartshill potteries (4) and the Oxford potteries (2). None are likely to be earlier than AD 150/170; four could well be within the period AD 170–220/240, while the reeded hammerhead is more likely to belong to the second half of the 3rd century or the 4th century, even possibly as late as the middle of the 4th century. No 8 is not closely datable.

Samian Pottery
by Steven Willis with Emily Bird

Introduction

A total of 32 sherds (404 g) of samian pottery (*terra sigillata*) were recovered during the Area B excavation. Some eleven contexts yielded samian. Approximately 28 vessels are represented. No stamps are present and there are no cases where decoration is represented. None of the samian items warrant drawing. The majority of the sherds are of 2nd-century AD date and from Lezoux; types associated with both pre- and post-*c* AD 150/160 dates are represented. Two items of earlier date occur, being from southern Gaul and lying within the date bracket *c* AD 40–100. No sherds of East Gaulish samian were present. This samian assemblage comprises sherds of various sizes. However, in all cases, the sherds demonstrate exposure to a malign soil environment which has resulted in their weathering and extensive loss of original gloss surfaces.

Catalogue

The catalogue lists all samian sherds from the fieldwork. The catalogue adheres to a consistent format. Sherds are listed in number order, then the following data are given: the number of sherds and their type (i.e. whether a sherd is from the rim, base – footring – or body of a vessel), the source of the item (South Gaulish is abbreviated to SG and Central Gaulish to CG), the vessel form (where identifiable), the weight of the sherds in grams, the percentage of any extant rim (i.e. the RE figure, where 1.00 would represent a complete circumference) or base (i.e. the BE figure) and the rim and base diameters, and an estimate of the date of the sherd in terms of calendar years (this being the date range of deposits with which like pieces are normally associated).

Ditch B6, F412.04, 4038, Phase 1

1 Base, CG Lezoux, Drag. 18/31R, 64g, BE: 0.36. Diam. 90mm, *c* AD 120–160. The sherd is abraded; none of the original interior surface survives and only about 30% of the exterior original slip survives.

Surface F420, 4042, Phase 2

2 Body, CG Lezoux, possibly Drag. 37, 2g, *c* AD 120–200. The sherd is fully excoriated.

Eaves-drip gully, Structure B1, F422, 4043, Phase 2

3 Body, CG Lezoux, form not identifiable, 2g, *c* AD 120–200. The sherd is fully excoriated and badly weathered.

Eaves-drip gully, Structure B2, F424, 4052, Phase 2

4 Rim, CG Lezoux, Drag. 18/31, 2g, RE: *c* 0.04. Diam. 170mm, *c* AD 120–150. The sherd is extensively excoriated and weathered.

5 Base, CG Lezoux, from a plain bowl or dish, 4g, BE: 0.10. Diam. 80mm, *c* AD 120–200. Burnt. Very badly weathered.

6 Body, CG Lezoux, form not identifiable, less than 1g, *c* AD 120–200. Severely weathered.

7–10 One rim sherd and three body sherds - all conjoining, CG Lezoux, Drag. 31, 8g, RE: 0.07. Diam. 170mm, *c* AD 150–200. Burnt. The exterior is excoriated and the original interior surface is also largely missing and the sherds are considerably weathered.

Pit F429, 4064, Phase 2

11 Rim, CG Lezoux, Drag. 18/31 or 31, 8g, RE: 0.12. Diam. 190mm, *c* AD 120–200. 99% excoriated and severely weathered.

Surface F420, 4041, Phase 2

Each entry represents an item apparently from a different vessel from other sherds recovered from this context. Just about all of the sherds are either fully or virtually excoriated and severely weathered.

12 Rim, CG Lezoux, Drag. 18/31 or 31, 5g, RE: 0.06. Diam. *c* 174mm, *c* AD 120–200.

13 Rim, CG Lezoux, Drag. 36, 3g, RE: 0.07. Diam. 160mm, *c* AD 120–200.

14 Body, CG Lezoux, Drag. 37, 24g, *c* AD 120–200. No decoration is represented.

15 Base, CG Lezoux, from a plain bowl or dish, 7g, BE: 0.13. Diam. 104mm, *c* AD 120–200.

16 Body, CG Lezoux, from a plain bowl or dish, 4g, *c* AD 120–200.

17 Body, CG Lezoux, from a bowl or dish, 5g, *c* AD 120–200.

18 Body, CG Lezoux, from a bowl or dish, 2g, *c* AD 120–200.

19 Body, probably CG Lezoux, from a bowl or dish, 2g, *c* AD 120–200.

20 Body, CG Lezoux, form not identifiable, 4g, *c* AD 120–200.

21 Body, CG Lezoux, form not identifiable, 1g, *c* AD 120–200.

22 Body, CG Lezoux, form not identifiable, less than 1g, *c* AD 120–200.

23 Rim, CG Lezoux, Pudding Pan Rock form 15, 51g, RE: 0.18. Diam. 190mm, *c* AD 150–200.

24 Base, CG Lezoux, Drag. 31R, 110g, BE: 0.23. Diam. 110mm, *c* AD 160–200.

25 Base, CG Lezoux, Drag. 31R, 35g, BE: 0.21. Diam. 100mm, *c* AD 160–200.

Ditch B4, F438, 2017, Phase 2

26 Rim, CG Lezoux, Drag. 18/31R, 5g, RE: 0.06. Diam. 260mm, *c* AD 120–160. Excoriated.

Pit F431, 4066, Phase 3A

27   Base, SG La Graufesenque, Drag. 15/17, 14g, BE: 0.07. Diam. *c* 84mm, *c* AD 40–100. Virtually excoriated and heavily weathered.

Surface F442, 4083, Phase 3B

28   Body, CG Lezoux, form not identifiable, 2g, *c* AD 120–200. Severely weathered.

29   Body, CG Lezoux, form not identifiable, 1g, *c* AD 120–200. Severely weathered. From a different vessel to the above item.

Surface F442, 4084, Phase 3B

30–31   Two conjoining body sherds, CG Lezoux, Drag. 38, 36g, *c* AD 130–200. Virtually excoriated, severely weathered.

Cleaning layer 4003, not phased

32   Body sherd (just a flake), SG Graufesenque, form not identifiable, 1g, *c* AD 40–100.

Discussion of the Samian Pottery

A samian assemblage of modest size was collected from Area B. Whilst this sample is small and the material in a poor state of preservation, the overall nature of the collection is strongly apparent. It is useful to compare this material with the assemblage from the Area A excavation (Willis, Chapter 2 above).

Table 8. Area B, samian composition of assemblage by date

Date Range	Number of Examples
c AD 40–100	2
c AD 120–150	1
c AD 120–160	1
c AD 120–200	18
c AD 130–200	1
c AD 150–200	2
c AD 160–200	2
Total	27

The time-span of the collection is *c* AD 40–200 (Table 8). There are two 1st-century items represented which are significant. Both date to the period *c* AD 40–100 (Table 9). One of these South Gaulish items is an example of the platter 15/17 which, although current until the end of the 1st century AD, was becoming less prominent by *c* AD 80/85. These two items hint that the site may have been receiving samian before the 2nd century AD, but this possibility has to be weighed in the light of other indicators of site dating. Moving on chronologically, there are no examples of samian datable to the period AD 100–120. This cannot be taken as a straightforward indicator of site chronology as this is a period when the supply of samian to Britain was comparatively moderate (Willis 2005). Overall, the great

Table 9. Area B, samian, composition of assemblage, number of examples represented

Form Type / Source	South Gaulish: La Graufesenque	Central Gaulish: Lezoux
Decorated Bowls		
Drag. 37	-	2
Plain Bowls		
Drag. 31R	-	2
Drag. 38	-	1
Pudding Pan Rock. 15	-	1
Bowls or Dishes		
Indeterminate	-	6
Dishes:		
Drag. 18/31	-	1
Drag. 18/31 or 31	-	2
Drag. 18/31R	-	1
Drag. 31	-	1
Drag. 36	-	1
Platter		
Drag. 15/17	1	-
Totals	1	18
(Form not identifiable)	1	7
Aggregate Totals	2	25

proportion of material is 2nd century in date, coming from the Lezoux workshops in Central Gaul, spanning the Hadrianic to Antonine period. Within this bracket there are items likely to date to the first half of the 2nd century and some likely to date to the second half. In fact, most of these Lezoux pieces cannot be dated more closely within the broad *c* AD 120–200 date range, in large part because of their denuded character. Hence there is no clear emphasis in date that can be detected within this 2nd-century AD band. No 3rd-century items are present, although it remains entirely possible that a proportion of the 2nd-century vessels remained in use beyond AD 200. Due to the weathered nature of the sherds it is not possible to discern a level of wear to these vessels which might otherwise be an indicator of their lifespan. No pieces show evidence of repair. The very small range of samian sherds from Area A are also heavily weathered but show a somewhat later emphasis in date than is apparent within the present group (Willis, Chapter 2 above). The chronology of the samian pottery must, of course, be viewed alongside that of the coarse pottery and other dating indicators.

Whilst the samian may not be especially helpful in dating contexts in this particular case, the sample nonetheless provides a record of supply/ acquisition over a defined period that is of value, particularly given the nature of the site. Table 9 summarises the composition of the sample by source, generic type and form class. Amongst the assemblage only 20 vessels could be classified to form. The range of types is as one might expect from a smaller settlement but does include an example of one unusual type, namely a Pudding Pan Rock form 15. Of the 20 vessels, two (*c* 10%) are decorated; this number, when considered against proportions from other rural sites, is low (Willis 2005). This may be an index of the status of the site.

Amongst the plain forms, bowls and dishes are to the fore, with no particular form being well represented – rather, there is a range of familiar plain forms. The absence of cups is potentially noteworthy.

The assemblage largely comprises quite fragmented small sherds, suggesting that sherds had been subject to attritional processes following the original breakage of the vessels.

Charred Plant Remains
by Pam Grinter

Archaeobotanical samples were collected from a range of features. One sample was selected for full analysis of the charred plant remains present.

Laboratory method

The sample selected for full analysis was 10 litres in volume, and environmental officers at Birmingham Archaeology used water flotation to process the sample. Due to the high clay content of the soil matrix, the sample was soaked in a solution of sodium hydrogen carbonate prior to processing. The flot and heavy residue was recovered on a 500μm sieve and the residue on a 1mm mesh. The resultant flot was analysed by the author under a low-power microscope at a magnification of x15. Identification was aided by use of a seed collection held by the author and with various seed identification manuals (Anderberg 1994; Berggren 1969 and 1981; Cappers *et al.* 2006). Nomenclature follows Stace (1997) for indigenous taxa and Zohary and Hopf (2000) for economic plants.

Results

Table 10 presents the results for the sample. Charred plant remains were present in low numbers. The charred plant remains comprised grains of barley (*Hordeum vulgare*) and spelt wheat (*Triticum spelta*), together with small quantities of spelt chaff. Some of the spelt grains showed signed of germination. Spelt wheat and barley are commonly recorded at sites of Roman date in Britain.

Discussion

The feature which produced the plant remains was a layer overlying a pebble surface. The cereal grains and spelt chaff clearly represent crop harvesting or processing activities (Hillman 1981) that may have taken place on the cobbled surface or near by, which became incorporated within the ashy layer on top of the feature. The number of grains present is limited and does not represent large-scale cereal processing on site. However, seven of the spelt grains were germinated; this may indicate that this deposit was the result of the disposal of spoiled grain, the consequence of a very wet summer which caused some of the grain to sprout. Alternatively, it may indicate that the malting of grain was taking place on the site as part of a beer-making process, in which case the sample may be the remains of the fire from a kiln which had been used to parch sprouted grains as part of the malting process (Hillman 1982). Several weed species were present and these included dock cf. sheep's sorrel (*Rumex* cf. *acetosella*) and knot grass (*Polygonum aviculare* L) these species are common on many soils including open and cultivated land.

Conclusions

The charred plant assemblage obtained from the sample is limited in size. It comprises a few wheat and barley grains together with a small quantity of crop-processing waste. This indicates that crop-processing activities were taking place near by. The sample probably represents the disposal of waste from processing activities; however, the germinated spelt grains could indicate that this activity was also associated with the beer-making process, but the size of the assemblages makes any interpretation uncertain.

Comparative evidence

This small assemblage is similar to those recovered from deposits at Metchley Roman Fort during various excavations carried out by Birmingham Archaeology (Ciaraldi 2005 and forthcoming; Smith forthcoming). These assemblages, also small, contained spelt and barley grains, although these samples did not contain any processing waste or sprouted grains. This indicates that, as would be expected, crop-processing activities were not taking place on the fort site.

Table 10. Area B, charred plant remains

Identification	Count
Fraction sorted	100%
Cereal	
Triticum spelta L. grain	18
Triticum spelta L. grain (germinated)	7
Hordeum vulgare L. grain indet.	7
Cereal grains indet.	27
Triticum spelta L. glume bases	128
Glume bases indet.	36
Detached plumules	2
Wild	
Polygonum aviculare L.	1
Rumex cf. acetocella	18
Small weeds indet.	5

AREA B THE LIVESTOCK HERDING STRUCTURES (FIELD 1)

Plate 7. Area B, general view of excavation, view: west

Plate 8. Area B, Phase 3B stone surface F442, view: south

Chapter 4

Area C–D, the Roadside Plots (Field 1)

RESULTS
by Bob Burrows and Alex Jones

Phasing

A scheme of two phases, specific to Area C–D (Fig. 4), has been defined, as follows:

Phase 1   Early Romano-British roadside plots, 2nd–early 3rd century
Phase 2   Later Romano-British activity, later 3rd–4th century

Further refinement of the phasing, based on the broader historic plot boundary alignments is considered in Chapter 6. The results of the Area B excavations, also in Field 1, are described in Chapter 3 (above).

In Area C–D the Phase 1 features were cut into the natural red-brown clay subsoil (6004/7002).

Phase 1: Early Romano-British roadside plots, 2nd–early 3rd century (Figs 27–31)

The main features excavated were a series of east-west aligned ditched plot boundaries, cut at a right-angle to Ryknild Street, some further defined by adjoining metalled roads. Many, but not all, ditched boundaries could be traced within both areas. The plots extended over 100m to the rear of the Ryknild Street frontage, assuming that the Roman road was roughly contiguous with the modern road. Excavation of Area C and D examined the full width of three plots (A, B and C) and part of a fourth (D). Plot A measured approximately 28m in width (measured centre to centre of the road surfaces). Plots B and C measured approximately 35m in width. Finally, Plot D was recorded for a width of 16m, but its northern limit was not recorded within the excavated area. Most of the recorded features belonged to Phase 1.

Description of Phase 1 features

Plot A

The southern boundary of Plot A was formed by a pebble road surface, 6147, measuring up to 4m in width. Towards the Roman road frontage, the road joined an east-west aligned pebble surface, 6147A, recorded for a maximum width of 5.5m, and a length of 21m. The only features recorded within Plot A were two adjoining pits, 6091 and 6095, each measuring an average of 0.65m in diameter, located to the rear of the frontage, and a single post-hole, 7033, recorded closer to the Roman road frontage. The features were backfilled with brown-grey silt-sand-clay.

Plot B

The northern limit of Plot A and the southern boundary of Plot B were defined by an east-west aligned metalled road, 6074 (Fig. 29.S.1, Plate 9), and two slightly misaligned, and offset, ditches to the north, D1 (Fig. 29.S.1) and D1a (Fig. 30). The alignment of the southern edge of this road varied, possibly as a result of resurfacing. The road was better preserved in Area D, being more truncated, perhaps as a result of ploughing, in the Roman roadside area. The metalled surface was composed of pebbles measuring 0.02–0.10m in diameter with occasional slightly larger sub-rounded stones. Road 6074 measured between 3.0 and 3.8m in width and survived to a depth of between 0.04 and 0.09m. A single post-hole, 7048, was cut into the road surface. In contrast to the road surface, the associated ditch, D1, was better preserved towards the road frontage area, D1a (Fig. 28.S.2–S.3). The ditches were cut to a U-shaped profile and measured an average of 0.8m in depth and between 0.16m and 0.26m in depth. They were backfilled with orange-brown sand-silt.

Within the excavated part of Plot B was recorded part of a rectangular enclosure, Enclosure E1, dug to the north of roadside ditch D1. The eastern, D4, western, D5, and parts of the northern side, D6, were recorded. The enclosure measured 22m (north-south) by a maximum of 50m (east-west). The eastern ditch, D4, was misaligned with the other sides of the enclosure and also with the Plot B boundaries.

The western enclosure ditch, D5 (Fig. 29.S.4–S.5) was cut to a U-shaped profile and measured a maximum of 0.7m in width and 0.32m in depth. The western edge of the ditch was cut by a post-hole, 6113, which measured 0.3m in diameter. An entry-gap measuring 0.7m in width was retained at the northwestern angle of the enclosure. This entry-gap was further defined by a north-south aligned gully, 6136, cut flush with the western terminal of the northern ditch of the enclosure, D6 (Fig. 29.S.6), and by a pit, 6134 (S.5), cutting ditch D5 towards its northern terminal. The pit measured 0.98m in diameter. Ditch D6 was cut to a U-shaped profile and measured an average of 0.35m in depth, varying from 0.5m to 0.8m in width at its western and eastern terminals respectively. The eastern enclosure ditch, D4 (Fig. 29.S.2 and S.7), measured an average of 0.43m in depth and between 0.8m and 0.52m in width at its northern and southern terminals respectively. The southern terminal of ditch D4 was cut by ditch D1a, the northern roadside ditch, or by its later surviving re-cut.

Within the Enclosure E1 interior, the main group of features – a circular ring-gully, R2 (7015, 7019 and 7026;

Fig. 29.S.8, Fig. 30, Plate 10) and associated features – were concentrated within its southeastern angle. Only the eastern half of the ring-gully survived later truncation. R2 measured approximately 8m in diameter. It measured 0.4–0.5m in width and 0.15m in depth, and was cut to a U-shaped profile. Three post-holes, 7060, 7062 and 7064, were cut along the line of R2. R2 was backfilled with charcoal-rich sand-silt-clay, 7025. An oval, east-west aligned hearth, 7017 (Fig. 29.S.9), was the only feature recorded within R2. 7017 was backfilled with grey-brown silt-sand-clay, 7016, flecked with charcoal.

To the east of R2 was a line of small stones, 7074, which may represent the base of a truncated gully, surviving to a depth of only 0.02m. This feature could possibly represent the eastwards continuation of D1, although this could not be proven. No relationship could be established between 7074 and R2. Also to the east of R2 was a pit, 7046, measuring 1.2m in diameter and cut to a U-shaped profile.

Ditch D5 was backfilled with light grey-brown silt-clay. D6 and D4 were backfilled with light grey silt-sand-clay.

Few features were located within Plot B outside the enclosure. A single small pit, 7033, measuring 0.4m in diameter, and a post-hole, 7039, were recorded to the east of Enclosure E1. To the west of the enclosure was a spread of stones, 6069/6103, curvilinear in plan, and recorded for a length of 10m. This feature may represent the base of a heavily truncated ditch or gully. This adjoined a single post-hole, 6115.

Plot C

The northern boundary of Plot B and the southern boundary of Plot C was formed by an east-west aligned metalled surface, 6109, with a ditch to its northern edge, D2 (Fig. 29.S.10, Fig. 31.S.11, Plate 11), similar to the arrangement recorded along the Plot A/ Plot B boundary further to the south. Surface 6109 measured a maximum of 5m in width, and comprised small sub-rounded pebbles. Two post-holes, 6011 and 6105, were cut into the surface. The post-holes averaged 0.6m in diameter and 0.18m in depth. Ditch D2 was heavily truncated by a post-medieval field boundary (not illustrated in plan).

The main feature identified within the Plot C interior was a ring-gully, R1 (Fig. 30, Fig. 31.S.12–S.13). Only the southeastern half of the feature was recorded – the remainder, perhaps originally less substantial in depth, had presumably been removed by truncation. It was cut in sections, with changes in angle. R1 measured approximately 10.3m in diameter. An entry-gap, measuring 0.6m in width, was recorded in the southeastern angle of the feature. The ring-gully was cut to a U-shaped profile. It measured a maximum of 0.6m in width and 0.18m in depth (in the southeast), changing to 0.26m in width and 0.05m in depth along its southwestern side. R1 was backfilled with grey-brown silt-sand-clay.

A number of features were recorded within the interior of R1. Two post-holes, 6071 and 6076, and a pit, 6119, were recorded in the west of the R1 interior. Traces of stone-packing survived within 6071, which was cut to a U-shaped profile and measured 0.38m in diameter and 0.18m in depth. Three post-holes, 6078 (Fig. 31.S.14), 6080 and 6082, following a northwest-southeast alignment in the southeast segment of R1, could have formed one side of an entrance structure not otherwise recorded. The post-holes measured an average of 0.35m in diameter and 0.18m in depth. A single pit, 6087, was also recorded in the north of the R1 interior.

The only other feature within Plot C was a large, flat-based pit, 6017 (Fig. 31.S.15), recorded to the southwest of R1. In plan, it measured 6.4m by 5.8m, and was cut to a maximum depth of 0.26m. It was backfilled with redeposited subsoil and light grey silt-clay, 6016. The sequence of backfills suggests gradual backfilling of the feature by trampling and it is interpreted as an animal watering hole. The feature was surrounded by a possible pebble surface (not illustrated). No internal features were recorded in this plot within Area C.

Plot D

The northern limit of Plot C, and the southern side of Plot D, was defined by an east-west aligned ditch, D3 (Fig. 31.S.16), and a metalled road, 6146, recorded immediately to the north. D3 was cut to a U-shaped profile and measured 0.5–0.65m in width and 0.1–0.23m in depth. In Area D the ditch became notably less substantial in the east of the excavated area, which might suggest its possible eastward continuation into Area C could have been entirely scoured-out by truncation. D3 was backfilled with brown sand-clay. In contrast to the other ditched plot boundaries, ditch D3 was slightly curvilinear in plan. This irregularity might suggest that it was not part of the original Romano-British layout. The small excavated sample of the Plot D interior contained no Phase 1 Romano-British features. This absence is not surprising given that more of the plot's interior was tested towards the Roman road frontage, which contained few features in Plots A–C to the south.

Dating evidence from Phase 1 features

The Enclosure E1 ditches contained pottery dating to the 2nd–3rd century, AD 120+, late 2nd century +, to the 2nd–3rd century from ditch D5 and to the 2nd–3rd century from ditch D4. Ditches D1 and D2 contained Romano-British pottery. Ditch D3 contained pottery dating AD 120+, to the mid-2nd–early 3rd century, and to the 2nd–3rd century, as well as material classed only as Romano-British. Road surface 6074 contained pottery dating to the 2nd–4th century. Pit 6017 in Plot C contained 2nd-century pottery.

Interpretation of Phase 1 features

Area C–D provided the opportunity for the only extensive examination of the roadside area during the 2002–2007 investigations. The precise alignment of Ryknild Street is not known, although it may reasonably be assumed to have followed the course of the modern road. The main features identified were a parallel series of boundary ditches and

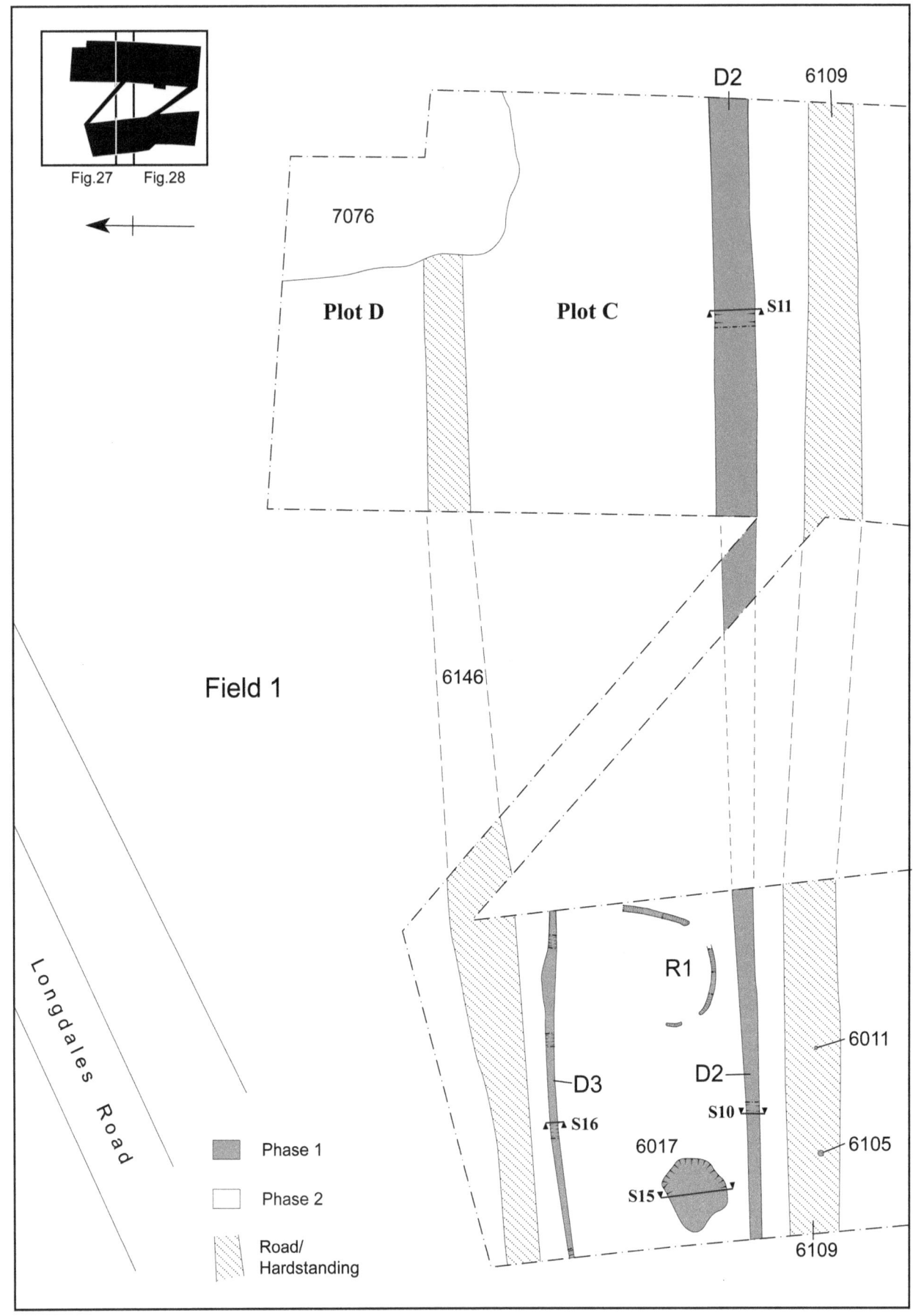

Figure 27. Area C–D, simplified plan, Phase 1–2 features north (overlaps with Fig. 28; scale 1:500)

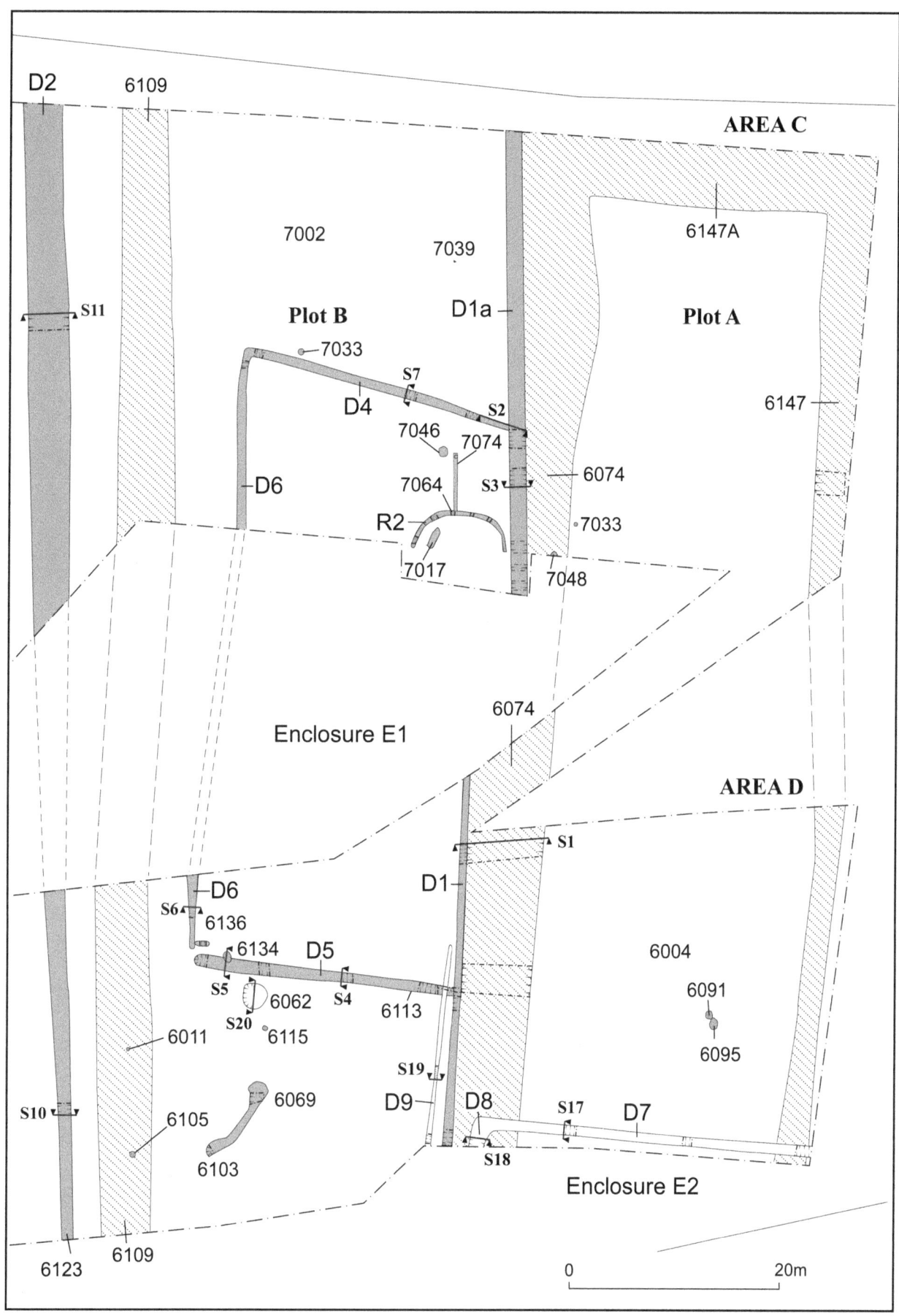

Figure 28. Area C–D, simplified plan, Phase 1–2 features south (overlaps with Fig. 27; scale 1:500)

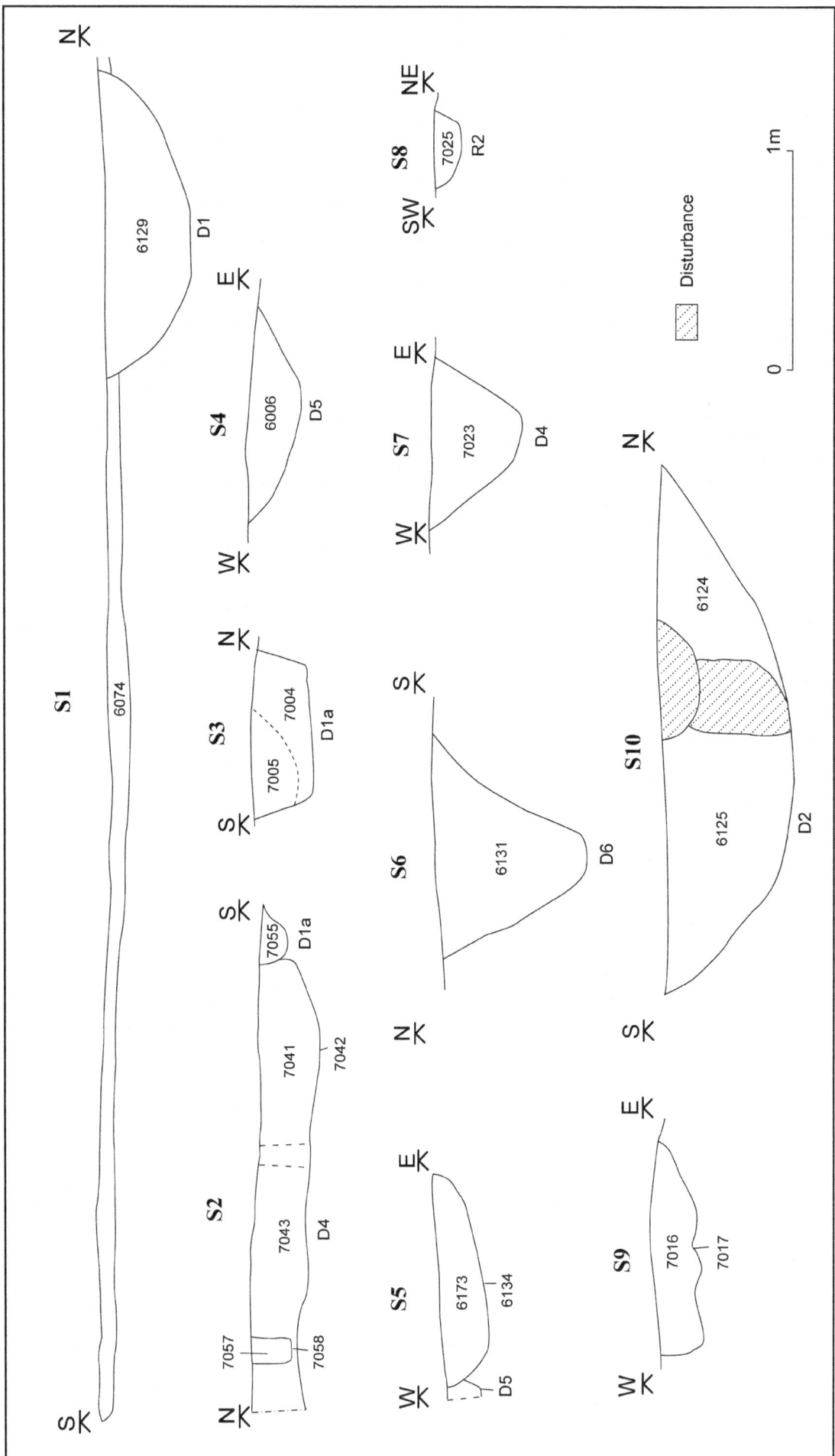

Figure 29. Area C–D Phase 1 sections (scale 1:25)

related metalled surfaces, defining four plots, cut at a right-angle to the Roman road. These plot boundaries were recorded for a distance of more than 100m to the rear of the presumed Roman road frontage. It is notable that in each case the immediate road frontage, which might have been expected to contain features, did not. The plot widths of 35m and 28m recorded at Longdales Road are roughly within the range of plot widths recorded at Hibaldstow (Smith 1987, 31: 15–30m), and Catsgore (Leech 1982: 26–46m). A plot width of 27m was recorded at Barnsley Park, Gloucestershire (McWhirr 1981, 101). At the roadside settlement of Birdlip quarry, Gloucestershire (Mudd 1999a, 239, and 1999b), plot widths of 30m and 35m were recorded. A 30m wide plot width was recorded at Ilchester Little Spittle (Leach 1982, fig. 34).

The trackway, 6074, defining the Plot A/ Plot B boundary followed the predominant east-west alignment. It is notable that the associated ditches, D1 and D1a, were offset and also cut on slightly different alignments, suggesting two stages of plot layout (see Chapter 6 below). This change in layout may be associated with Enclosure E1, which was cut towards the south of Plot B. At the southwestern angle of the enclosure, ditches D5 and D1 appear to have been contemporary. At the southeastern angle, D4 was cut by D1a (or by its surviving re-cut), in which case D1a may be later than D1, assuming that the entire Enclosure E1 circuit belonged to one phase. The maintenance of an entrance at the northwestern angle of the enclosure and, in particular, its partial closure (by 6136), suggests that the enclosure contained livestock. Ring-gully R2, contemporary with D1a, could have formed part of a later sub-phase, possibly after the livestock enclosure went out of use. Ring-gully R2 contained post-holes cut along the trench, a native type of construction recorded at Alcester (e.g. Mahany 1994, 148, structure ea). A further ring-gully, R1, was recorded within Plot C. Finally, 6091 and 6095, adjoining post-holes in Plot A, could have retained the two uprights of a loom measuring 1m in width.

Correlation of the results of excavation in Area B (Chapter 3 above) with the Area C–D investigations is difficult. Road 6147 was found in Area C–D and its western continuation was also found in Area B (as F442, Chapter 3 above), as well in the 2004 watching brief (F119, Chapter 5 below). The Plot A/ Plot B boundary, 6074 and D1/D1a was positioned flush with the northeastern angle of Field 2, which respected a Romano-British land-division. Conversely, it is impossible to correlate the northern boundaries of Plots B and C within the results from Area B to the east. This suggests that the western limits of these plots lay somewhere between the two excavated areas. It is possible that stone surface F400 (Area B) could have formed part of the westwards continuation of surface 6109 (Area C–D), between Plots B and C.

R1 and the associated features could have been in use in late Phase 1, or early Phase 2, as suggested by the pottery dating evidence (termed Phase 1/2 in the pottery report, Evans below). The circular hut form – which may have persisted into Phase 2 (see below) may have been an expression of the social traditions of the inhabitants, as suggested at Birdlip quarry (Mudd 1999b).

Pit 6017 could have been used for watering cattle if it reached the seasonal water-table, by analogy with similar features from Orton Hall Farm, Cambridgeshire (Mackreth 1996, 61).

Phase 2: Later Romano-British activity, later 3rd–4th century

Phase 2 activity was less intense than that of the preceding phase, and also largely confined to the area of abandoned Phase 1 Plot A. The main Phase 2 feature was the northeastern corner of an enclosure, Enclosure E2, associated with a parallel ditch to the north.

Description of Phase 2 features (Figs 27–28, and 31)

The metalled roads, 6147 and 6074, defining the southern and northern limits of Phase 1 Plot A, had gone out of use by the end of Phase 1. It is possible that the other plot boundaries, formed by ditches and metalled roads, had also gone out of use at the same time.

The main Phase 2 feature was the northeastern angle of a ditched enclosure, Enclosure E2. Only part of the eastern side, and a very short length of the northern side of this enclosure, were recorded at excavation; its other sides lay outside the excavated area. The eastern ditch of the enclosure, D7 (Fig. 31.S.17), was cut through Phase 1 roads 6147 and 6074, and the northern ditch, D8 (Fig. 31.S.18), was also cut into surface 6074. The eastern ditch, D7, was dug to a stepped, U-shaped profile, and measured between 0.8–1m in width and 0.36m–0.5m in depth. It was backfilled with grey silt-sand-clay. The short excavated length of D8 was cut to a V-shaped profile, and measured a maximum of 1.58m in width and 0.5m in depth. It was backfilled with mid grey-brown silt-sand-clay, 6072.

An east-west aligned ditch, D9 (Fig. 31.S.19), dug 5m (measured centre to centre) to the north of Enclosure E2, may have been associated. D9 was cut for a distance of 20m, extending 15m to the east of D7. Ditch D9 was cut through the backfilled Phase 1 ditch D5 (Enclosure E1) and into the subsoil, 6004. Ditch D9 was cut to a U-shaped profile and measured a maximum of 0.63m in width and 0.15m in depth. It was backfilled with grey-brown silt-sand-clay.

Further to the north was a pit, 6062 (Fig. 31.S.20), sub-circular in plan, measuring a maximum of 2.5m in width and 0.5m in depth. It was backfilled with charcoal-flecked silt-clay. In the extreme northeastern angle of Area C was an irregular pebble spread, 7076, which sealed the backfilled Phase 1 plot boundary, D3.

As noted above, Phase 1 ring-gully R1 in Plot C could also have continued in use into Phase 2.

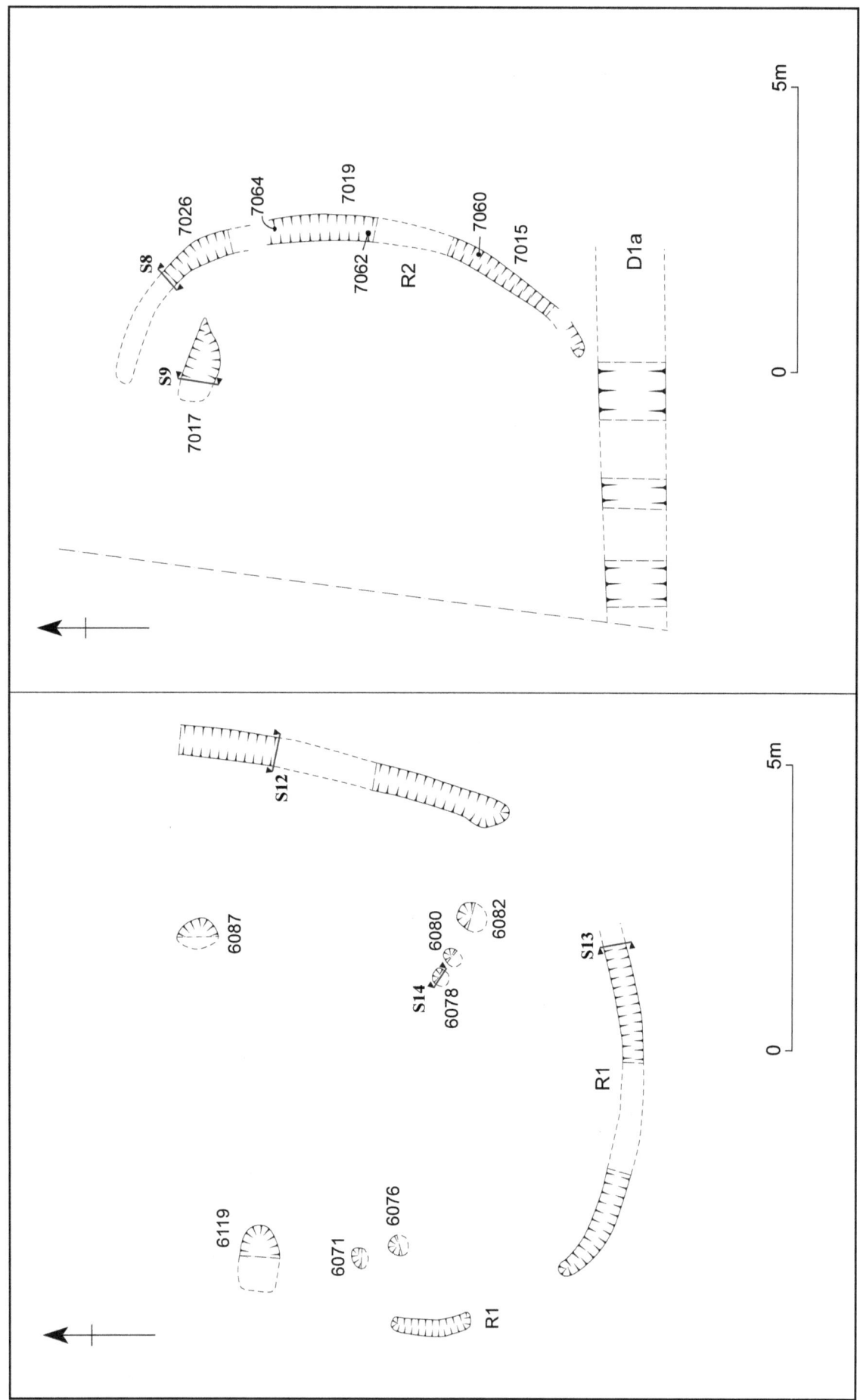

Figure 30. Area C–D detailed ring-gully R1–R2 plans (scale 1:100)

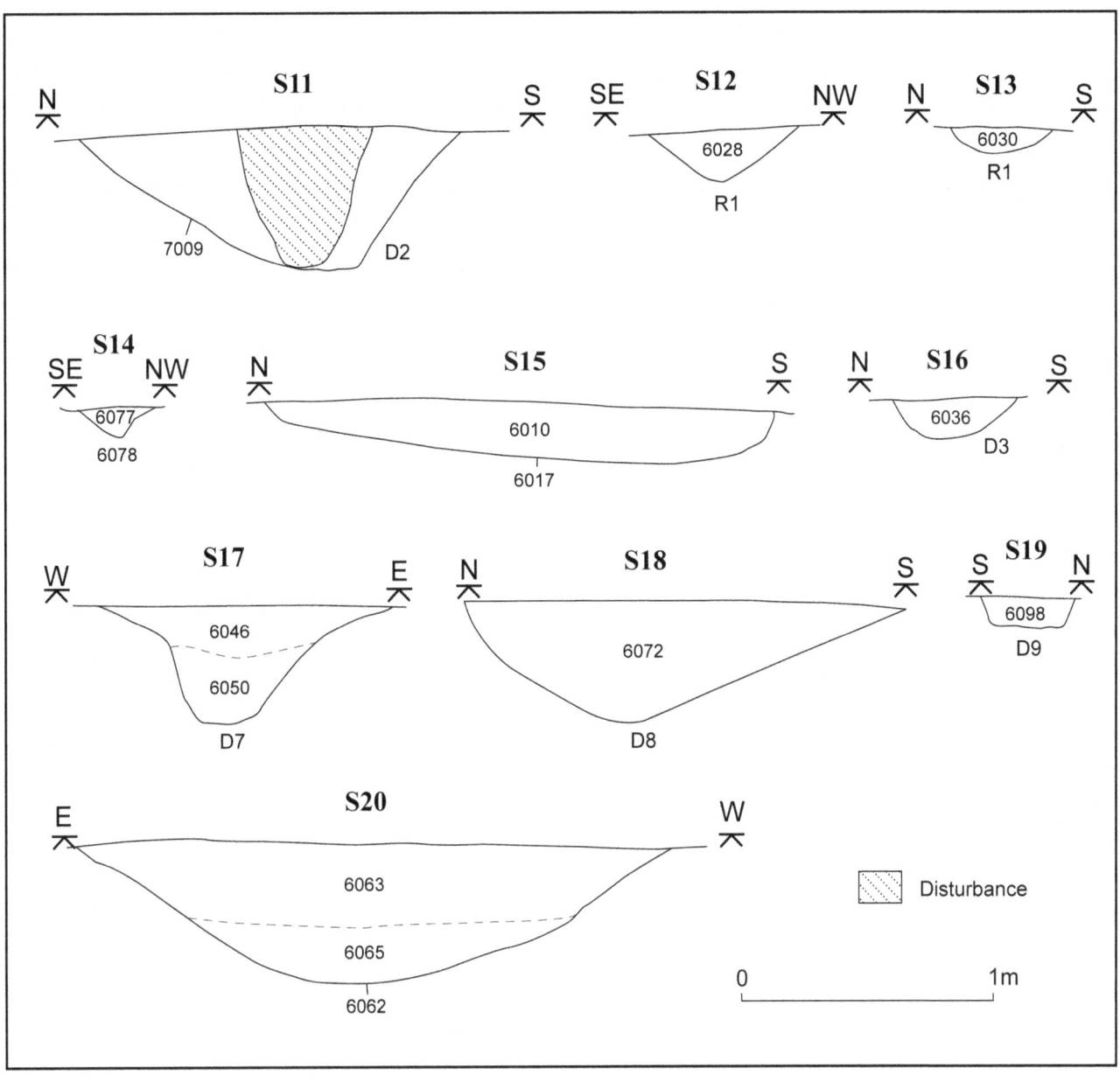

Figure 31. Area C–D Phase 1–2 sections (scale 1:25)

Dating evidence from Phase 2 features

Ditch D7 contained a 3rd-century mortarium fragment and pottery dating to AD 240+, with residual material dating to AD 120+; of 2nd- to 3rd-century date and of 3rd- to 4th-century date. Ditch D8 contained pottery of late 3rd- to 4th-century date. Ring-gully R1 contained pottery dating to AD 240+, and associated feature 6082 contained pottery dating to the 3rd–4th century which may suggest the features continued in use into Phase 2. Ditch D9 contained a mortarium fragment dating to the mid–late 3rd century. Finally, pit 6062 contained pottery dating to the 3rd–4th century.

Interpretation of Phase 2 features

The eastern side of Phase 1 Enclosure E2 was cut across Phase 1 Plot A. A possible narrow trackway may have been retained between the northern side of the enclosure, D8, and ditch D9 further to the north. Part of the width of Phase 1 road 6074 could have remained in use after this rearrangement, as is suggested by the recovery of pottery dated to the 2nd–4th century from its surface. The northern boundary of Plot D, 6146, was sealed by a stone surface, 7076, which is also attributed to Phase 2. The other Phase 1 plot boundaries may also have gone out of use during Phase 2.

These Phase 2 arrangements were not recorded as continuing within Area B to the west (Fig. 4), which suggests that the western side of the enclosure lay between the Areas D and B. Phase 1 road 6147 was cut by the eastern ditch, D7, of Enclosure E2, and went out of use. The projected continuation of the same road (F442, Area B) went out of use around AD 250–350+, as is indicated by the deposition of quantities of pottery, burnt grain and ash, which were not cleared away to maintain the roadway.

FINDS

Romano-British pottery by
C Jane Evans

Introduction

The Area C–D excavations produced 483 sherds of Romano-British pottery, weighing 3.7kg and dating from the 2nd–3rd century to the 4th century. The pottery came from 42 stratified contexts, 31 of which produced less than ten sherds. A further 18 sherds (208g, 0.05% rim EVE) were recovered during subsequent salvage excavation of a ring-gully and ditch in 2007. Overall, 95% of the pottery by weight came from stratified contexts. The assemblage adds yet another body of data from an area for which few Romano-British pottery assemblages have previously been published.

Methodology

The pottery from the 2006 and 2007 fieldwork is treated as a single assemblage for the purposes of this report. The pottery was recorded using the same Birmingham Archaeology coding system used during analysis of the Area A (Hancocks, Chapter 2 above), and Area B (Evans, Chapter 3 above) pottery from Longdales Road. Fabrics were recorded with reference to the Area A and Area B fabric series, cross referenced where possible with the National Roman Fabric Reference Collection (NRFRC, Tomber and Dore 1998) and the Metchley fabric and form series (Green *et al.* 2001; Hancocks *et al.* 2005, appendix 2, 90–2; Evans and Hancocks 2005, appendix 6, 110). Precise form types and broad vessel classes (for example bowl, flagon, mortarium) were both recorded where identifiable. The fabrics and forms are listed, illustrated and described below (Tables 11–12, Fig. 32, and Appendix C1–C3). Evidence for manufacture (wasters), use (sooting) and repair (rivets and rivet holes) was sought. However, as with the other pottery assemblages from this area, sherds were extremely abraded by the acidic soils with little surface evidence surviving. Diagnostic forms provided some dating evidence for activity. These are illustrated below (Fig. 33) by fabric, published parallels being cited for more fragmentary rims. The assemblage was quantified by sherd count, weight and rim EVE. Data for base EVEs are included in the archive. The pottery data were recorded and analysed using Microsoft Access and Excel, in relation to stratigraphic data provided by Birmingham Archaeology.

Taphonomy

The majority of the assemblage came from Phase 1 deposits (Table 11). This contrasts with the evidence from previous excavations at Longdales Road (Hancocks, Chapter 2 above; Evans, Chapter 3 above), which produced Romano-British pottery predominantly from later Romano-British features. The unphased material in Table 11 below includes 18 sherds from the 2007 salvage recording.

Table 11. Area C–D, Romano-British coarse ware pottery, summary of the assemblage by phase

Phase	Qty	% Qty	Wt (g)	% Wt	Rim EVE	% Rim EVE	Av Wt
Various	56	11.6%	415	11.2%	0.05	1.6%	7
1	319	66.0%	2,289	61.6%	2.62	84.0%	7
1/ 2	58	12.0%	475	12.8%	0.11	3.5%	8
2	37	7.7%	477	12.8%	0.32	10.3%	13
3	13	2.7%	59	1.6%	0.02	0.6%	5
Totals	483	100.0%	3,715	100.0%	3.12	100.0%	8

Table 12. Area C–D, Romano-British coarse ware pottery, summary of the assemblage by feature type

Feature type	Qty	% Qty	Wt (g)	% Wt	Rim EVE	% Rim EVE	Av. Wt
Other	58	12.0%	418	11.3%	0.07	2.2%	7
Ditch	160	33.1%	1,588	42.7%	1.54	49.4%	10
Ditch/ Gully	37	7.7%	278	7.5%	0.18	5.8%	8
Gully	99	20.5%	598	16.1%	0.44	14.1%	6
Hearth	9	1.9%	145	3.9%	0.02	0.6%	16
Layer	7	1.4%	26	0.7%	-	-	4
Pit	43	8.9%	373	10.0%	0.45	14.4%	9
Plough furrow	2	0.4%	2	0.1%	-	-	1
Post-hole	14	2.9%	38	1.0%	0.03	1.0%	3
Surface	54	11.2%	249	6.7%	0.39	12.5%	5
Total	483	100.0%	3,715	100.0%	3.12	100.0%	8

Table 13. Area C–D, Romano-British coarse ware pottery, summary of the assemblage by ditch (D), or ring-gully (R)

Construct No	Qty	% Qty	Wt (g)	% Wt	Rim EVE	% Rim EVE
Other	226	46.9%	1,771	47.5%	1.44	46.3%
D1a	16	3.3%	43	1.2%	0.16	5.1%
D2	59	12.2%	319	8.6%	0.54	17.3%
D4	16	3.3%	100	2.7%	0.14	4.5%
D5	8	1.7%	163	4.4%	0.25	8.0%
D6	29	6.0%	147	4.0%	0.14	4.5%
D7	33	6.8%	382	10.3%	0.16	5.1%
D8	4	0.8%	95	2.6%	0.16	5.1%
R1	58	12.0%	475	12.8%	0.11	3.5%
R2	34	7.0%	220	5.9%	0.02	0.6%
Total	**483**	**100.0%**	**3,715**	**100.0%**	**3.12**	**100.0%**

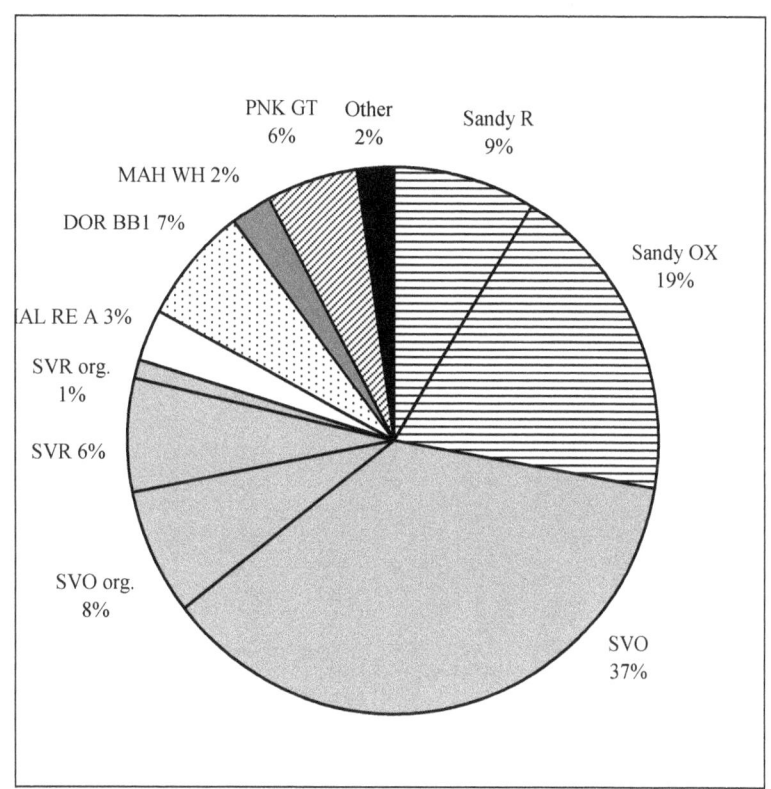

Figure 32. Area C–D pottery, fabric groups by percentage weight

The pottery was very abraded, reflecting the soil conditions on site, and was in most cases very fragmentary. The overall average sherd weight was 8g, although there was variation between features. Pit 6062, which produced a more substantial fragment of a Severn Valley ware tankard (Fig. 33.9), had an average sherd weight of 30g. The ditches in general produced the least fragmentary assemblages (Table 12); pottery from ditches D5 and D6 had an average weight of, respectively, 45g and 49g. Hearth 7017 appears to have had a relatively high average sherd weight, but included a single sherd of grog-tempered storage jar (Fabric F018) weighing 127g. The most fragmentary pottery came from layers, plough furrows, post-holes and surfaces. Just over half of the assemblage came from ditches and ring-gullies (Table 13), in particular ditch D2, forming the boundary between Plots B and C, and ring-gully R1 within Plot C.

Chronology

The dating of the assemblage is heavily reliant on coarse wares, and many of the forms were not closely datable. Sufficient evidence was recovered, however, to indicate a chronological framework for the site. Detailed lists of forms and fabrics by phase can be found in Appendices CD3–CD4.

Phase 1

The largest assemblage came from deposits associated with Phase 1 (Table 11). This included the majority of the identifiable forms (Appendix C3). These provided evidence for 2nd- to 3rd-century activity. Ditch D2 produced a sherd of Central Gaulish samian of Antonine date (Wild below). Some coarse ware forms dated broadly to the 2nd century, including a Malvernian tubby cooking pot (Fig. 33.8, 11, 12). Another dated to the 2nd–3rd century (Fig. 33.10). However, some of the diagnostic vessels dated to the late 3rd or 4th centuries, and are, presumably, intrusive from Phase 2 activity. Ditch D5 produced a Mancetter-Hartshill mortarium dating to the mid–late 3rd century (Timby below). Ditch D7 produced a typically late BB1 flanged bowl (Fig. 33.9) and pit 6062 a characteristically late Severn Valley ware tankard type (Fig. 33.6). A hearth in ring-gully R2 (feature 7017), produced a body sherd in pink grog-tempered ware (Fabric F018). This fabric is also typically associated with late 3rd- and 4th-century assemblages (Booth and Green 1989).

Phase 1/2

Phase 1/2 produced a much smaller assemblage, with only two identifiable Severn Valley ware forms (Appendix C3). One (Fig. 33.9) was a diagnostically late 3rd- to 4th-century type. The other was less closely datable (Fig. 33.4), but does have a parallel in a late 3rd-century context at Droitwich. Some residual Phase 1 material was included, notably a fragment from a form 38 or 44 bowl in Central Gaulish samian (Wild below) from pit 6087. This dated to the second half of the 2nd century AD. Some typically earlier Romano-British fabrics decreased or disappeared in this phase. The proportion of organic-tempered Severn Valley ware (Fabrics O02.13, O03.1 and O03.4) declined, and handmade Malvernian ware (Fabric N02.1) was absent from this and later phase assemblages (Appendix C5).

Phase 2

Phase 2 produced only 37 sherds of pottery. The diagnostic forms dated broadly to the 2nd to 3rd centuries, including a Severn Valley ware bowl (not illustrated) and a jar (Fig. 33.13).

Phase 3

Only 13 sherds of Romano-British pottery came from Phase 3 deposits, all residual.

Fabrics/ forms

Twenty-one wheelmade, and two handmade, fabrics were identified (Table 14; Appendix C1). The occurrence of fabrics by phase is detailed in Appendix C4. The divisions between some of the coarse wares may be rather subjective, reflecting varying proportions of a range of inclusions rather than absolute differences.

Over half of the assemblage comprised Severn Valley wares (Fig. 32), mainly oxidised (O02.1, O02.13, O03.1, O03.4) but including some reduced variants (G04, G04v, G05). Plain Severn Valley ware (O02.1, G04) was most common, though a significant proportion also had some level of organic inclusions (O02.13, O03.1, O03.4, G05). This latter group had distinctive black inclusions, rather than the burnt-out voids noted in some organic-tempered wares. One fabric had sand and organic inclusions (O02.13). These are all characteristics noted in the assemblages previously studied from Longdales Road (Evans, Chapter 3 above). The assemblage included a 4th-century Severn Valley ware tankard with a warped rim, an indication that it may have been produced in the vicinity of the site. This supports the evidence from the Area B excavation at Longdales Road, which produced a warped rim from a 3rd- to 4th-century Severn Valley ware jar (Evans, Chapter 3 above).

The various oxidised (O06.01, O06.05, O06.07, O06.09) and reduced (G06.05, G06.06, G06.07, G06.08) sandy wares occurred in a very limited range of forms (Appendix C4). The reduced sandy wares included copies of BB1 plain rimmed dishes, and a jar. These are all likely to be fairly local products.

The assemblage reflected a similar range of trade contacts as the previously studied groups: the Malvern area (a tubby cooking pot in Fabric N02.1), Dorset (bowls, dishes and a jar in BB1, Fabric B02), Mancetter Hartshill (Fabric M02) and Oxfordshire (Fabric P09). Additionally, the pink grog-tempered ware (Fabric F018) indicated trade links with the Milton Keynes area (Booth and Green 1989). Once again, there were no amphorae, the only imports being the Central Gaulish samian bowls.

Table 14. Area C–D, Romano-British coarse ware pottery, fabrics, sources and quantities

Common Name, NRFRC Fabric Code	Fabric Code	Qty	% Qty	Wt (g)	% Wt	Rim EVE	% Rim EVE
Reduced ware, Sandy	G06.05	27	5.6%	156	4.2%	0.17	5.4%
	G06.06	3	0.6%	115	3.1%	-	-
	G06.07	2	0.4%	37	1.0%	0.04	1.3%
	G06.08	2	0.4%	15	0.4%	0.05	1.6%
Oxidised ware, Sandy	O06.01	1	0.2%	87	2.3%	0.16	5.1%
	O06.05	8	1.7%	56	1.5%	-	-
	O06.07	8	1.7%	68	1.8%	-	-
	O06.09	34	7.0%	494	13.3%	0.08	2.6%
Severn Valley ware	O02.1	157	32.5%	808	21.7%	0.83	26.6%
	O02.13	109	22.6%	558	15.0%	0.75	24.0%
Organic variant	O03.1	15	3.1%	204	5.5%	0.31	9.9%
	O03.4	9	1.9%	74	2.0%	-	-
Reduced variant	G04	38	7.9%	234	6.3%	0.08	2.6%
	G04v	1	0.2%	5	0.1%	-	-
	G05	10	2.1%	48	1.3%	0.05	1.6%
Total Severn Valley ware		339	70.2%	1,931	52.0%	2.02	64.7%
Total Local / Regional wares		**424**	**87.8%**	**2,959**	**79.7%**	**2.52**	**80.8%**
Malvernian metamorphic, MAL RE A	N02.1	6	1.2%	116	3.1%	0.08	2.6%
Black Burnished ware, DOR BB 1	B02	43	8.9%	257	6.9%	0.34	10.9%
Mancetter-Hartshill mortaria, MAH WH	M02	1	0.2%	89	2.4%	0.08	2.6%
Oxfordshire white ware OXF WH	P09	3	0.6%	6	0.2%	-	-
Pink Grog-tempered ware PNK GT	F018	2	0.4%	207	5.6%	-	-
Total Traded wares		**55**	**11.4%**	**675**	**18.2%**	**0.5**	**16.0%**
White ware	W16	1	0.2%	23	0.6%	-	-
Mortaria (Timby, below)	M	1	0.2%	49	1.3%	0.1	3.2%
Total uncertain source		**2**	**0.4%**	**72**	**1.9%**	**0.1**	**3.2%**
CG Samian, Lezoux 2, LEZ SA 2	S03	2	0.4%	9	0.2%	-	-
Total Imported		**2**	**0.4%**	**9**	**0.2%**	**-**	**-**
TOTAL POTTERY		**483**		**3,715**		**3.12**	

See Appendix CD 1 for details of the fabrics.

Catalogue of illustrated pottery (percentage of rim surviving appears in brackets)

Fig. 33.1–13

B02

1 BI8.25. Rim from a conical bowl with a dropped flange, WA type 25 (Seager Smith and Davies 1993, 235, fig. 124), broadly dating to the late 3rd or 4th century. Diam. uncertain, (3%). Ring-gully R1, post-hole 6082, context 6081, Phase 1/2.

2 BI8.22. Rim from a conical bowl with a grooved, flange rim, WA type 24 (Seager Smith and Davies 1993, 235, fig. 123), broadly dating to the late 2nd to early 3rd century. Diam. 18cm (10%). Ditch D2, 6025, context 6024, Phase 1.

3 DA1.01. Rim from a straight-sided dish, WA type 20 (Seager Smith and Davies 1993, 233, fig. 123), produced throughout the Romano-British period but particularly common from the late 2nd century onwards. Diam. 18cm (4%). Ditch D7, 6085, context 6083, Phase 1.

G04

4 JN1.2. Severn Valley ware jar with a well defined bead rim. Not a closely dated form, although a similar jar rim was found at Bays Meadow, Droitwich in a late 3rd-century context (Barfield 2006, fig. 96, 73a), which might be consistent with other dating evidence from the site. Diam. 16cm (8%). Ring-gully R1, 6029, context 6028, Phase 1/2.

G06.05

5 JW19.1. Thickened, near triangular rim from a jar. Diam. 18cm (5%). Ring-gully R2, 7019, context 7018, Phase 1.

6 JLS19.1. Out-curving, slightly triangular rim from a large storage jar. Possibly copying a BB1 form. Diam. 30cm (8%). Ditch D6, 6130, context 6129, Phase 1.

G06.07

7 DA1.01. Rim from a straight sided dish, copying a BB1 form (see No 3 above). Diam. 24cm (4%). Ditch D6, 6132, context 6131, Phase 1.

N02.1

8 JK22.05. Near upright rim from a Malvernian tubby cooking pot. This form is dated to the 2nd century by Peacock (1967, fig. 1.1, 2), though it has subsequently been found in 1st century contexts (Green *et al.* 2001, 105). Diam. 19cm (8%). Pit 6017, context 6016, Phase 1.

O02.1

9 NC1.01. Rim and profile from a splayed tankard, a type dated to the 4th century by Webster (Webster 1976, fig. 7, E44). The rim is warped so the diameter is not reliable. Diam. 14cm (32%). Pit 6062, context 6065, Phase 1.

10 BC8.33. Fragmentary rim from a flanged bowl with a slight internal lip, Webster type F dating to the late 2nd or 3rd century (Webster 1976, fig. 8.50, 51). Diam. 22cm (16%). Pebble road surface, context 6074. Phase 1.

O02.13

11 JW19.1. Triangular rim from a wide-mouthed jar, a form dated by Webster to the mid to late 2nd century (Webster 1976, fig. 4, C22). Diam. 25cm (5%). Post-hole 6056, context 6016. Phase 1.

C/BKC7.01. Not illustrated: very abraded, everted rim from a small cup or beaker. Diam. 12cm (10%). Ditch D2, 6049, context 6048, Phase 1.

O03.1

12 JW19.1. Rounded, triangular rim from a wide-mouthed jar, mid to late 2nd century (Webster 1976, fig. 4, C22). Diam. 28cm (14%). Ditch D4, 7024, context 7023. Phase 1.

O06.01

13 JW20.01. Hooked rim from a wide-mouthed jar, a 2nd- to 3rd-century type (Webster 1976, C24, 25). Diam. 31cm (16%). Ditch D8, 6073, context 6072. Phase 2.

Function

The emphasis was once again on jars (45% by rim EVE), predominantly suitable for storage, although bowls (28%) were proportionately more common than in the Area B assemblage (Fig. 34). The bowls and dishes, in Severn Valley ware and BB1, could have been used for both food preparation and storage. Other forms comprised a tankard, a colander represented by a body sherd, a lid, a small cup or beaker, and two mortaria. There were no flagons, and the only table wares comprised the three sherds of samian (Wild below), all from 2nd-century bowls.

Discussion

The wider significance of pottery from Longdales Road has been discussed by Hancocks (Chapter 2 above) and by Evans (Chapter 3 above). More pottery from Area C–D was associated with earlier Romano-British deposits. However, the other assemblages also produced a quantity of 1st–2nd and 2nd–3rd-century pottery, often residual in Phase 2 features. Once again there is clear evidence for late 3rd–4th-century activity. The absence of shell-tempered ware, associated with the latest Romano-British deposits elsewhere in the region (Barfield 2006, 154; Evans 2004; Symonds 1997, figs 366 and 372), indicated that the site may have been abandoned by the mid–late 4th century. Otherwise, this assemblage reflects a similar range of utilitarian vessels to the previously analysed groups, and a similar range of sources.

Mortaria
by Jane Timby

Two sherds of mortaria (not illustrated) were recovered from Area C–D.

Catalogue

1 Rimsherd from Mancetter-Hartshill mortarium (Tomber and Dore 1998, 189 MAH, WH). Diam. 340mm. Fine white paste with sparse, mainly fine, black, angular trituration grits. Upstanding rim with downward projecting corrugated flange. Mid–late 3rd century. Ditch D5, 6097, context 6096, Phase 1.

2 Rimsherd from mortarium in pale brown fabric. Diam. 320mm. The vessel has an upright rim and a flat, horizontal, flange thickened at the edge. The sherd is in worn condition. At x20 magnification the paste contains a dense frequency of fine sub-angular to rounded quartz sand (less 0.5mm) with rare brown sub-angular grains protruding from the surface along with a scatter of red-brown argillaceous inclusions ranging from fine up to 2.5mm. Source uncertain. Typologically the sherd is likely to date to the 3rd century. Ditch D2, 6050, context 6047, Phase 1.

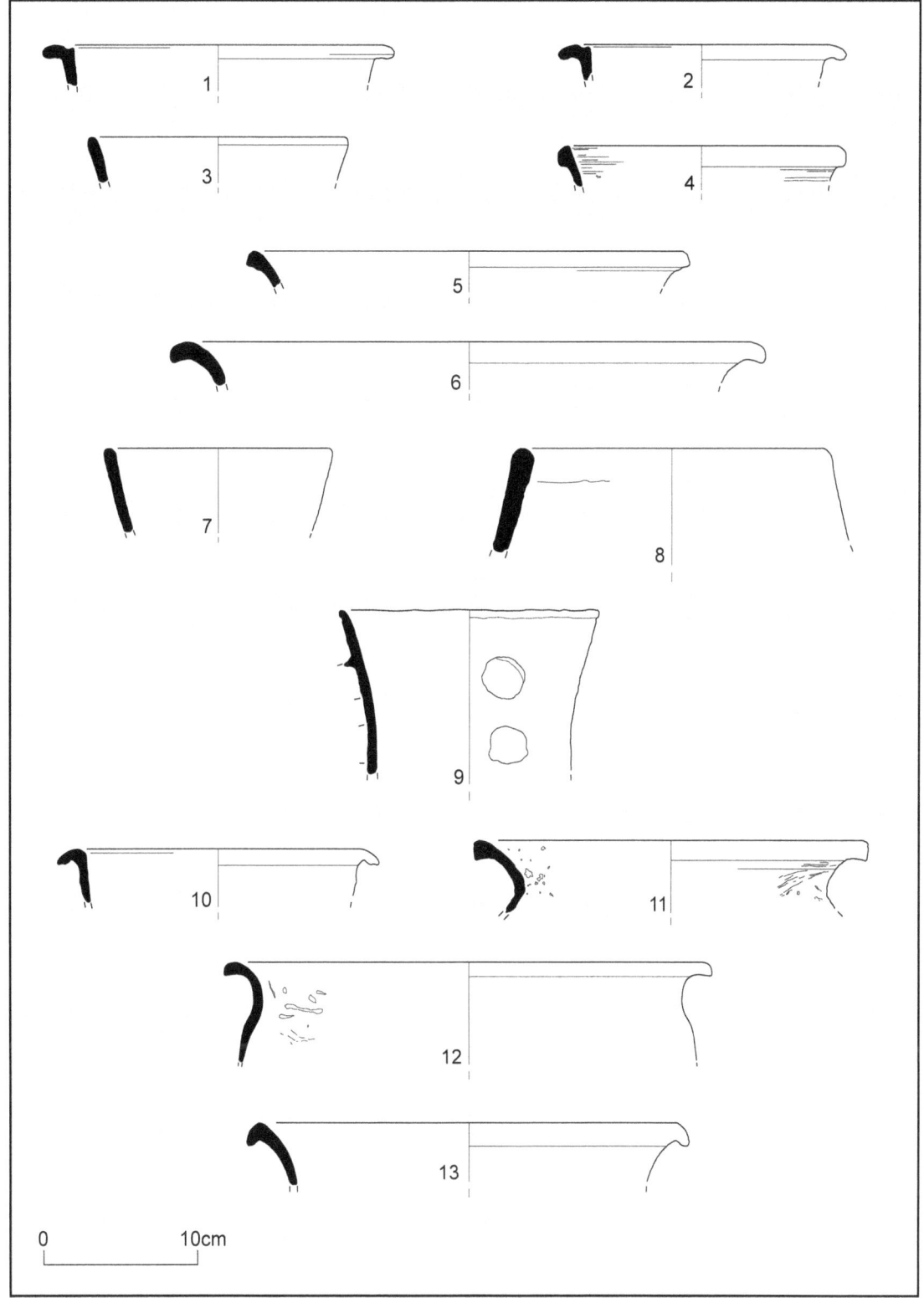

Figure 33. Area C–D pottery, nos 1–13 (scale 1:4)

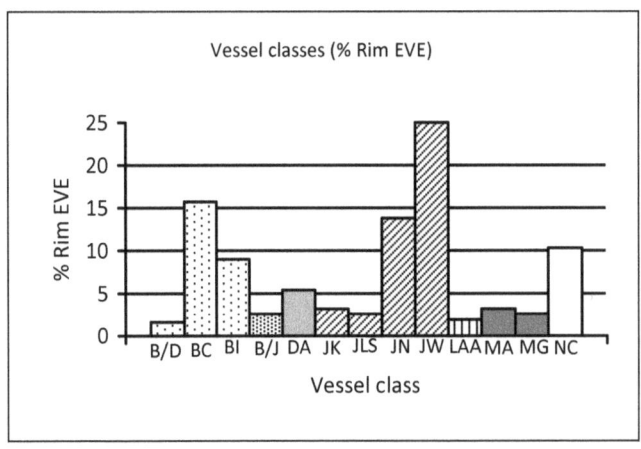

Figure 34. Area C–D pottery, vessel classes (percentage rim EVE)

Samian pottery
by Felicity Wild

The Area C–D fieldwork produced three sherds of samian ware (not illustrated), all heavily abraded. All are likely to be Central Gaulish and Antonine in date.

1–2   Two heavily abraded sherds, with the surface slip almost entirely gone, possibly from the same vessel, a possible bowl. Central Gaulish, probably Antonine. Ditch D2, 6009, context 6008, Phase 1.

3   Abraded footstand from a bowl such as form 38 or 44, Central Gaulish. The form of the footstand is typical of the second half of the 2nd century AD. Pit 6087, context 6086, Phase 1.

CHARRED PLANT REMAINS
by Val Fryer

A total of 22 samples from datable contexts were assessed (Fryer 2006).

With the exception of charcoal fragments, plant macrofossils were exceedingly scarce. Single grains of barley (Hordeum sp.) and wheat (Triticum sp.) were recorded along with a spelt wheat (T. spelta) glume base and individual seeds of persicaria (Persicaria maculosa/lapathifolia) and dock (Rumex sp.). Preservation was quite poor, with most remains being puffed and distorted (possibly as a result of combustion at very high temperatures).

The assemblages are all extremely small. There is no evidence for the primary deposition of material within any of the features recorded, and it would appear most likely that the assemblages are largely derived from scattered or wind-blown hearth waste, which accidentally became incorporated into the feature fills. As none of the assemblages are quantifiably viable (i.e. containing more than 100 specimens), no full analysis was worthwhile.

Plate 9. Area C–D, road Plot A/B boundary, view: east

Plate 10. Area C–D, Plot B, ring-gully R1 R2, view: northeast

Plate 11. Area C–D, detail of gully D2, view: south

Chapter 5

Other Investigations

This chapter summarises the results of the watching brief (2004) and trial-trenching (1998–2007), outside the excavated areas.

WATCHING BRIEF 2004, FIELDS 1–4 (Fig. 4)
by Alex Jones and Paul Mason

The results (Mason 2004) are described in field number order. There is insufficient data, in particular datable pottery, to phase the watching brief results.

Field 1 (Figs 35–36)

Description

A red/ brown clay subsoil with dispersed patches of pale yellow sand and gravel was recorded at a depth of 0.2–0.4m below the modern surface. Most of the features identified during the watching brief were found within this field. The main area of groundworks observed in this field adjoined, and slightly overlapped with, the Area B excavation (Chapter 3, above). The main feature groups were in the north and in the south of the areas recorded during the watching brief – and are described in that order.

The northern feature group comprised two small ditches (F109, F110) and a post-hole (F111). Feature F110 (Fig. 36.S.1) was curvilinear in plan, measuring a maximum of 0.5m in width and 0.25m in depth, and was cut to a U-shaped profile. It was backfilled with light grey clay-silt (1008). Ditch F109 was not excavated.

The southern group of features comprised areas of pebble surfacing (F102, F107, F112, F125), post-holes (F104, F105), a small pit (F103), and three ditches (F106, F108, F117/ F119). The pebble surfaces may originally have formed part of the same continuous feature. Detailed archaeological recording in this area was hampered by surface water and machine tyre ruts.

The post-holes (F104, F105) and the small pit (F103) together formed a southwest-northeast alignment, perhaps defining part of a fence. Ditch F117/ F119, recorded for an approximate length of 15m, was located to the south of the pebble surface. Both the surface and the ditch were aligned northwest-southeast. The ditch measured a maximum of 0.7m in width and 0.4m in depth and was cut to a V-shaped profile. It was backfilled with grey-brown clay-sand (1022). Northwest-southeast aligned ditch F117 (Fig. 36.S.2) was sealed by pebble surface F125. It was cut to a U-shaped profile and measured a maximum of 0.4m in depth. It was backfilled with mottled red-brown-grey clay-silt (1020), sealed by light grey silt-clay (1019, not illustrated).

Interpretation

Pebble surfaces F102, F107 and F112 probably formed part of the eastward continuation of surface F442 recorded within Area B (Fig. 21), which may have been extended to the east to form the southern boundary of Plot A (Area C–D, Fig. 28). The road probably extended across the full width of Field 1. Evidence from Area B suggests that the surface may have turned to the south, following the eastern boundary of Field 2 (Fig. 4).

Ditch F117/F119 could have formed part of the southern boundary of Plot A (Fig. 28). Ditch F119 was backfilled with a quantity of pottery, including late 3rd- to 4th-century forms, which may place the feature in Phase 3 (as defined in Area B) and Phase 2 (as defined in Area C–D). If this is the case, the overlying surface (F125) may be of slightly later date, contemporary with Phase 3B (Area B, Fig. 22) during which a quantity of pottery was deposited over the road surface when it went out of use. A possibility is that ditch F117/F119 formed part of the southern side of Enclosure E2, the eastern part of this side being formed by feature 306 (Vaughan 2002, fig. 10). Backfilled ditch F117/F119 was sealed by surface F125, which would suggest that, although itself undated, it was one of the latest Romano-British features found in Field 1.

Feature F110, a curvilinear ditch recorded towards the north of the watching brief area, probably formed part of one side of an enclosure; its diameter (over 30m) was too large to be interpreted as an eaves-drip gully. This feature is difficult to interpret as it was not recorded as extending into Area B to the west.

Lengths of Phase 1 ditches B6 (F108) and B5 (F109) in Area B (Fig. 22) were also recorded during the watching brief.

Field 2

Description

Previous investigations within the northern part of this field had been limited to a single trial-trench. A red/ brown clay subsoil with dispersed patches of pale yellow sand and gravel was recorded at a depth of 0.2–0.4m below the modern surface. In the extreme north of this field the subsoil was a light yellow-brown clay-sand. Three groups of archaeological features were identified, in the east, south and southeast of the areas recorded during the watching brief – described in that order.

The eastern feature (F120) was a curvilinear ditch, recorded for a distance of 4m. The ditch was cut to a V-shaped profile, measuring a maximum of 0.3m in width and 0.2m

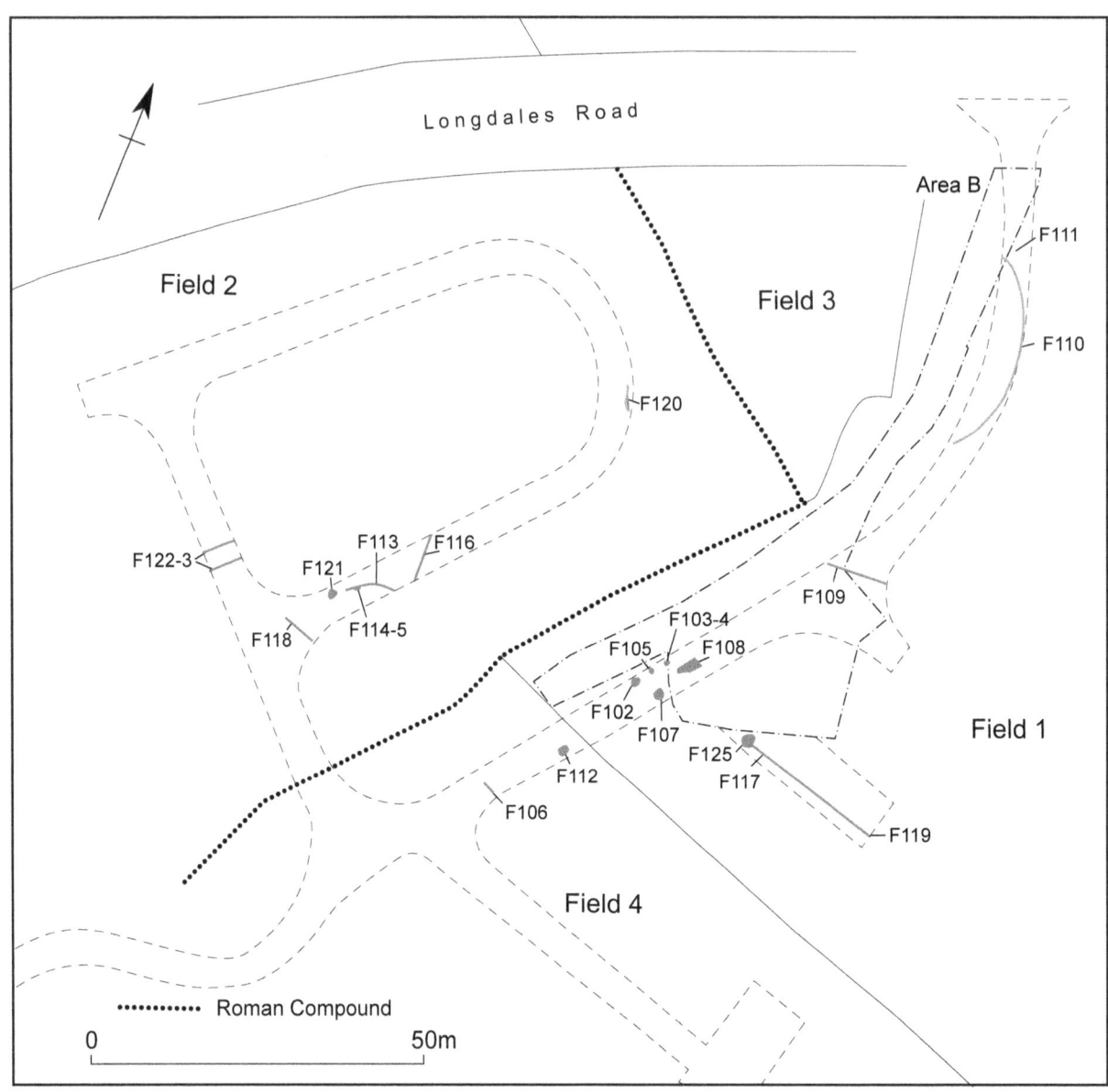

Figure 35. Watching brief, plan (scale 1:1000)

in depth. It was backfilled with grey clay-sand (1023). A number of curvilinear gullies, S-shaped in plan, were recorded during the Area A excavation (Chapter 2 above).

The southern feature group comprised ditches (F113, Fig. 36.S.3; F116, Fig. 36.S.S.4; F118) cut on different alignments, and a re-cut pit (F114–5). The northernmost feature of this group was a northwest-southeast aligned ditch (F116). It was cut to a V-shaped profile and measured a maximum of 0.6m in width and 0.3m in depth. The ditch was backfilled with mottled clay-sand (1016), sealed by mid-grey clay-sand (1015). To the south was a curvilinear ditch (F113), mainly aligned southwest-northeast. This ditch measured a maximum of 1.3m in width and 0.3m in depth. It was backfilled with mottled red/ brown/ grey clay-sand with frequent small stones and flecks of charcoal (1014), sealed by a mid-grey clay-sand with frequent small to medium stones (1010). This ditch may have cut two small pits: an oval pit (F114) backfilled with many small–medium stones in a sand-clay (1012), which was in turn cut by a smaller semi-circular feature (F115) backfilled with grey silt-clay (1013); neither was excavated. A spread of pebbles (1012) forming a yard surface (F121) was recorded to the west of ditch F113, also overlying it. The southernmost feature of the group was an approximately east-west aligned ditch (F118), recorded for a distance of 4m. It measured a maximum of 0.6m in width and 0.4m in depth and was dug to a V-shaped profile. It was backfilled with mid-grey clay-sand with occasional pockets of orange/ brown sand with flecks of charcoal (1021).

The southwestern feature group comprised two adjoining ditches (F122–3, Fig. 36.S.5), aligned southwest-northeast. Both were cut with flat-based profiles and measured an average of 1.6m in width and 0.3m in depth. Ditch F122 was backfilled with brown-yellow silt-clay (1024) and ditch F123 was backfilled with orange-yellow silt-clay (1025). No clear relationship could be recorded between the two ditches.

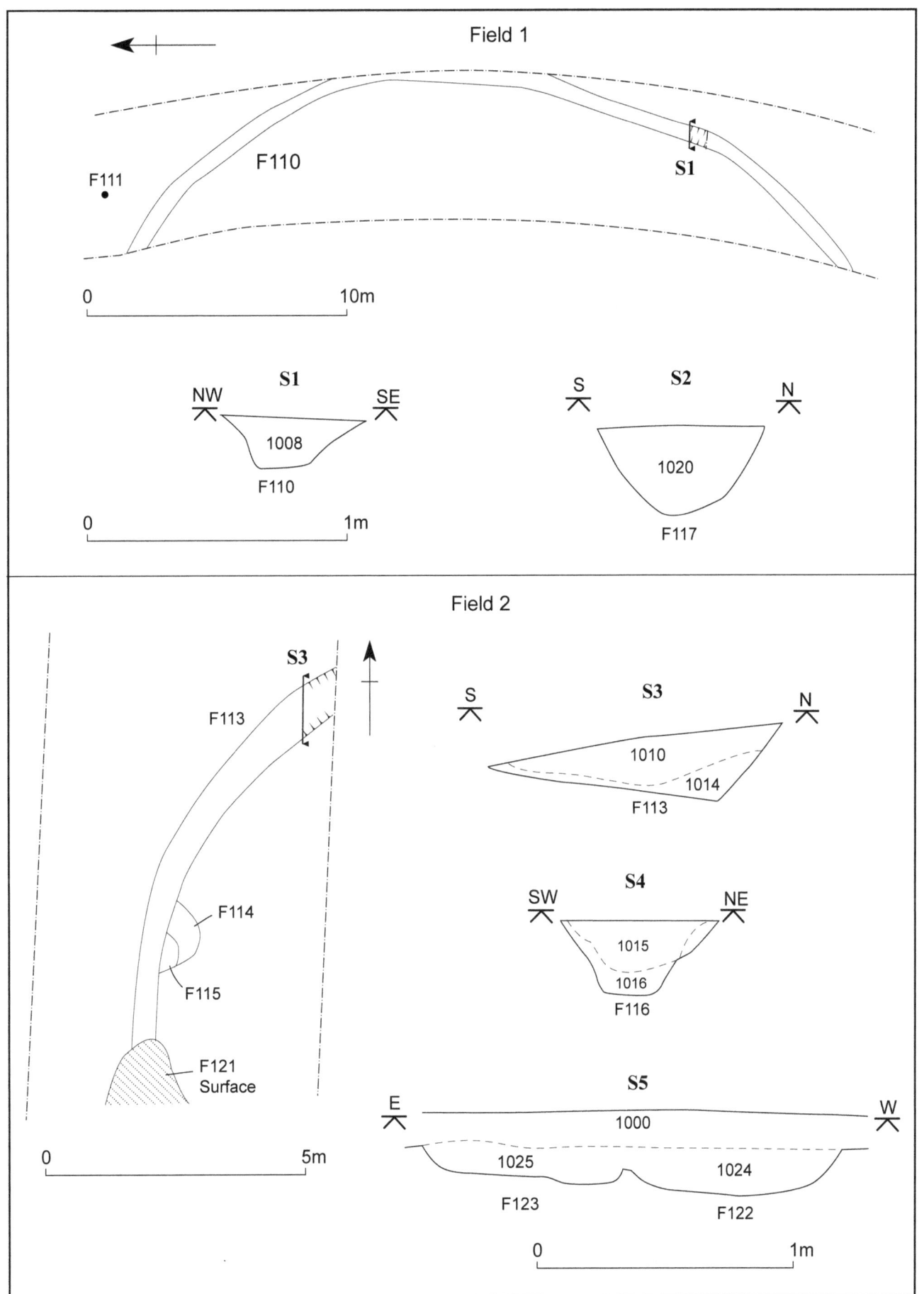

Figure 36. Watching brief, plan and sections (scales 1:200 and 1:20)

Table 15. Watching brief, summary of the Romano-British coarse ware pottery

Feature/ Context	Roman Sherd Count	Spot Date	Comments
F110/1008	3	Late 3rd–4th	Oxfordshire mortarium
F116/1015	5	Roman	SV ware bases and bodies
Layer 1017	2	Roman	Reduced SV ware body sherds
Layer 1018	1	Roman	Reduced SV ware body sherd
F119/1022	31	Late 3rd–4th	Good diagnostic group (see below)
F120/1023	3	Roman	SV ware body sherds
U/S	2	Roman	(Field 1) SV body sherds
U/S	1	Roman	(Field 2) SV body sherd
U/S	1	Roman/ post-med	(Furrow)
U/S	1	Roman/ post-med	(Field 2)
Total	50		

Key: SV = Severn Valley

Archaeological observation was also maintained during the partial stripping of topsoil along the line of a temporary access road in the south of this field – but, in the event, only the upper part of the topsoil was removed and no features of archaeological interest could be identified.

Interpretation

The results of the watching brief indicate a focus of settlement within the Romano-British compound perpetuated by the modern Field 2 boundaries (Chapter 3 above). Two curvilinear features (F120 and F113) were recorded, both of which may be too large in diameter to represent eaves-drip gullies. A large diameter curvilinear gully at Metchley (Jones 2001, Area 2) was interpreted as a possible animal compound. At Birdlip quarry (Mudd 1999b, 528) the excavator underlined the importance of the circular hut form – which persisted to the late 3rd century – as being important for the social life of the inhabitants. If the Longdales Road inhabitants were culturally accustomed to domestic architecture in the round, larger structures, such as animal enclosures built with the same form, may have fitted the traditional mindset. The two pits (F114–F115), cut by feature F113, could belong to Phase 1–2, as defined in Area A. Ditch F106 appeared to follow the same alignment as ditch F118 in Field 2.

The identified ditches followed a variety of orientations. Ditch F116 did not follow any of the Phase 1–Phase 3 ditch alignments in the field. Ditch F118 was roughly parallel with the northern side of Phase 1–2 Enclosures A1–A2, and may have been a contemporary feature. Parallel ditches F122–F123 were cut at an approximate right-angle to the alignment of Phase 3 ditch A5 (Fig. 12). They could represent a re-cut boundary, although the relationship could not be established during the watching brief.

Field 4

Description and interpretation

The removal of 0.2–0.4m of topsoil over the line of the main access road revealed a red-brown clay subsoil with dispersed patches of pale yellow sand and gravel. Work in this field was undertaken in very wet conditions, making the identification of potential features difficult.

A spread of pebbles sealed in a dark soil matrix (F112), observed in the northwest corner of the field, may relate to the cobbled surface recorded to the northwest during the Area B excavation (Chapter 3 above). The other feature identified during the watching brief comprised a ditch (F106), aligned northwest-southeast, which measured 0.4m in width. It was recorded for a length of 1.5m, but was not excavated. These features demonstrated that Romano-British activity extended into the northwestern corner of this field. Other observations included the excavation of a service trench, following the line of the road, and, within the footprint of a building, to the east of the road – both with negative results.

A total of five trenches were excavated to test the area adjoining the Ryknild Street in 2007 (Fig. 4; Burrows 2007). The only feature recorded was a pebble surface recorded in the southeast of Trench 1. This feature could have defined an area of pebble hardstanding adjoining the Roman road, or a trackway laid out at a right-angle to the road, by analogy with the evidence from Area C–D (Chapter 4 above). No finds of Roman date were recovered from this trenching.

Romano-British pottery
by C Jane Evans

A total of 50 sherds of pottery were recovered from the watching brief, as detailed in Table 15. Most deposits only produced only handfuls of undiagnostic sherds. The largest assemblage came from feature F119. This included some diagnostically later Romano-British forms: a late 3rd- to 4th-century BB1 jar, WA type 3 (Seager Smith and Davies 1993, fig. 122) and a Severn Valley ware wide-mouthed jar, similar to one dated by Webster to the 4th century (Webster 1976, fig. 6.31). Feature F110 produced fragments from an Oxfordshire mortarium (Type 22, dating AD 300–400+: Young 2000, 68).

TRIAL-TRENCHING OUTSIDE AREAS EXCAVATED (Fig. 3)
by Alex Jones

East of Ryknild Street (Edwards and Jackson 1998)

No Romano-British features were found, possibly indicating that area remained woodland. Three parallel gullies, a shallow pit, a pebble surface, and two possible post-holes were revealed in Trench 21 (Fig. 3). The features were associated with a quantity of cooking pot of 13th–14th century date. A single dwelling may have been located here. Trench 22 revealed a layer of pebbles, interpreted as a medieval holloway. Ridge and furrow earthworks recorded extensively to the east of Ryknild Street. In Trench 21 the ridge and furrow cut the recorded features.

Fields A–B (Patrick and Darch 2002; Fig. 3)

Two east-west aligned gullies, 6m apart, were recorded in Field A. They measured an average of 0.5m in width, and 0.16m in depth. The gullies may be interpreted as drainage features flanking a pebble surface.

A group of features of Romano-British date were recorded in Field B. These comprised possible pits, three post-holes forming part of a timber-framed building or fence, a pebble surface, and a gully. The heat-fractured stones found in the post-hole backfills were interpreted as pot boilers for heating water. Most of the pottery was dated in the broad range from 1st–4th century AD. The features represent *in situ* Romano-British activity, but are difficult to interpret further. This trenching demonstrates that Romano-British settlement extended to the south of Primrose Hill.

Chapter 6

Discussion and Conclusion

by Alex Jones

CHRONOLOGY AND SEQUENCE

In common with most Romano-British roadside settlements (Smith 1987, 3), there was no evidence of pre-Roman occupation at Longdales Road. The results of excavation along the line of the M6 Toll (Booth 2006, 506) suggest Iron Age–Roman continuity away from Wall. Sites 19 and 29 in particular may have originated in the Mid–Late Iron Age (*ibid.*).

The Roman army reached the west midlands around AD 47 (Todd 2004, 50). Forts of Claudian date are recorded at Metchley (Jones 2001, see Chapter 1 above for a summary of the military sequence), at Lower Alvesley Lodge, Alcester (Booth and Evans 2001, 301), and elsewhere (Fig. 1). The earliest Roman feature at Longdales Road would have been Ryknild Street, located beyond the eastern boundary of the areas investigated 2002–2007. This road formed part of the military communication networks laid out towards the later 1st century AD. Although undated, it is believed to post-date Watling Street (Booth 2006, 503), for which a date in the AD 70s is suggested by Gould (1966; 1997, 351). Despite 1st-century military activity along Ryknild Street, locally linking Alcester with Metchley, very little 1st-century pottery was recovered from the Longdales Road excavations. A few sherds of residual coarse ware pottery dating to the 1st century were found in Area A (Fig. 4, Chapter 2 above), and two sherds of residual samian, both dated AD 40–100, from Area B (Chapter 3 above). Perhaps most surprising was the lack of early Romano-British material from Area C–D (Chapter 4, above), adjoining the road. Excavations in the 1950s and more recently at Parsons Hill, King's Norton (Fig. 2), have produced evidence of later 1st–2nd-century AD Romano-British activity. This comprised gravel surfaces overlain by burnt deposits containing pottery, and a nearby re-cut ditch (Foard Colby 2007; Fig. 2).

Continued military occupation at Alcester is suggested into the first quarter of the 2nd century (Booth and Evans 2001, 303) – significantly around the time that the first settlement is recorded at Longdales Road. This timing is interesting, since such a military garrison might be expected to provide a ready market for surplus production in their hinterland. Alcester developed in the 2nd century from the Bleachfield Street fort (Booth 1994, 164). The pattern of pottery supply to Alcester indicates a 2nd-century re-alignment of suppliers and dislocation of trading patterns (Booth and Evans 2001, 308) which may help to provide a context for the establishment of the Longdales Road settlement. The Late Iron Age settlement at Tiddington, Warwickshire (Palmer 1983), was reorganised in the early 2nd century. In upland Derbyshire, for example at Roystone Grange, Staden, and Rainster Rocks, new sites were founded in the 2nd century as a result of the reorganisation of rural settlement after the redeployment of military garrisons further to the north (Branigan 1991).

It was the location of the site along the road network, the raised plateau on which it was located, the availability of pasture, and a nearby water supply, which provided a catalyst for the establishment of a settlement here, possibly together with local factors now unrecoverable. The first double-ditched enclosure at Longdales Road (A1) was laid out in the 2nd century (Fig. 37), but more precise dating is not possible because early finewares were absent. More precise dating from samian of AD 120–160 is provided by the Area B livestock funnel in the northwestern angle of the Romano-British compound (modern Field 2, Fig. 4) within which Enclosure A1 was set, as well as by the absence of earlier finewares from later Area A contexts. Although dating evidence is sparse from the roadside plots, a similar chronology for their first layout may be suggested. Enclosures A1–A2 and the surrounding Romano-British compound continued in use during the 3rd century, during which time the livestock funnel (Area B) continued to be remodelled.

The latest, small-scale episode of settlement in Area A (Phase 3) and Area B (Phase 3A–B) is dated to the later 3rd–early 4th century. This later activity is mainly represented by soils deposited over earlier pebble surfaces. These deposits contained mortaria dated to the second half of the 3rd century, and to the late 3rd–early 4th century (F141, Area A), by pottery dated AD 280–370 (ditch re-cut A33 in Area A), and by a mortarium dated AD 250–350+ (overlying surface F442 in Area B). The only later enclosure (Enclosure E2) in Area C–D (Figs 26–27) contained pottery dated to the late 3rd–4th century, by which time the roadside frontage may have been given up. The later 3rd–4th century-activity may have been limited, and possibly sporadic. Evans (Chapter 4 above) notes that the absence of shelly wares, common on settlements post-AD 350, indicates that all activity at Longdales Road had probably ceased by that time, although Ryknild Street may have continued in use.

LAYOUT

The archaeological evidence for plot width, depth, alignment and sequence (Fig. 38)

Three plots, and part of a fourth, were excavated along the western road frontage (Figs 27–28, Chapter 4 above). The

DISCUSSION AND CONCLUSION

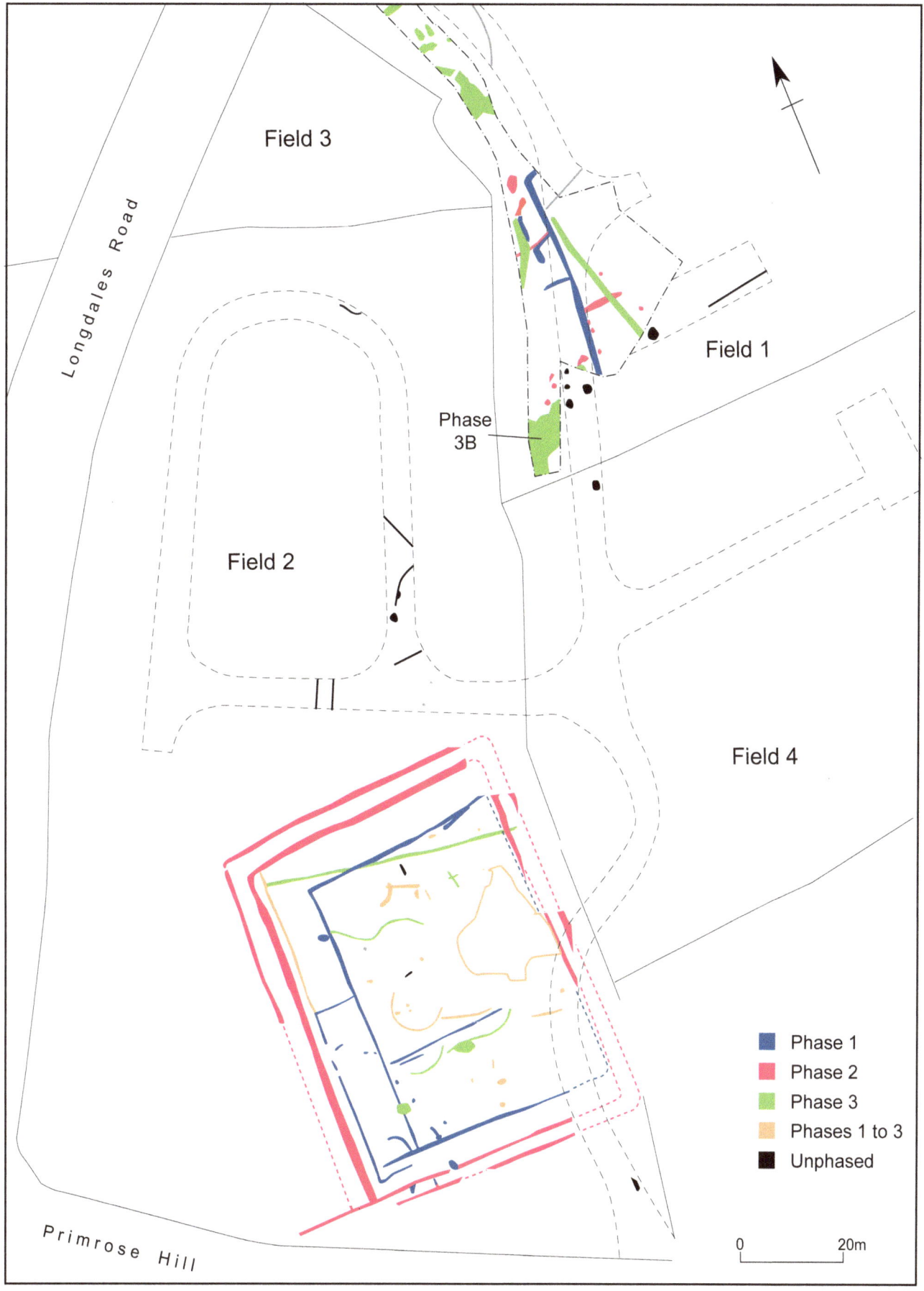

Figure 37. Areas A and B, simplified plan of phasing

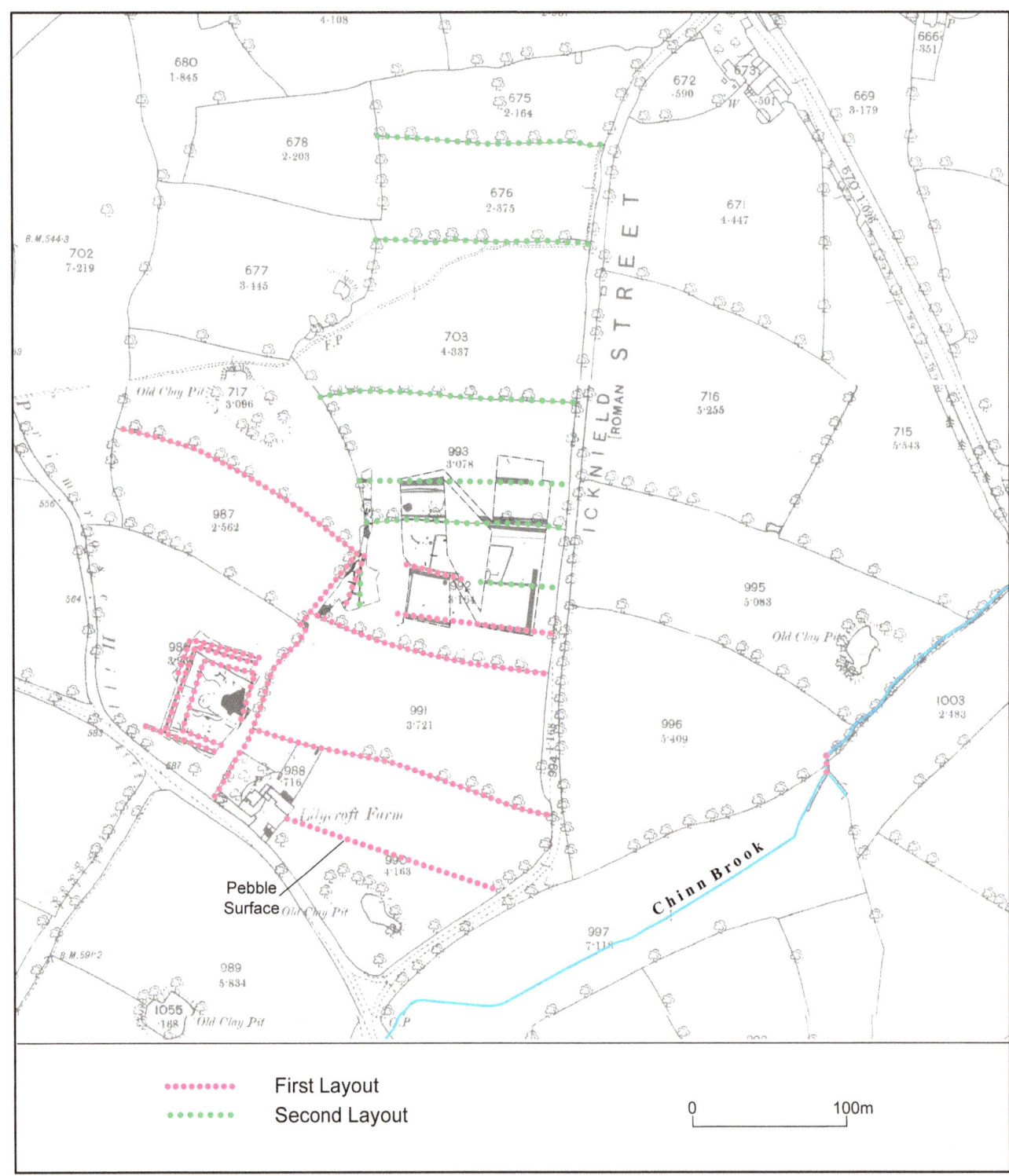

Figure 38. First Edition Ordance Survey map, the evidence for the first and second stages of plot layouts

plots were of differing widths (A, 28m; B and C, 35m), which may suggest that the land was not laid out as one event or, if it was, that the allotment was unequal (Smith 1987, 31). Although the excavated sample is admittedly very small, the location of ring-gullies within the broader Plots B and C may suggest that the narrower plots (e.g. A) could have been unoccupied.

The 35m-wide plot boundaries may have been laid following Roman measurements, in units of 120 *pes monetalis* (0.295m: Rawes 1981), or half an *actus*. Plots 35m wide identified at Duncote Farm, Shropshire, were interpreted as market gardens (Jones 1994, 67). The 28m-wide plots at Longdales Rod corresponded to 94 *pes monetalis*, which is not a recognised Roman unit of measurement, although plots 29m wide were recorded at Birdlip quarry, Gloucestershire (Mudd 1999a; Fig. 39). The

DISCUSSION AND CONCLUSION

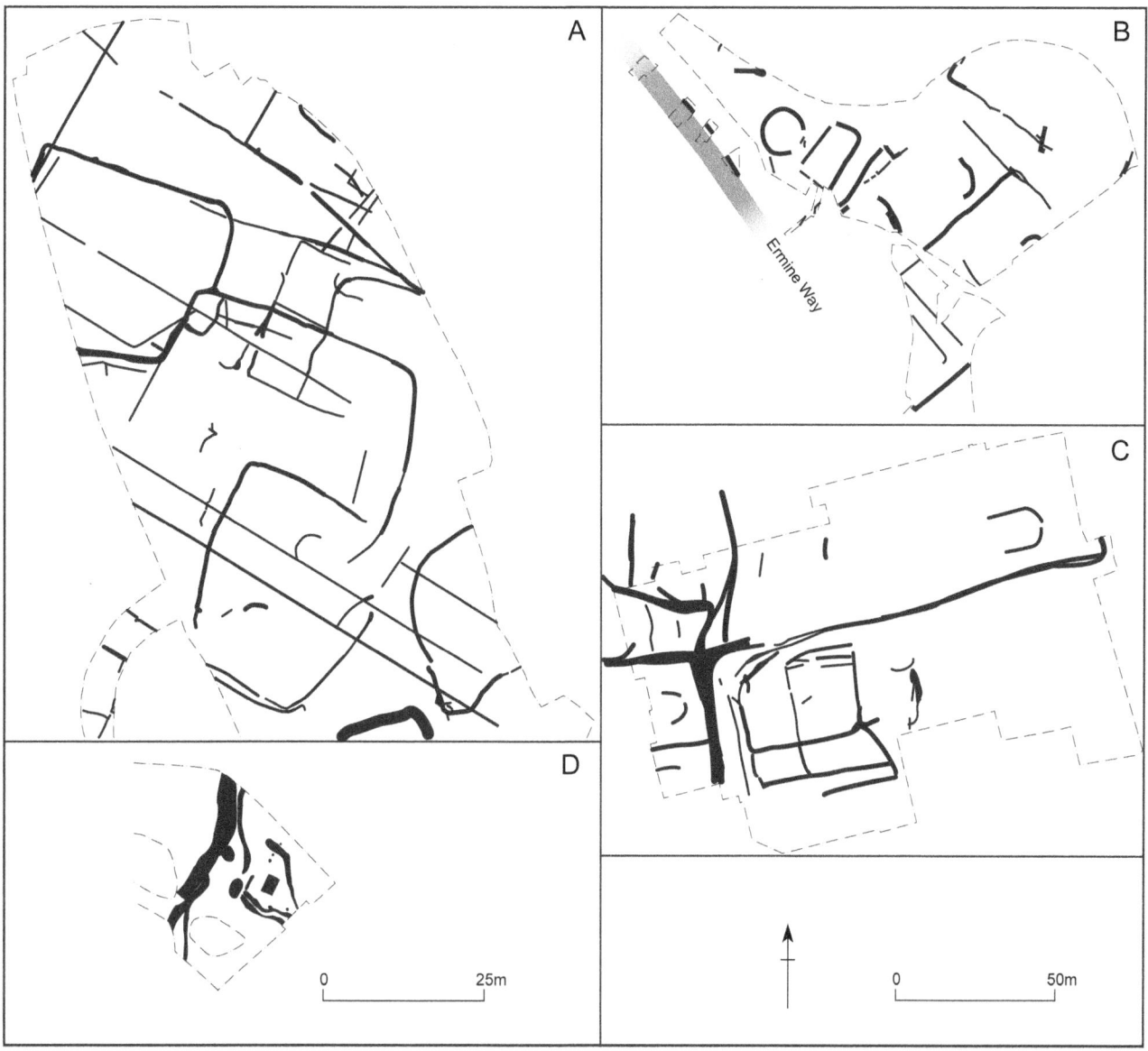

Figure 39. Simplified comparative plans of Romano-British livestock complexes, (A) Site 29, M6 Toll, (B) Birdlip quarry, (C) Orton Hall Farm, Cambridgeshire, (D) Metchley Roman fort, Birmingham, Area 9

roadside plot boundaries at Tort Hill West, Cambridgeshire (Ellis *et al.* 1998, 110 and fig. 9), measured 25m and 35m in width. They were interpreted as market garden plots, or temporary stock enclosures, in which case the ditches would have functioned as trenches for solid stockades, forming corrals for horses, an interpretation based on the number of horse bones found.

Within the excavated features two alignments are represented: the first defined by the Area A enclosure, the second by the majority of the roadside plot boundaries. In Area B (Figs 21–22), where the two alignments intersect, the Enclosure A1–A2 alignment (ditch B6) is cut by the north-south alignment (ditch B3) – which suggests that the former belonged to the earlier layout. Less clear is the excavated evidence from Area C–D. Here, plot boundary ditch D1a is cut at a right-angle to Ryknild Street, while ditch D1 to the west is cut on an alignment closer to that of Enclosure A1–A2; but no direct relationship between the two ditches could be recorded (Figs 27–28). However, the eastern ditch (D5) of adjoining Enclosure E1 respected ditch D1, while the eastern enclosure ditch (D4) was cut by ditch D1a, which could suggest that it was also later than ditch D1 to the west. Significantly, this follows the same sequence as that recorded in Area B.

Historic map evidence (Fig. 38)

Consideration of the excavated evidence in tandem with historic mapping (e.g. Fig. 6), could allow some tentative deductions to be made concerning the broader layout of the Romano-British roadside plot series associated with the settlement. Modern field layouts often follow a similar alignment to their Romano-British predecessors, for example around Wroxeter (e.g. Ellis *et al.* 1994, 109) and also elsewhere (Taylor 2007, 61). In addition to the Field 1 and 4 boundaries on the western Ryknild Street frontage

(Fig. 4), other field boundaries to the north (C–D) and to the south (A, Figs 6 and 38) are mapped at, or close to, a right-angle to the Roman road. These could have originated as plot boundaries associated with the Romano-British settlement. Away from the road frontage, the northern and southern Field E boundaries also form an approximate right-angle to the road. Ryknild Street will, of course, have been the dominant factor in the local landscape, influencing the pattern of field boundaries up to the present. Whilst it cannot be proved that the post-medieval boundaries (with the exception of the boundary perpetuating the line of Romano-British ditch 6109, Figs 27–8) respected Romano-British plot boundaries, it is possible, although by no means proven, that the modern field pattern could in part respect Romano-British field boundaries.

The excavated roadside plot boundaries (Area C–D, Figs 27–28, excluding ditch D1) (Fig. 35), Field C and D boundaries, and the northern boundary of Field 1 were laid out at a right-angle to the Roman road. A second alignment, at ten degrees off the former, is evident in Field 4, in Field A, and also in the boundaries of Field E to the northwest. Significantly, this second alignment follows that of the shorter axis of Enclosures A1–A2 and ditch B6 in Area B (Fig. 4). This alignment could have included a minimum of seven roadside plots, three in Field 4, two in Field 1, and two in Field A.

As noted above, the combined evidence from the Area B and Area C–D excavations therefore suggests that Enclosures A1–A2 and the parallel plot boundaries pre-dated the plot boundaries aligned at an exact right-angle to the road.

Could this suggested sequence allow a hypothetical model of the broader development of the Longdales Road settlement to be proposed? The recorded sequence would suggest that Enclosure A1–A2, its integral compound (Field 1), Field E, and several roadside plots to the east of the enclosure following the common alignment, were laid out during the earliest Romano-British occupation of the Longdales Road site. The northernmost recorded limit of this early settlement was defined by ditch D1 (Plot A/B boundary), which, significantly, was approximately flush with the northwestern angle of Field 2 (the Romano-British compound, Fig. 4) that formed part of the same layout. It is also notable that the east-west bounds of Field E, to the rear of the road frontage, follow the Enclosure A1–A2 alignment, although this was not recorded elsewhere to the rear of the road frontage. This earlier layout followed the topography rather than the Ryknild Street alignment.

The second stage in roadside layout may have been formed by the plots arranged at an exact right-angle to the Roman road. The southern limit of this later plot series was formed by ditch D1a. It is assumed that the two alignments were in contemporary use.

SETTLEMENT MORPHOLOGY

The three elements of Romano-British activity at Longdales Road comprise the Roman road, the double-ditched enclosures (A1–A2) and associated compound and, thirdly, the roadside plots. Topographically, Ryknild Street was aligned following, and slightly downslope of, the eastern edge of the natural ridge (Figs 4–5).

The double-ditched enclosures and associated roadside plots formed the earliest settlement at Longdales Road. The enclosures were located at, or near the crest of, the natural ridge, which would have provided better drainage than the Roman road frontage. The first double-ditched enclosure (A1) was characterised by the regularity of its ditched layout as well as by the complex treatment of the various entrances, which indicate an association with animal husbandry although animal bone did not survive in the acid subsoil. A feature of Enclosure A1 was the wide spacing between the enclosure ditches, which may have been intended to facilitate herding or driving livestock around the enclosure perimeter. A sub-enclosure, possibly used for penning animals, was recorded along its western side. Enclosure A1 and its successor (Enclosure A2) were located within the ditched compound defined by the surviving Field 2 boundaries. Enclosure A2 was re-sited slightly to the west of its predecessor, possibly to create a droveway between the eastern side of the enclosure and the same side of the compound. A number of curvilinear ring-gullies were recorded within the enclosure interiors, indicating occupation, which could not be securely stratigraphically or chronologically related to the enclosure ditch sequence. The quantity of pottery deposited in Enclosures A1–A2 (417 sherds), compared with the number of sherds recovered from the 'funnel' compound complex (Area B, 726 sherds, excluding Phase 3B), suggests only limited occupation, rubbish disposal within the enclosures, or correspondingly higher quantities of pottery loss within the Area B complex.

Overall, the most notable feature of the excavations was the limited evidence for roadside activity. This area was also the first to be given up, possibly because of its poor drainage. Whilst the immediate Ryknild Street frontage was not available for investigation, the evidence from Area C–D suggests that most activity within the roadside plots was located at some distance from the road. Although temporary structures built on earth-fast foundations would be difficult to detect archaeologically, associated activity would undoubtedly result in the accumulation of considerable debris, including pottery – which would be identified at excavation. Only comparatively small quantities of pottery were collected from Area C–D (483 sherds from investigations of approximately 9,500 square metres, equivalent to 0.05 sherds per metre). The adjoining eastern Ryknild Street frontage occupied a steeply sloping southeast-facing scarp which may have been unsuitable for settlement.

A parallel for the limited roadside activity at Longdales Road is provided by excavations at the settlement of Birdlip quarry, Gloucestershire, established alongside Ermine

Street in the later 2nd century (Mudd 1999a, 238; Fig. 39). Here the roadside frontage was never at a premium, and strip buildings were not laid out adjoining Ermine Street (*ibid.*, 238). While the faunal remains and plant remains suggest that mixed farming was practised here, many of the ditched enclosures may have functioned as animal paddocks, with cattle and horses used for traction as well as long-distance transport (Mudd 1999b, 242), suggesting an association with the *cursus publicus*. In contrast, the layout of the Meole Brace settlement, established in the mid-2nd century, was more typical of Romano-British roadside settlements. Settlement here occupied a length of approximately 190m with properties strung out along the road frontage, forming a zone of occupation not extending more than 40m from the frontage (Hughes 1994, 53), with strip buildings fronting directly onto the road. Excavation here (Evans *et al.* 1994) produced 3,705 sherds of pottery (amounting to approximately 0.39 sherds per square metre).

FUNCTION AND ECONOMY

The excavated evidence presents a paradox. While the enclosures and plots had presumably been established here because of the roadside location, as well as to take advantage of the natural plateau, the immediate roadside zone – usually providing the greatest opportunities for trade – was largely ignored. A range of agricultural, industrial and service industries was typically carried out from roadside settlements (Burnham and Wacher 1990; Smith 1987, 59; Crickmore 1984, 71 and 199), exploiting the economic potential of the roadside. This section of the discussion considers the evidence from Longdales Road in order to ascribe a function, or functions, to the settlement. The finds evidence, principally pottery, is next considered; bone did not survive at all because of the acid subsoil.

Origins

The earliest economic stimulus to the establishment of roadside settlements was often provided by the military – with settlement developing from a *vicus* established outside a fort (Millett 1990, table 1, model 1), as for example at Greensforge (Jones 1999), Alcester (Booth and Evans 2001), Wall (Gould 1964), and elsewhere. At Longdales Road there is no evidence of military occupation, however shortlived. Similarly, the *vicus* at Metchley fort, only 3km distant from Longdales Road, was small and only briefly occupied (Jones 2002). Recent reinterpretation of the evidence from Leintwardine (Brown 1996) illustrates economic dependency between the civilian settlement established there, first with the earlier fort established at Jay Lane, 0.6km distant, and also with the later fort at Brandon, 1.6km distant (*ibid.*, 564). There is no such evidence for economic interdependence between Metchley and Longdales Road, although the Metchley annexes in particular (Jones 2005), in use until the end of the 2nd century, could have functioned for coralling animals.

Livestock rearing or corralling, the 'animal management system'

The most likely function of the Longdales Road settlement is one associated with livestock rearing, collection or management. Some rural settlements (e.g. Orton Hall Farm: Mackreth 1996) have been attributed to livestock farming on the basis of the excavated layouts and the associated animal bone. Elsewhere, where animal bone does not survive in the soil conditions, as at Longdales Road, and Site 19 (Wishaw Hall Farm) and Site 29 (Langley Mill Farm) along the M6 Toll (Booth 2006), enclosures have been attributed a function associated with livestock farming based on the recorded layouts alone. The suggested physical evidence for livestock husbandry at Longdales Road is summarised in Table 16. In summary, this includes the layout of entrances at the enclosure corners to facilitate livestock herding (Pryor 1998, 101; e.g. Site 19, M6 Toll: Trevarthen 2006, fig. 19.6), the subdivision of Enclosure A1 to create possible subsidiary livestock pens, and the provision of 'funnel-type' ditched arrangements usually associated with livestock farming. 'Funnel' entrances, such as the examples recorded in Area B at Longdales Road and adjoining the Metchley military stores depot (Jones 2002), are a typical feature of livestock enclosures (e.g. Fasham 1987).

Ditched droveways are also typically associated with livestock farming (e.g. Whitemoor Haye, Staffordshire (Coates 2002 and Hewson 2006), and Site 19 M6 Toll (Trevarthen 2006, 287–324, fig. 19.6)). Their possible absence from the archaeological record at Longdales Road does not preclude interpretation of the site as associated with animal husbandry, in particular because they could have been located in areas which were not excavated or not excavated in detail. Parallel ditches B1 and B2 in Area B may perhaps be interpreted as a droveway (Fig. 22).

The closest excavated parallel for the Longdales Road layout – in particular the Area A enclosures, integral animal compound (Field 2) and its funnel entrance arrangement (Area B) – is the arrangement of small enclosures, droveways and animal compounds at Orton Hall Farm, Cambridgeshire (Mackreth 1996; Fig. 39). Here the excavator identified a stockyard maintained through most of the Romano-British period, accessed by ditched droveways and containing a variety of enclosures, including complex or funnel-shaped entrances. These arrangements were interpreted by the excavator as forming an 'animal management system' (*ibid.*, 220) containing specialised side areas in the main stockyard for feeding, watering, lambing, breeding and culling animals. This amounted to a more complex overall arrangement than that required for the collection or processing of cereal crops (*ibid.*, 221). Each species would have required its own handling/management set-up (Pryor 1998, 98), for diverse activities including droving, batching, confining, inspection and sorting. In order to be stockproof, the ditches would have been complemented with banks and hedges (*ibid.*, 85 and 87), which have left no trace in the archaeological record at Longdales Road. Such a stockyard would also have functioned to keep wild animals out (*ibid.*, 82).

Table 16. Suggested physical evidence for animal husbandry at Longdales Road

Phase/ Group	Feature	Interpretation
AREA A		
1 Enclosure A1	A16, A26, associated pits	Livestock entrance at corner of enclosure
1 Enclosure A1	A15, A26	Entrance to sub-enclosure
1 Enclosure A1	A17, F380–1, F383	Entrance to enclosure
1 Enclosure A1	A9, A10/a, A26, A15, A12, A6	Sub-enclosure for corralling livestock
1 Enclosure A1	Outer and inner ditches	Separation of 9m retained to run stock between?
1 Enclosure	A27, A28	Subdivisions of enclosure interior, ?retaining gap for running of stock
2 Enclosure A2	A8, A1, entrance gap at NW angle	Livestock entrance
1	Field 2	Modern field boundaries respect Roman livestock compound with entrance arrangement in Area B
2 Enclosure A2	A18–19, A20, F387	Livestock driven between ditches, and into southern entrance
AREA B		
1 Enclosure B1	B5–B6 and B7–8 and B10	Entrance 'funnel' for livestock integral with Field 2 livestock compound
2	Ditches B9 and B4	Entrance 'funnel' for livestock
3 Enclosure B2	B3 and B11	Entrance 'funnel' for livestock
AREA C–D		
1	Plots A–D	Depth of plots to rear of road frontage
1 Enclosure E1	D5–D6, 6134 and 6136	Entrance at NW corner of enclosure, further defined by pit and 6136

The faunal remains from Orton Hall Farm were typical of a production site with a considerable animal population (Mackreth 1996, 222). A viable herd size of 20–40 cattle was suggested, based on 0.6ha of the pasture per animal, plus additional pasture for hay, a total of approximately 23ha, including pasture for hay (*ibid.*, 223), would have been required. The composition and age profile of the animal population at Longdales Road cannot be known, although some of the entrance features are notably narrow, perhaps suggesting sheep rather than cattle. Pryor (1998, 106) suggests a ratio of 10 sheep plus their lambs to the hectare, so that a total area of 3ha would be required for a minimum viable herd size of 30 sheep.

Barn type accommodation would have been required for calving/ lambing (Mackreth 1996, 226), or at least a secure stock enclosure, such as that provided at Longdales Road by the Romano-British compound (modern Field 2, Fig. 4). It is possible that Area A pebble surface F141 could have formed the floor of one or more barns. The livestock herders would have been presumably housed within circular dwellings (Area A, and Area C–D), and at least one circular dwelling was recorded at Site 29 (Langley Mill Farm) along the M6 Toll (Powell and Ritchie 2006, fig. 29.6). The elaborate entrance arrangements at Orton Hall Farm and Longdales Road suggest a connection with the sorting and separation of livestock. Similarly, the out-turned enclosure ditch terminal, partly closing an entry-gap at M6 Toll Site 29 (*ibid.*, fig. 29.6), would have facilitated control of livestock driven along outlying ditches (*ibid.*). The Orton Hall Farm animal management system was interpreted as a livestock collection and storage point rather than a single livestock holding because of the complexity in the arrangements (Mackreth 1996, 230).

The complexes recorded at Longdales Road, on the M6 Toll and at Orton Hall Farm may be distinguished from individual Romano-British enclosures (e.g. Meole Brace, Shropshire: Bain and Evans forthcoming; Werrington, Cambridgeshire: Mackreth 1988, Whitemoor Haye, Staffordshire: Coates 2002 and Hewson 2006). These sites formed the foci of individual family groups which were engaged in livestock farming, part of a basic pattern of the exploitation of the countryside, termed 'family farms' by Hingley (1989, 55). Single enclosures are a recurring feature of rural settlement layout (Booth 2006, 507; Gaffney and White 2007; Taylor 2007, 24, fig. 4.3). It is notable that the analysis of faunal assemblages from Orton Hall Farm indicates that two systems of animal husbandry were running in parallel – on the one hand, native self-sufficiency and, at a larger scale, estate owners producing surplus for a market (Mackreth 1996, 381).

The animal bone assemblages from Alcester provide an indication of the profile of the animals being consumed there, which are likely to have been supplied from the surrounding countryside, possibly including the Longdales Road settlement. The large animal bone assemblage from the Explosion site (Maltby 2001) was dominated by cattle, then sheep/ goat and then pig. The high numbers of cattle emphasise the high proportion of beef overall in the Roman diet (King 1984), while the predominance of adult cows at Alcester could indicate that dairying was also important (Maltby 2001, 284). It is suggested that animals were slaughtered in the town, having been driven on the hoof from the surrounding countryside. The sheep and goats could have been mainly raised for their meat, with some older animals also being kept for breeding or for their wool. The town's status as a market centre could have encouraged farmers to send flocks of sheep, deliberately raised for their meat, to Alcester (*ibid.*, 287). Gaffney and White (2007, 256) have suggested that the enclosures closer to Wroxeter may have been supplying dairy products to the town, which would have been able to arrive at their destination in peak condition because the distance travelled was short.

At the roadside settlement of Wilcote in Oxfordshire (Hamshaw-Thomas *et al.* 1993), established like Longdales Road in the 2nd century, sheep proportions were high into the 2nd century – a pattern typical of Iron Age animal husbandry. More broadly, it is suggested that, at sites with ready access to main roads, the increase in cattle at the expense of sheep may have been relatively accelerated, for example at Dragonby, Humberside (Harman in May 1996, 141–61). Here the animals recorded in the 1st century were two-thirds sheep and one quarter cattle, with cattle and sheep in equal proportions in the following century. The faunal remains from Wavendon Gate, Buckinghamshire (Dobney *et al.* 1996), also illustrate the change in emphasis from sheep to cattle in the early Romano-British period, with a gradual increase in the size of herds recorded along with the larger size of farming estates (Grant 2004, 376).

Other interpretations

Another possibility is that the settlement functioned as a local market centre, perhaps with a specialist function associated with a large livestock herd, or livestock trading centre. During the earlier part of the Romano-British period the *civitas* elite would have maintained close control over marketing activities (Millett 1990, 124). The Meole Brace roadside settlement was placed by the excavator at the edge of Wroxeter's hinterland – an ideal location for 'lower order' marketing activities, at the lowest level of Hodder and Hassall's hierarchy of market and service centres (1971, 405–6). Analysis of the distribution of enclosures around Wroxeter has led to the identification of an economic or other 'boundary' approximately 6km distant from Wroxeter (Gaffney and White 2007, 254). Longdales Road, located approximately 15km from Alcester, is less likely to have functioned as a local market centre for Alcester because of its distance from the town. However, Gaffney and White (*ibid.*) note that caution is required in the interpretation of optimal spacing between towns and market centres (Hingley 1989, 114). Other possible local market centres sites in the west midlands have also been identified (Crickmore 1984, 71 and 119). This interpretation is considered further later in this chapter.

Another possibility to be considered is that the settlement formed a collection point for livestock requisitioned for military supply. Esmonde Cleary (n.d.) has suggested that the west midlands may have formed a 'resource procurement zone', which could have included livestock for military supply. Analysis of the patterns of age-at-death, and the recovery of all parts of the carcase together, have indicated that animals were often requisitioned locally and butchered on site or near by (Davies 1989, 187–206; King 1999, 146; Webster 1998, 262–4). Study of the dimensions of livestock from several regions shows similarities between animals from civilian and military contexts within the same region, suggesting (King 1999, 144–5) a common and local source of supply. King (*ibid.*, 146) draws a distinction between the more wealthy and prestigious legionary sites which may have been able to be at least partly selective in meat supply, and the auxiliary garrisons that may have mostly relied on animals which were locally reared and slaughtered. This interpretation of the Longdales Road settlement is therefore unlikely unless animals were being transported long distances – because there were no sizeable military garrisons in the close proximity during the floreat of the Longdales Road settlement.

More widely, Millett (1990, 56) emphasises the importance of the local supply of commodities in the post-conquest period, using existing social and political systems, to avoid excessive demands on the native population. Early military requisitions caused disruption to the pre-existing husbandry arrangements (Grant 2004, 372) which provided only limited potential for the creation of a surplus. Earlier military assemblages contained more cattle than the contemporary native assemblages (King 1999, 139), in part because cattle were prized for traction and leather as well as for their meat. The evidence from Exeter fortress (Maltby 1981) suggests that animals were driven there on the hoof from the surrounding countryside, to be slaughtered beside the defences.

The finds evidence

Analysis of the finds, primarily pottery, provides another method of subjecting the function and status of the Longdales Road settlement to objective scrutiny. Located alongside Ryknild Street, it might be expected that a wide range of pottery, such as that recorded at Meole Brace, Shropshire (Evans 1994), might be recovered from Longdales Road, reflecting the site's ready access to the wider trading network. In fact, the broadly contemporary pottery assemblage from Meole Brace (Evans *et al.* 1994, table 9) shows that site to have had access to a far broader range of finewares than Longdales Road, probably due to its proximity to Wroxeter.

Finewares from Longdales Road comprised 1.6% of the whole assemblage, compared to between 1% and 7% recorded at rural sites in Warwickshire (Evans 2001, fig. 10: Abbots Salford and Salford Priors villa, respectively). No amphorae were found at the rural settlements of Longdales Road, Ling Hall, Crewe Farm, Bidford Grange and at the roadside settlement of Princethorpe (all Warwickshire), in contrast to military sites which show proportions of 1–11%, and small towns which show proportions of 1–1.5% (*ibid.*, fig. 11). The almost complete platter of Ludowici Th found in ditch A7 at Longdales Road (Phase 2, Area A) was a rare discovery suggesting a degree of wealth – not supported by analysis of the coarseware pottery. Overall, the proportions of samian from Longdales Road are consistent with assemblages from other rural sites – indicating that samian was not being used to advertise wealth, with occupation being typical of low-status, small-scale Romano-British rural sites (Willis,

Chapter 3, above). Such a pastoral community would have valued livestock above all other possessions (White 2007, 123), with the surpluses generated from the sale of excess livestock invested in the purchase of additional beasts (Taylor 2001, 56). Livestock would also have been suitable for exchange – for example as a dowry (Esmonde Cleary 1989, 104).

A larger quantity of pottery was recovered from Longdales Road (Table 17, 3,344 sherds) compared with M6 Toll Site 19 (Wishaw Hall Farm, 823 sherds: Booth 2006, 517) and Site 29 (Langley Mill Farm, 745 sherds). The pottery from Site 19 at M6 Toll (Leary 2006a, 313) contained high numbers of bowls, dishes and flagons, and also included amphorae. Despite a location, furthest from Wall, of all the sites excavated along the M6 Toll, and an economy probably based on livestock herding, the pottery suggests a relatively high status for the settlement – suggested to derive from the sale of surplus livestock. In contrast, Site 29 (M6 Toll: Leary 2006b), also interpreted as associated with animal husbandry, produced a pottery assemblage indicating a modest status for the settlement, and a comparatively low, or occasional, level of occupation. The main focus of occupation here could, of course, have been located outside the excavated area.

Evans (2001, 30) has noted that a notable regional identity can be discerned at rural sites within the Severn Valley which have high levels of drinking vessels, often tankards (*ibid.*, fig. 5). The Area A assemblage (Hancocks, Chapter 2 above) reflects the dominance of locally and regionally traded Severn Valley and Malvernian wares along with smaller quantities of Black Burnished ware. The Area B assemblage (Evans, Chapter 3 above) has a particular emphasis on jars (67% of the assemblage by rim EVE). Other forms recorded include bowls and dishes, a colander, mortaria and tankards. This narrow pottery repertoire is typical of a low-status rural assemblage. There is some limited evidence of links to more distant trade networks, provided for example by jars from Malvern, mortaria from Mancetter-Harshill and Oxfordshire, and Black Burnished Ware from Dorset. Pottery from the near roadside area (Area C–D, Evans, Chapter 4 above) was dominated by jars and then bowls, which may have been used for food preparation and storage, indicating settlement, albeit on a small scale.

The Area B assemblage produced at least one waster (Evans, Chapter 3 above) and the range of fabric variants also suggests a local source. It is possible that pottery production was undertaken on a seasonal basis at Longdales Road, echoing the disparate sources of pottery production recorded more generally within the Severn Valley area (Taylor 2007, fig. 4.13). Historic mapping (Fig. 6) indicates several clay pits in the locality – suggesting that the local clay was suitable for post-medieval brick and tile production.

There was only limited finds or environmental evidence for other activities at Longdales Road. The recovered loom-weight (post-hole F357 within Enclosure A1 interior: Macey-Bracken, Chapter 2 above), and excavated paired post-hole arrangements in Area A and Area C–D (Figs 12, 14, and 27–8) could suggest that weaving was another activity undertaken on site, probably at a domestic scale. This object is suggested to be Anglo-Saxon in its morphology. No evidence of ironworking was found at Longdales Road. A small quantity of cereal grains were found in a deposit overlying surface F442 (Phase 3B, Area B) indicating crop harvesting or processing, although the number of grains did not suggest large-scale crop processing. An oven was recorded in Area A (F313, Fig. 14) but there was no evidence of its particular function.

REGIONAL CONTEXT

Writing in the regional research agenda, Esmonde Cleary (n.d.) highlights one of the distinguishing features of the Romano-British west midlands as potentially being a resource procurement zone – in particular to feed, clothe and equip troops during the first two centuries of Roman rule. The natural resources exploited included livestock, cereals, minerals and timber. He argues that these resources could have been supplied to Wales, Chester and also the northwest, with the supply of Severn Valley wares to Hadrian's Wall being interpreted as a 'proxy' for a trade in livestock, cereals and other resources from the same region. By contrast, King (1999, 144) has argued for the mainly local sourcing of military livestock requisitions.

The Romano-British west midlands was not, of course, a single coherent territory. It was divided into two *civitas* groups (White 2007, fig. 12; Magilton 2006, 101; Fig. 1), the *Cornovii* to the northwest, and the *Dobunni* to the southeast, with the *Corieltauvi* to the northeast. The 'junction' between the three *civitates* is suggested to be in the vicinity of Coleshill (Magilton 2006, 101), by analogy with other temple complexes placed at *civitas* boundaries. Following this suggested boundary mapping, the Longdales Road settlement, along with Alcester, Droitwich and Metchley, would be located within the extreme north of the *Dobunnic civitates*. Millett (1990, fig. 17) placed the junction just to the west of Metchley.

This division into *civitates* also resonated with broader cultural and economic meanings. According to this interpretation, the *Dobunni* occupied a zone of innovation, easily assimilating Roman cultural identity - represented by small towns, small villages, villas, and material culture, exhibiting close cultural affinities with the south and east of *Britannia* (Esmonde Cleary n.d.). By contrast, the zone to the northwest, occupied by the *Cornovii*, suggests an opposite trend, with only limited incorporation of Roman settlement forms and material culture (Gaffney and White 2007). This was either the result of an ongoing 'conservative' tradition which limited the uptake of innovation – or could be explained in terms of the relatively thin and poor soils of the upland areas being more suited to pastoralism than the more fertile river valleys (Esmonde Cleary n.d.). Exceptionally, the Meole Brace roadside settlement produced a significant group of pottery upon excavation (Evans *et al.* 1994) because of its position on the

Discussion and Conclusion

Table 17. Composition of the pottery assemblages, Longdales Road and other Romano-British rural sites

Pottery type	Longdales Road (Areas A–D and watching brief)		M6 Toll Site 19 (% count, after Booth and Powell 2006, table 19.9)		M6 Toll Site 29 (% count, after Booth and Powell 2006, table 29.4)		Meole Brace, Shropshire (Evans et al. 1994)	
All pottery	3,344	100.00%	823	100.00%	745	100.00%	3,705	100.00%
Coarse wares	3,249	97.15%	734	89.19%	675	90.60%	2,864	77.30%
Samian	61	1.82%	12	1.46%	33	4.43%	380	10.26%
Amphora	-	-	35	4.25%	18	2.42%	365	9.85%
Mortaria	34	1.01%	42	5.10%	19	2.55%	96	2.59%

road network, but elsewhere pottery was relatively rare (Gaffney and White 2007, 241).

The Longdales Road settlement was located on soils of the Brockhurst 2 association, comprising stagnogleyic soils in fine loamy drift (Ragg *et al.* 1984), wet and heavy to work, which may have been suited to pastoralism. Analysis of enclosures in the Wroxeter Hinterland in comparison with land classification suggests that many were located on relatively heavy soils (land categories 3 and 4), both moisture retentive and usable for good pasture (Gaffney and White 2007, 255, fig. 6.7). The damper climate of Britain, in particular the western side of the country, was generally well suited to pastoralism (Pryor 1998).

This apparent lack of up-take of Roman culture and settlement forms may also have been the result of deliberate choices. Esmonde Cleary (n.d.) has suggested a parallel with the province of *Germania Inferior*, a heavily militarised zone exhibiting little evidence of the assimilation of Roman culture, whose pre-existing Iron Age society was based on warfare and cattle rearing. Following this suggested model, the *Cornovii* may have maintained the economic dominance of pastoralism during the Roman period as a result of positive cultural choices. Booth (2006, 517–8) has observed that the limited use of pottery during the M6 Toll excavations exhibits a pattern of limited material culture also seen in Shropshire. The larger quantities of pottery from the Longdales Road investigations (Table 17) has been noted above (p.88). The M6 Toll excavations have also suggested that arable farming may not have been particularly important away from Wall (*ibid.*, 511, 527), with pastoral farming, including large-scale livestock farming at Site 29 (Langley Mill Farm), predominant in the surrounding landscape.

Several important small towns such as, for example, Wall, centrally placed between Wroxeter and Leicester, developed at economically favourable points towards the *civitas* margins (Millett 1990, 148–9). These small towns, where located away from large towns, were able to exert a powerful local economic influence as market centres, particularly in the later Roman period (Booth 2006, 524). In the case of Alcester, this function is underlined by the layout of a surfaced area interpreted as a market (Booth 1994, 173), thought to be associated with temporary 'booths'. Droitwich, Chesterton and Alcester may have also developed in this way in the later Roman period (Booth 1996, 53). Similarly, smaller settlements could have been placed at, or close to, tribal boundaries to take advantage of the trading opportunities. The possible market at Plas Coch, Wrexham (Arnold and Davies 2000, 71), was located at the edge of a territory, possibly to take advantage of the monetary economy of Roman Britain and also the native barter economy (Gaffney and White 2007, 51). Is it possible that Longdales Road could have fulfilled a similar dual function, related to the different economies of the *Cornovii* and the *Dobunni*?

The location of Longdales Road at, or towards, the junction of the *Dobunni* with *Cornovii* may also be a metaphor for its diverging cultural influences. The dominance of animal husbandry within the later 2nd- and 3rd-century site economy reflects the pastoral tradition of the *Cornovii*. The apparent low status of the pottery assemblage (but not its quantity) may suggest that the surplus generated by the sale of livestock was re-invested in the purchase of stock. The persistence of circular ring-gullies also suggests an un-Romanised architectural tradition. The complex layout of the settlement, and its suggested association with livestock, rearing and management, place Longdales Road within the Romanised tradition, along with the quantity of pottery recovered (Table 17). Despite the tradition of pastoralism within Roman Shropshire there is a lack of large agricultural holdings, estates or estate centres (Gaffney and White 2007, 239). The regular layout of the enclosures and roadside plots, and in particular the adoption of half-*actus* units for some of the plot widths at Longdales Road, provides further evidence of 'Romanised' influences. The adoption of half *actus* plots width at Duncote Farm, Shropshire (Jones 1994), has been interpreted by White and Barker (1998, 66–7) to suggest land allotment to a veteran. Similarly, Arnold and Davies (2000, 71) have suggested that Plas Coch, Wrexham, was settled by veterans of *Legio* XX. Any association between veterans and the Longdales Road settlement – despite its proximity to Metchley, is, of course, pure speculation.

As a possible local market centre, Longdales Road will have formed part of the embedded Roman market economy of the *Dobunni*. The finds from Alcester further underline its 'Romanised' cultural affinities. They demonstrate (Booth and Evans 2001, 306) access to a widespread trade network and include unusual and high-status items. These suggest a closer connection with Cirencester (Cracknell 1994, 258), near to good-quality farming land, at the periphery of the Romanised lowland zone.

LATE ROMANO-BRITISH ACTIVITY AND ABANDONMENT

In the later 3rd century the site ceased its livestock rearing, collection or management function when Enclosure A2, its associated compound and entrance complex (Area B), together with the roadside plots, went out of use. This reduction in activity mirrors that of the roadside settlement at Meole Brace, Shropshire (Hughes 1994, 54), which suffered a decline in service and marketing activities, before being finally abandoned in the early 4th century. Similarly, at Tiddington, Warwickshire, further building is not recorded after the later 3rd century (Palmer 1983; Burnham and Wacher 1990) – although burial there continued into the 4th century.

The later 3rd–early 4th-century settlement in Area A at Longdales Road (Fig. 12) was represented by the accumulation of soils over an earlier pebble surface (F141), and by curvilinear gullies, interpreted as providing drainage to circular roundhouses, which have not survived later truncation. Similarly, in Area B, soil deposits overlying surface F442 are recorded. To the east (Area C–D) was recorded the corner of a ditched enclosure (Phase 2, Enclosure E2) of unknown extent. In the same excavation, earlier ring-gully R1 may have continued in use after the roadside plots were abandoned. It has been noted above that the roadside zone was the first to be given up, either because it was comparatively lowlying, or because the economic activities of the settlement were not focused on the economic potential of roadside trade.

In this latest phase, a single farmstead may have been sited at Longdales Road. The quantities of pottery recovered from this latest Romano-British activity suggest *in situ* occupation. Interestingly, the charred plant remains from a deposit overlying surface F442 (Area B) suggest possible grain processing, albeit on a small scale. This evidence needs to be treated with caution since it derives from one sample only – but this may be significant as the only interpretatable deposit of charred plant remains from Longdales Road. The absence of shell-tempered wares suggests that the site was finally abandoned by AD 350.

Nationally, the evidence suggests intensification in the exploitation of the countryside in the later Romano-British period (Esmonde Cleary 1989, 105). This may have been caused by the demands of taxation and the urban population, and an increasing population level overall, as well as by the desirability of creating agricultural surpluses to purchase goods and services (*ibid.*).

A more local explanation for this decline and then abandonment must therefore be sought. A peak of Severn Valley ware supply was recorded at Alcester in the mid-3rd century, whilst during that century there was a reliance on fewer, more distant, sources for pottery supply (Booth and Evans 2001, 307). If this re-alignment of suppliers also included livestock, it could provide the context for the apparent cessation of organised animal husbandry at Longdales Road – if the site lost access to key local markets such as Alcester.

The abandonment of Longdales Road could also have resulted from changes in later Romano-British animal husbandry, although nationally effective systems for stock distribution continued into the 4th century (Grant 2004, 382). More widely, there was an increase in the size of estates (Millett 1990, 203) which could possibly have made the Longdales Road landholding too small to be economically viable. The relationship between the tribal aristocracy and tribesmen may have broken down, leading to a purely economic relationship which may have left those farming smaller units exposed to market forces and embedded in a near feudal system (White 2007, 129). Furthermore, increased taxation by the state calculated on the basis of the area under cultivation would have increased the indebtedness of the peasant farmer (*ibid.*). This increased taxation could have also made the network of local centres unable to meet their targets and so to become economically unviable (Booth 2006, 526). Booth (2006, 526) draws a distinction between the Trent and Avon valleys, with a longer tradition of settlement which may have continued up to the end of the Roman period, and other areas lacking such extended settlement continuity, which, possibly including Longdales Road, could have been abandoned earlier towards the end of the Roman period.

Other excavations in the region provide clear evidence for 4th-century decline. For example, the M6 Toll excavations identified little evidence of 4th-century activity (Booth 2006, 524). The earlier Romano-British enclosure sites may have been abandoned by the middle of the 4th century (*ibid.*, 526), mirroring the later Romano-British decline of Wall itself (Burnham and Wacher 1990, 278). The later history of Wall is dominated by the enclosure laid out across Watling Street (Gould 1999, 185), one of a chain of sites suggested to have provided protection for goods in transit. Alcester also suffered a 4th-century economic decline (Booth and Evans 2001, 307) which could have curtailed or removed opportunities for trade with smaller centres in the surrounding countryside, such as Longdales Road.

POST-ROMAN ACTIVITY

It is suggested above that the final Romano-British settlement at Longdales Road had been abandoned by the mid–late 4th century, although Ryknild Street remained in use into the post-Roman period. There are, nevertheless, a few tantalising hints of post-Roman activity. The rim from a perforated bowl, caused by repair (Fig. 25.1), is paralleled by examples from Wroxeter dated AD 367–450 (Area B,

F442) and even AD 500–660 (Evans, Chapter 3, above). A single loom-weight of rounded, possible Anglo-Saxon, type is recorded from a Romano-British context. The only other evidence for Anglo-Saxon activity in Birmingham is an iron spearhead from Edgbaston and a possible pottery vessel from King's Norton (Hodder 2004, 77). Therefore, any finds of Anglo-Saxon date in the city are of particular importance. Evidence of renewed cultivation in the Anglo-Saxon period, with a corresponding decline in tree pollen, is recorded at Metchley Roman fort (Greig 2005, 79). Archaeological investigations at Longbridge (Mann *et al.* 2006) have revealed a palaeochannel or drainage gully, dated 890–920 cal AD to 940–1040 cal AD. Environmental evidence from this site suggests clearance of a wooded, riverine landscape, which was replaced by grassland.

An alternative phasing of post-hole F357 is that it was Anglo-Saxon in date. This feature was originally interpreted as forming part of the entrance arrangements in the southwest of Enclosure A2, as were the surrounding post-holes (F377, F358). Other nearby features (Phase 1–Phase 3, Fig. 14), particularly the line of stake-holes (F166) cut at a tangent to the Romano-British enclosure, may also belong to this suggested post-Roman episode.

Hodder (2004, 83) notes the potential survival of several later Romano-British sites in Birmingham, including Over Green and Wiggins Hill, into the Anglo-Saxon period, as well as a possible Anglo-Saxon origin for the Parsonage Moat (*ibid.*, 79). The Longdales Road site lies towards the centre of the Anglo-Saxon *Hellerelege* estate (Fig. 6), described in the charter dated AD 669, but any continuity of settlement is difficult to prove, principally because of the evidence for mid–late 4th-century Romano-British abandonment. Settlement in the adjoining area is recorded in the medieval period, with the adjoining Lilycroft Farm being first mentioned in 1314. Trenching to the east of Ryknild Street (Edwards and Jackson 1998) has also provided evidence for medieval agriculture, a possible structure and industrial activity. The most obvious survivor of the Roman landscape is, of course, Ryknild Street, which remains in use, forming the eastern boundary of the new cemetery, along with the surviving field boundaries corresponding to Romano-British plot divisions.

CONCLUSION

The excavation results are important for three reasons. Firstly, they contribute towards an understanding of the pattern of Romano-British rural exploitation of the countryside, which may be related in particular to the extensively investigated military complex at Metchley (Jones 2001; Jones 2005; Jones forthcoming), and the nearby well-researched Roman small town of Alcester (Cracknell 1994; Booth and Evans 2001). Secondly, despite the absence of animal bone, the extensive excavations have provided evidence of specialisation in livestock farming, which is poorly represented in the literature (Booth 1996, 46) with the exception of the faunal assemblages. Finally, the location of the site at, or close to, the *civitas* boundary may have been deliberate, to take advantage of trading opportunities with the *Cornovii*, as well as the more Romanised market economy of the northern *Dobunni* centred on Alcester.

For the post-Roman period, the site provides tantalising finds evidence and possible associations with a documented Anglo-Saxon charter dated AD 669, as well as the tangible survival of Romano-British field or plot boundaries up to the present.

Acknowledgements

The project was funded by Birmingham City Council, through its Urban Design Department. We would like to acknowledge the help and support from Chris Sheriff of the department throughout the project. Assistance from the staff of Kings Norton cemetery during the 2006–7 fieldwork is gratefully acknowledged.

The Worcestershire County Council Archaeology Service 2002 evaluation was supervised by Tom Vaughan, and managed by Simon Woodiwiss. Other fieldwork undertaken by the same organisation at Longdales Road was supervised by Chris Patrick, Rachel Edwards and Robin Jackson. The BUFAU trial-trenching and Area A excavation was supervised by Josh Williams and Bob Burrows, with the assistance of Kate Bain, Helena Biek, Suzy Blake, Bob Bracken, Melissa Conway, Maurice Hopper, Emma Hancox, Vicky Hudson, Ruth Leak, Phil Mann, Helen Martin, Derek Moscrop, Dave Priestley, Ellie Ramsey, Andy Walsh and Steve Williams. The Area B excavation was supervised by Josh Williams with assistance from Mark Hewson, Ioannis Alsitzoglou, Kate Bain, Dharminder Chuhan, Mark Kincey and Kristina Krawiec. The Area C–D investigation was led by Bob Burrows, with the assistance of Ros McKenna, Shaun Daly, Emily Hamilton, Liz Bishop and Jenny White. The 2004 watching brief was undertaken by Paul Mason. Bob Burrows also supervised the 2007 evaluation. Administrative support was provided by Jo Adams during the fieldwork. Peter Leather is thanked for permission to reproduce Plate 2.

The illustrations were prepared by John Halsted, Bryony Ryder and Nigel Dodds. The GIS-based illustrations (Figs 3 and 5) were prepared by Kristina Krawiec. Co-ordination with specialists was undertaken by Erica Macey-Bracken. The published results sections of this volume are based on earlier drafts prepared by Josh Williams (Areas A and B, Chapters 2 and 3), Bob Burrows (Area C–D, Chapter 4), and Paul Mason (Watching Brief, Chapter 5), revised for publication by Alex Jones. Alex Jones would like to thank the staff of OLRC, University of Birmingham for their help. The project manager throughout was Alex Jones, who also edited and compiled this report. Dr Simon Esmonde Cleary is thanked for his academic comments on the text. The text was proof edited for publication by Dr Della Hooke. The project was monitored for Birmingham City Council by Dr Michael Hodder.

Bibliography

Anderberg, A L, 1994 *Atlas of Seeds and Small Fruits of Northwest-European Plant Species. Part 4, Resedaceae-Umbelliferae*. Stockholm: Swedish Museum of Natural History

Arnold, C J, and Davies, J L, 2000 *Roman and Early Medieval Wales*. Stroud: Sutton

Bain, K, and Evans, C J, forthcoming A later Iron Age and Roman enclosure at Meole Brace, Shropshire, *Transactions of the Shropshire Archaeological and Historical Society*

Barfield, L, 2006 Bays Meadow villa, Droitwich: excavations 1967–77, in Hurst (ed.) 2006 *Roman Droitwich*, 78-242

Barker, P, White, R, Pretty, K, Bird, H, and Corbishley, M, 1997 *The Baths basilica Wroxeter Excavations 1966–90*, English Heritage Archaeological Report No 8. London: English Heritage

Berggren, G, 1969 *Atlas of Seeds and Small Fruits of Northwest-European Plant Species. Part 2, Cyperaceae*. Stockholm: Swedish Natural Science Research Council

Berggren, G, 1981 *Atlas of Seeds and Small Fruits of Northwest-European Plant Species with Morphological Descriptions. Part 3, Salicaceae-Cruciferae*. Stockholm: Swedish Museum of Natural History

Black, E W, 1995 *Cursus Publicus: the infrastructure of Government in Roman Britain*, British Archaeological Reports, Brit ser 241. Oxford: BAR Publishing

Booth, P M, 1987 Sutton Coldfield kiln, *West Midlands Archaeology*, 30, 75

Booth, P M, 1994 The excavations in the context of the Roman town, in Mahany (ed) 1994 *Buildings*, 164–75

Booth, P M, 1996 Warwickshire in the Roman period: a review of recent work, *Transactions of the Birmingham and Warwickshire Archaeological Society*, 110, 25–57

Booth, P M, 2006 The Roman period discussion, in Booth and Powell 2006 *The Archaeology of the M6 Toll*, 503–28

Booth, P, and Evans, J, 2001 *Roman Alcester: northern extramural area, 1969-1988 excavations*, Roman Alcester Series Vol. 3, CBA Report 127. York: Council for British Archaeology

Booth, P M, and Green, S, 1989 The nature and distribution of certain pink, grog tempered vessels', *Journal of Roman Pottery Studies*, 2, Study Group for Roman Pottery

Booth, P, and Powell, A, 2006 *The archaeology of the M6 Toll, 2000–2002*, Oxford Wessex Archaeology Report no 2, draft, unpublished

Branigan, R, 1991 Civilian development in a military zone: the Peak AD 43-400, in R Hodges and K Smith (eds) *Recent Developments in the Archaeology of the Peak District*. Sheffield: Sheffield University Press, 57–68

Brown, D L, 1996 The Roman small town at Leintwardine, excavations and other fieldwork 1971–1981, *Transactions of the Woolhope Naturalists Field Club*, 48, part 3, 510–73

Bryant, V, 2004 Fired clay artifacts, in H Dalwood and R Edwards *Excavations at Deansway, Worcester 1988-89: Romano-British small town to late medieval city*, CBA Research Report 139. York: Council for British Archaeology

Burnham, B C, and Wacher, J, 1990 *The Small Towns of Roman Britain*. London: Batsford

Burrows, B, 2006 *Longdales Road, Kings Norton, Birmingham, excavations 2006, post-excavation assessment*, BA report no 1485

Burrows, B, 2007 *Longdales Road, Kings Norton, Birmingham, an archaeological evaluation 2007*, BA report no 1552

Cappers, R, Bekker, R, and Jans, J, 2006 *Digitalezadenatlas Van Nederland*. Groningen: Barhuis Publishing and Groningen University Library

Charles, M, Duncan, M, and Hislop, M, 2007 *Archaeological Investigations at the Saracen's Head, Kings Norton, Birmingham, post-excavation assessment*, BA report no 1609

Ciaraldi, M, 2005 Charred plant remains, in Jones 2005 *Roman Birmingham 2*, 72–5

Ciaraldi, M, forthcoming Charred plant remains, in Jones forthcoming *Roman Birmingham 3*

Clarke, G, 1979 *The Roman Cemetery at Lankhills*, Winchester Studies 3, Pre-Roman and Roman Winchester. Oxford: Clarendon Press

Coates, G, 2002 *A Prehistoric and Romano-British Landscape: excavations at Whitemoor Haye Quarry, Staffordshire 1997–1999*, British Archaeological Reports, Brit Ser 340. Oxford: BAR Publishing

Cool, H E M, and Philo, C (eds), 1998 Roman Castleford, Excavations 1974–85, Vol. I The Small Finds, Yorkshire Archaeology, 4

Cracknell, S, 1994 Discussion, in S Cracknell and C Mahany (eds) *Roman Alcester: Southern extramural area, 1964–1966 excavations*, Roman Alcester Series: Vol. 1, Part 2: Finds and discussion, CBA Research report 97. York: Council for British Archaeology, 249–59

Crickmore, J, 1984 *Romano-British Urban Settlements in the West Midlands*, British Archaeological Reports, Brit ser 127. Oxford: British Archaeological Reports

Darlington, J, and Evans, C J, 1992 Roman Sidbury, Worcester: Excavations 1959–1989, *Transactions of the Worcestershire Archaeological Society*, 3rd Ser 13, 5–104

Davies, R W, 1989 *Service in the Roman Army*. Edinburgh: Edinburgh University Press

Demidowicz, G, 2003 The lost Lint Brook. A solution to the *Hellerelege* Anglo-Saxon charter and other explorations of King's Norton history, *Transactions of the Birmingham and Warwickshire Archaeological Society* 107, 111–29

Dobney, K M, and Jacques, S D, 1996 The mammal bone, in R J Williams, P J Hart and A T L Williams

Wavendon Gate, A Late Iron Age and Roman Rural Settlement in Milton Keynes, Buckinghamshire Archaeological Monograph Series 10. Aylesbury: Buckinghamshire Archaeological Society

Edwards, R, and Jackson, R, 1998 *Evaluation at Walker's Heath, Icknield Street, King's Norton, Birmingham and Wythall, Worcestershire,* Field Section, County Archaeological Service, Worcestershire County Council, report no 660

Ellis, P, Evans, C J, Hannaford, H, Hughes, E G, and Jones, A E, 1994 Excavations in the Wroxeter hinterland, 1988-1990: the archaeology of the A5/A49 Shrewsbury Bypass, *Transactions of the Shropshire Archaeological and Historical Society*, 69

Ellis, P, Hughes, E G, Leach, P J, Mould, C, and Sterenberg, J, 1998 *Excavations along Roman Ermine Street, Cambridgeshire, 1996: the archaeology of the A(1)M Alconbury to Peterborough Road Scheme,* British Archaeological Reports, Brit ser 276. Oxford: BAR Publishing

Esmonde Cleary, A S, 1989 *The Ending of Roman Britain.* London: Batsford

Esmonde Cleary, A S, n.d. West Midlands Archaeological Resarch Framework: the Romano-British period, draft, unpublished: www.iaa.bham.ac.uk/research/fieldwork_research_themes/projects/wmrrfa/intro.htm

Evans, C J, 1994 The Roman pottery, in Ellis *et al.* 1994 Excavations in the Wroxeter hinterland, 76–91

Evans, C J, 2004 The pottery, in M Napthan *Archaeological works at 1 The Butts, Worcester. WCM 101107, 101108, 101109.* Mike Napthan Archaeology, 12–16, 21–24

Evans, C J, with Dickinson, B, Hartley, K, and Williams, D, 1994 The Roman pottery, in Ellis *et al.* 1994 Excavations in the Wroxeter hinterland, 76–91

Evans, C J and Hancocks, A, 2005 Romano-British pottery, in Jones 2005 *Roman Birmingham 2,* 104–8, 110–11

Evans, C J, Hancocks, A, Hartley, K, Tomlin, R, Willis, S and Wilson, D, forthcoming *The Romano-British pottery,* in Jones forthcoming *Roman Birmingham 3*

Evans, C J, Jones, L, and Ellis, P, 2000 *Severn Valley Ware Production at Newland Hopfields: excavation of a Romano-British kiln site at North End Farm, Great Malvern, Worcestershire in 1992 and 1994,* British Archaeological Reports, Brit ser 313, BUFAU Monograph series 2. Oxford: BAR Publishing

Evans, J, 2001 Material approaches to the identification of different Romano-British site types, in S James and M Millet (eds) *Britons and Romans: advancing an archaeological agenda,* CBA Research Report 125. York: Council for British Archaeology, 19–25

Fasham, P J, 1987 A 'banjo' enclosure at Micheldever Wood, Hampshire: MARC 3, site R27. Hampshire Field Club and Archaeological Society Monograph. Winchester: Hampshire Field Club

Foard-Colby, A, 2007 *Archaeological excavation at the Old Bowling Green, Parsons Hill, Kings Norton, July 2006,* unpublished archive report

Frere, S S, 1972 *Verulamium Excavations, Vol. 1,* Reports of the Research Committee of the Society of Antiquaries of London 28. London: The Society of Antiquaries of London

Frere, S S, 1983 *Verulamium Excavations, Vol. 2,* Reports of the Research Committee of the Society of Antiquaries of London 41. London: The Society of Antiquaries of London

Frere S S, 1984 *Verulamium Excavations, Vol. 3,* Oxford University Committee for Archaeology Monograph 1. Oxford: Oxford University Committee for Archaeology

Frere, S S, 1987 *Britannia: a history of Roman Britain,* 3rd edition. London: Guild

Fryer, V, 2006 Charred plant remains, in Burrows 2006 *Longdales Road, Kings Norton,* 14–17

Gaffney, V L, and White, R H, with Goodchild, H, 2007 Integrating the evidence, in *Wroxeter, The Cornovii, and the Urban Process: final report on the Wroxeter Hinterland Project 1994-1997, Vol. 1, Researching the Hinterland,* Journal of Roman Archaeology, Supplementary series, No 68. Portsmouth, Rhode Island US: Journal of Roman Archaeology, 237–86

Golsworthy, A, and Haynes, I, (eds), 1999 *The Roman Army as a Community,* Journal of Roman Archaeology Supplementary series 34. Portsmouth: Journal of Roman Archaeology, 139–49

Gould, J T, 1964 Excavations at Wall, Staffs, *Transactions of the Lichfield and South Staffordshire Archaeological and Historical Society,* 5, 1–50

Gould, J T, 1966 Excavation in advance of road construction at Shenstone and Wall (Staffordshire), *Transactions of the Lichfield and South Staffordshire Archaeological and Historical Society,* 6, 1–19

Gould, J T, 1968 Excavations at Wall, Staffordshire, 1964-6, on the site of the Roman Forts, *Transactions of the Lichfield and South Staffordshire Archaeological and Historical Society,* 8, 1–38

Gould, J T, 1997 Letocetum, an early vexillation fortress, *Britannia,* 28, 350–2

Gould, J T, 1999 The Watling Street Burgi, *Britannia,* 30, 185–97

Grant, A, 2004 Domestic animals and their uses, in Todd (ed) 2004 *A Companion to Roman Britain,* 371–92

Green, S, Dickinson, B, Evans, J, Hancocks, A, Hartley, B, Hartley, K, Pengelly, H, and Williams, D, 2001 Pottery (Areas 1–6), in Jones 2001 *Roman Birmingham 1,* 90–7

Greig, J R A, 2005 Pollen and waterlogged seeds, in Jones 2005 *Roman Birmingham 2,* 75–80

Hamshaw-Thomas, J F, and Bermingham, N, 1993 Analysis of faunal remains, in A R Hands *The Romano-British Roadside Settlement at Wilcote, Oxfordshire: I, excavation 1990–1992,* British Archaeological Reports, British series 232. Oxford: BAR Publishing

Hancocks, A, 1997 *BUFAU Roman pottery recording system,* BUFAU

Hancocks, A, with Hartley, K, Williams, D and Willis, S, 2005 Romano-British pottery, in Jones 2005 *Roman Birmingham 2,* 47–67, 90–3

Harman, M, 1996 Mammalian bones, in May (ed) 1996 *Dragonby: report on excavations at an Iron Age and Romano-British settlement in North Lincolnshire,*

Oxbow Monograph 61. Oxford: Oxbow Books, 141–61

Hartley, B R, 1959 Notes on pottery from some Romano-British kilns in the Cambridge area, *Proceedings of the Cambridge Antiquarian Society*, 53, 23–8

Hewson, M, 2006 *Excavations at Whitemoor Haye, Staffordshire, 2000–2004, a prehistoric and Romano-British landscape*, British Archaeological Reports, Brit ser 428. Oxford: BAR Publishing

Hillman, G C, 1981 Reconstructing crop processing from charred remains of crops, in R Mercer (ed) *Farming Practice in British Prehistory*. Edinburgh: Edinburgh University Press, 123–62

Hillman, G C, 1982 Evidence for spelting malt, in Leech 1982 *Excavations at Catsgore*, 137–40

Hingley, R, 1989 *Rural Settlement in Roman Britain*. London: Seaby

Hobley, B, 1969 A Neronian-Vespasian military site at The Lunt, Baginton, Warwickshire, *Birmingham Archaeological Society, Transactions and Proceedings*, 83, 65–129

Hodder, I R, and Hassall, M W C, 1971 The non random spacing of Romano-British walled towns, *Man*, 6, 391–407

Hodder, M A, 2004 *Birmingham: the hidden history*. Stroud: Tempus

Hodgkinson, H R, and Chatwin, P B, 1944 The Roman site at Shenstone, Staffordshire, *Birmingham Archaeological Society, Transactions and Proceedings*, for 1939-1940, 63, 1–14

Hughes, G, 1994 A Roman roadside settlement at Meole Brace, in Ellis *et al.* 1994, Excavations in the Wroxeter Hinterland, 31–55

Hughes, H V, 1959 A Romano-British kiln site at Perry Barr, *Transactions of the Birmingham and Warwickshire Archaeological Society*, 77, 33–9

Hurst, J D, 2006 Overall conclusions, in Hurst (ed) 2006 *Roman Droitwich*, 243–5

Hurst, J D, (ed.) 2006 *Roman Droitwich: Dodderhill fort, Bays Meadow villa, and roadside settlement*, CBA Research Report 146. York: Council for British Archaeology

Jackson, R, and Hancocks, A, 1996 *Salvage recording on the Frankley to Norton Link Main*, Hereford and Worcestershire County Council County Archaeological Service internal report, 482

Jackson, R, Hurst, J D, and Pearson, E A, 1996a A Romano-British settlement at Leylanndii House Farm and Lenchwick, *Transactions of the Worcestershire Archaeological Society*, 3rd ser, 15, 63–73

Jackson, R, Bevan, L, Hurst, J D, and de Rouffignac, C, 1996b Salvage recording on the Trimpley to Blackstone Aqueduct, *Transactions of the Worcestershire Archaeological Society*, 3rd ser, 15, 93–126

Jones, A E, 1994 A Romano-British field system and enclosure at Duncote Farm, in Ellis *et al.* 1994 Excavations in the Wroxeter hinterland, 55–68

Jones, A E, 1998 Excavations at Wall (Staffordshire) by E. Greenfield in 1962 and 1964 (Wall Excavation Report No 15), *Transactions of the Staffordshire Archaeological and Historical Society*, 37, 1–57

Jones, A E, 1999 Greensforge: investigations in the Romano-British civilian settlement, 1994, *Transactions of the Staffordshire Archaeological and Historical Society*, 38, 12–30

Jones, A E, 2001 Roman Birmingham 1, Metchley Roman Forts Excavations 1963-4, 1967-9 and 1997, *Transactions of the Birmingham and Warwickshire Archaeological Society*, 105

Jones, A E, 2002 *Vincent Drive, Birmingham, archaeological investigations 1999-2000, post-excavation assessment*, BUFAU report no 751

Jones, A E, 2005 Roman Birmingham 2, Metchley Roman Forts, Excavations 1998–2000 and 2002, The Eastern and Southern Annexes and other Investigations, *Transactions of the Birmingham and Warwickshire Archaeological Society*, 108

Jones, A E, forthcoming Roman Birmingham 3, Metchley Roman Forts, the southwestern defences and extra-mural area

Jones, L, Ratkai, S, and Ellis, P, 2001 Excavations at No 15, The Green, Kings Norton 1992, *Transactions of the Birmingham and Warwickshire Archaeological Society*, 104, 101–21

King, A, 1984 Animal bones and the dietary identity of military and civilian groups in Roman Britain, Germany and Gaul, in T F C Blagg and A C King (eds) *Military and Civilian in Roman Britain*, British Archaeological Reports, British ser 137. Oxford: British Archaeological Reports, 187–217

King, A, 1999 Animals and the Roman army: the evidence of animal bones, in Golsworthy and Haynes (eds) 1999 *The Roman Army as a Community*, 139–49

Leach, P J, 1982 *Ilchester Volume 1, Excavations 1974–1975*, Western Archaeological Trust Excavation Monograph 3. Bristol: Western Archaeological Trust

Leary, R S, 2003 The Romano-British pottery from the kilns at Lumb Brook, Hazelwood, Derbyshire, *Derbyshire Archaeological Journal*, 123, 71–110

Leary, R S, 2006a Romano-British pottery, in Trevarthen 2006 Wishaw Hall Farm, 307–14

Leary, R S, 2006b Romano-British pottery, in Powell and Ritchie 2006 North of Langley Mill, 397–404

Leech, R H, 1982 *Excavations at Catsgore 1970-1973: a Romano-British village*, Western Archaeological Trust Excavation Monograph 2. Bristol: Western Archaeological Trust

Lyons, F H, and Gould, J, 1964 A section through the defences of the Roman forts at Wall, Staffordshire, *Transactions and Proceedings of the Birmingham Archaeological Society*, 79, 11–23

Mackreth, D F, 1988 Excavation of an Iron Age and Roman enclosure at Werrington, Cambridgeshire, *Britannia* 19, 59–151

Mackreth, D F, 1996 *Orton Hall Farm: a Roman and early Anglo-Saxon farmstead*, East Anglian Archaeology 76

McWhirr, A 1981 *Roman Gloucestershire*. Gloucester: Sutton

Mahany, C, 1994 *Buildings: summary description of building types*, in C Mahany (ed) 1994 *Roman Alcester Series*, 148–53

Mahany, C, (ed), 1994 *Roman Alcester Series, Vol. 1, part 1: Southern extramural area, 1964-1966 excavations: stratigraphy and structures*, CBA Report 96. York: Council for British Archaeology

Magilton, J, 2006 A Romano-Celtic temple and settlement at Grimstock Hill, Coleshill, Warwickshire, *Transactions of the Birmingham and Warwickshire Archaeological Society*, 110

Maltby, M, 2001 Faunal remains, 265–293, in Explosion site excavations, in Booth and Evans 2001 *Roman Alcester Series 3*, 92–293

Mann, A, Patrick, C, and Hurst, D, 2006 *Archaeological investigations at the former Longbridge North Works Car Park*, Worcestershire Archaeological Service, unpublished report

Margary, I D, 1967 *Roman Roads in Britain*. London: Baker

Marsh, G D, 1981 London's samian supply and its relationship to the development of the Gallic samian industry, in A C and A S Anderson (eds) *Roman Pottery Research in Britain and North-West Europe: papers presented to Graham Webster*, British Archaeological Reports, International ser 123. Oxford: British Archaeological Reports, 173–238

Mason, P, 2004 *Longdales Road, Birmingham, an archaeological watching brief*, BA report no 1167

Millett, M, 1990 *The Romanisation of Britain: an essay in archaeological interpretation*. Cambridge: Cambridge University Press

Mudd, A, 1999a Discussion: the Roman period, in A Mudd, R J Williams and A Lupton *Excavations Alongside Roman Ermine Street, Gloucestershire and Wiltshire: the archaeology of the A419/A417 Swindon to Gloucester road scheme, Vol. 2, Medieval and post-medieval activity, finds and environmental evidence*. Oxford: Oxford Archaeological Unit, 523–28

Mudd, A, 1999b Birdlip quarry, in A Mudd, R J Williams and A Lupton *Excavations Alongside Roman Ermine Street, Gloucestershire and Wiltshire: the archaeology of the A419/A417 Swindon to Gloucester road scheme, Vol. 1, Prehistoric and Roman activity*. Oxford: Oxford Archaeological Unit, 153–227

Oswald, F and Pryce, T D, 1920 *An Introduction to the Study of Terra Sigillata*. London: Longmans, Green and Co

Palmer, N, 1983 Tiddington Roman settlement, *West Midlands Archaeology*, 26, 37–47

Patrick, C, and Darch, E, 2002 *Archaeological evaluation of a proposed new cemetery site, Longdales Road, Birmingham (Area 2)*, Archaeological Service, Worcestershire County Council, report 1002

Peacock, D P S, 1967 Romano-British pottery production in the Malvern district of Worcestershire, *Transactions of the Worcestershire Archaeological Society*, 3rd Ser, 1 (1965–7), 15–28

Powell, A, and Ritchie, K, 2006 North of Langley Mill (Site 29), in Booth and Powell 2006 *The Archaeology of the M6 Toll*, 381–414

Pryor, F M M, 1998 *Farmers in Prehistoric Britain*. Stroud: Tempus

Ragg, J M, Beard, G R, George, H, Heaven, F W, Hollis, J M, Jones, R J A, Palmer, R C, Reeve, M J, Robson, J D, and Whitfield, W A D, 1984 *Soils and their Use in Midland and Western England*, Soil Survey of England and Wales Bulletin 12. Harpenden: Soil Survey of England and Wales

Rankov, B, 1999 The governor's men: the *officium consularis* in provincial administration, in Golsworthy and Haynes (eds) 1999 *The Roman Army as a Community*, 16–34

Rawes, B, 1981 The Romano-British site at Brockworth, Gloucestershire, *Britannia*, 12, 45–77

Rawes, B, 1982 Gloucester Severn Valley ware, *Transactions of the Bristol and Gloucestershire Archaological Society*, 100, 33–46

Round, A A, 1983 Excavations at Wall (Staffordshire), 1968-1972 on the site of the Roman Forts (Wall Excavation report no 12*)*, *Transactions of the South Staffordshire Archaeological and Historical Society* 1981-2, 23, 1–14

Round, A A, 1992 Excavations on the *mansio* site at Wall (*Letocetum*), Staffordshire, 1972-78 (Wall Excavation report no 14), *Transactions of the South Staffordshire Archaeological and Historical Society*, 33, 4–6

Sawyer, P H, 1968 *Anglo-Saxon Charters: an annotated list and bibliography*. London: Royal Historical Society

Seager Smith, R, and Davies, S M, 1993 Black Burnished Ware Type Series: the Roman pottery from excavations at Greyhound Yard, Dorchester, Dorset. Wessex Archaeology, in P J Woodward, S M Davies, and A H Graham, *Excavations at the Old Methodist Chapel and Greyhound Yard, Dorchester 1981-1984*, Dorset Natural Historical and Archaeological and Society Monograph Series 12. Dorchester: Dorset Natural History and Archaeology Society, 229–89

Scott, K, 1984 Mancetter village: first century fort, *Transactions of the Birmingham and Warwickshire Archaeological Society*, 91, 1–24

Smith, R F, 1987 *Roadside Settlements in Lowland Britain*, British Archaeological Reports, Brit ser 157. Oxford: British Archaeological Reports

Smith, W, forthcoming Charred plant remains in Jones, in preparation *Roman Birmingham 3*

Stace, C, 1997 *New Flora of the British Isles*, 2nd edition. Cambridge: Cambridge University Press

Symonds, R P, 1997 The Roman pottery, in P Barker, R White, K Pretty, H Bird and M Corbishley, *The Baths Basilica Wroxeter: excavations 1966-90*, English Heritage Archaeological Report 8. London: English Heritage, 269–318

Taylor, J, 2001 Rural society in Roman Britain, in James and Millett (eds) 2001 *Britons and Romans*, 46–59

Taylor, J, 2007 *An Atlas of Roman Rural Settlement in England*, CBA Research Report 151. York: Council for British Archaeology

Todd, M, 2004 The Claudian conquest and its consequences, in Todd (ed) 2004 *A Companion to Roman Britain*, 42–59

Todd, M, (ed), 2004 *A Companion to Roman Britain*. Malden, MA: Blackwell

Tomber, R, and Dore, J, 1998 *The National Roman Fabric Reference Collection. A handbook*, MoLAS Monograph 2. London: Museum of London Archaeology Service

Trevarthen, M, 2006 Wishaw Hall Farm (Site 19), in Booth and Powell 2006 *The Archaeology of the M6 Toll*, 287–324

Tyers, P, 1996 *Roman Pottery in Britain*. London: Batsford

Vaughan, T, 2002 *Archaeological evaluation at proposed new cemetery site, Longdales Road, Birmingham*, Worcestershire County Council report no 960

Webster, G, 1981 *Rome Against Caratacus, the Roman Campaigns in Britain AD 48-58*. London: Batsford.

Webster, G, 1998 *The Roman Imperial Army of the First and Second Centuries AD* London: Constable

Webster, P V, 1976 Severn Valley Ware: a preliminary study, *Transactions of the Bristol and Gloucestershire Archaeological Society*, 94, 18–46

Welfare, H, and Swann, V, 1995 *Roman Marching Camps: the field archaeology*. London: RCHME

White, R, 2007 *Britannia Prima, Britain's Last Roman Province*. London: Batsford

White, R, and Barker, P, 1998 *Wroxeter: life and death of a Roman city*. Stroud: Tempus

Williams, D F, 1977 The Romano-British Black-Burnished industry: an essay on characterization by heavy mineral analysis, in D P S Peacock (ed) *Pottery and Early Commerce: characterization and trade in Roman and later ceramics*. London: Academic Press, 163–220

Williams, J, 2003a *Longdales Road, King's Norton, Birmingham, archaeological investigations 2002, post-excavation assessment*, BUFAU report no 958

Williams, J, 2003b *Longdales Road, King's Norton, Birmingham, archaeological investigations 2003, post-excavation assessment*, BA report no 958.01

Willis, S H, 1997 *Research Frameworks for the Study of Roman Pottery*, Study Group for Roman Pottery

Willis, S H 1998 Samian pottery in Britain: exploring its distribution and archaeological potential, *Archaeological Journal*, 155, 82–133

Willis, S H, 2005 *An e-monograph: Samian pottery, a resource for the study of Roman Britain and beyond: the results of the English Heritage funded Samian Project*, in *Internet Archaeology*, 17: www.intarch.ac.uk/journal/issue17/willis_toc.html

Young, C J, 1977 *The Roman Pottery Industry of the Oxford Region*, British Archaeological Reports, Brit ser 43. Oxford: British Archaeological Reports

Zohary, D, and Hopf, M, 2000 *Domestication of Plants in the Old World: the origin and spread of cultivated plants in West Asia, Europe, and the Nile Valley*, 3rd edition. Oxford: Oxford University Press

Appendices

Appendix A

Appendix A1: Pottery, list of fabrics

B02
C02
G04
G05 fabric 7.2 Roman Birmingham 1 (Green *et al*. 2001)
G06.5 fabric 7.5 Roman Birmingham 1
G06.7 fabric 7.6 Roman Birmingham 2 (Hancocks *et al.* 2005)
G06.8 fabric 7.7 Roman Birmingham 2
G06.9 fabric 7.8 Roman Birmingham 2
G06.12 fabric 7.11 Roman Birmingham 2
M02
M04c
M04cv
N02.1 fabric 7.1 Roman Birmingham 1
N02.2 fabric 7.1 Roman Birmingham 1
O02 fabric 6.2 Roman Birmingham 1
O02.1 fabric 6.2 Roman Birmingham 1
O02.12
O02.13
O03.1 fabric 7.2 Roman Birmingham 2
O03.2
O03.3
O06.01
O06.09 fabric 6.5 Roman Birmingham 2
O06.10 fabric 6.6 Roman Birmingham 2
O06.11 fabric 6.7 Roman Birmingham 2
O06.22
O06.91
S03 Central Gaul (Lezoux) Roman Birmingham 2
S04R
W11 fabric 5.3 Roman Birmingham 1
W11.2

Fabrics in normal condition

M02 Fabric 3 (normal fabric)Mancetter-Hartshill potteries
A usually fine-textured, cream fabric, varying from softish to very hard, sometimes with pink core. Inclusions usually moderate, smallish, transparent and translucent white and pinkish quartz with sparse opaque orange-brown fragments and occasionally white clay pellets (or re-fired pottery). The range in fabric is, in fact, quite wide, from that with scarcely any inclusions to fabrics with a fair quantity and fabrics with hard, ill-sorted black inclusions. The trituration grit after AD 130/140 consisted of hard red-brown and/ or hard blackish, re-fired pottery fragments (Drs D P S Peacock and D F Williams, pers. comm.) with only very rare quartz fragments. Earlier mortaria usually have a mixed trituration grit in which quartz and sandstone are normal components and some early 2nd-century mortaria probably have entirely quartz trituration grit.

M04c Fabric 1 Oxford potteries (Cowley, Headington, Sandford, etc: Young 1977; Tomber and Dore 1998, 174–5)
Self-coloured, slightly sandy, off-white fabric, occasionally with pink core. The very distinctive trituration grit, associated with all Oxford fabrics, consists entirely of mixed pink, brownish and transparent quartz. The texture of Fabric 1 varies according to the amount of tempering added; mortaria dated *c* AD 100–140 often have abundant, well-sorted quartz inclusions and, if the distinctive trituration grit is missing, the fabric can be difficult to distinguish from Fabric produced in the Verulamium region. Mortaria produced in potteries in the vicinity of Oxford after *c* AD 140 are mostly, but not invariably in a fine-textured fabric.

M04cv Fabric 2 Oxford potteries (Balsdon, Cowley, Dorchester, Sandford etc: Young 1977)
Fine-textured, micaceous, red-brown fabric, sometimes with grey core; some tiny quartz and sparse red-brown inclusions. Trituration grit as in Fabric 1. In normal circumstances the fabric has a red-brown slip, comparable to the slip on samian but not as good.

Note that only fabric descriptions not previously published are described

Appendix A2: Pottery, vessel classes within assemblage

Form Name	
B	Bowl type
B/DA	Straight-sided bowl/dish
BI	Flanged bowl
BK	Beaker
BKD	Globular/Bulbous Beaker
CC	Conical Cup
DA	Straight-sided dish
F	Flagon type
FG	Disc-mouthed flagon
J	Jar type
JE	Squat, high-shouldered jar
JG	Globular/Bulbous jar
JJ	Lid-seated jar
JK	Cooking pot jar
JL	Storage jar
JN	Narrow-mouthed jar
JW	Wide-mouthed jar
MB	Hammerhead mortaria
NA	Upright Tankard

Appendix A3: Pottery, occurrence of vessel forms by fabric and phase

Unphased
G05   JN7.01

Phase 1
G05   **JE1.01**
G06.5   JK7.03
O02.1   JW1.04

Phase 2
G05   JX1, JE1.01
G06.5   JX1
GO6.8   JG7.01
GO6.9   BKDX1, JJX1
O02.1   J1.01, JE7.01, JJ13.02, JL2.01, JW1.04X2, NA1.12X2
O03.1   BI8.31, JE1.01
S03   CC20.04
W11   BK

Phase 1–2
N02.1   JK1.01
O02.1   NA1.12
O02.13   JE7.01

Phase 1–3
B02   DA1.01
N02.1   DA8.31
O02.1   JW1.04X2, NA1.12

Phase 3
B02   BI8.25, BI8.31, DA1.01X3, DA1.12, JK7.01, JK7.3X2
C02   BKD5.01
G04   NA1.12
G05   JX2, J1.01, JE1.01, JN7.01
GO6.5   J, JE7.01, JN7.01, BI8.04X2
M02   MB, MB17.08, MB17.09
N02.1   JK22.05, JL7.01
O02.1   B1.01, B1.04, BI, BI1.04, BI8.25, F2.11, FG, JX2, JE1.01, JE1.04X2, JG7.01, JL1.04, JN7.01, JW1.04X4, NA1.12X2
O03.1   BI8.31, JE1.01, JW1.04

Phase 4
O02.1   JE1.01, JW1.04

Appendix A4: Pottery, occurrence of fabrics by phase (by count)

Fabric/ Phase	Un-phased	Phase 1	Phase 1-2	Phase 1-Phase 3	Phase 2	Phase 3	Phase 4	Total
B02	0.49%	0.21%	0.07%	0.07%	0.21%	5.21%	-	**6.26%**
C02	-	-	-	-	-	0.07%	-	**0.07%**
G04	0.35%	-	-	-	-	-	-	**0.35%**
G05	0.07%	0.14%	-	0.14%	0.97%	1.95%	-	**3.27%**
G06.5	-	0.28%	-	-	1.88%	2.85%	-	**5.01%**
G06.7	-	0.14%	0.35%	-	-	-	-	**0.49%**
G06.8	-	-	-	-	0.07%	-	-	**0.07%**
G06.9	-	-	-	-	0.62%	-	-	**0.62%**
G06.12	-	0.69%	-	-	-	-	-	**0.69%**
M02	-	-	-	-	-	0.35%	-	**0.35%**
M04c	-	-	-	-	-	0.49%	-	**0.49%**
M04cv	-	-	-	-	-	0.28%	-	**0.28%**
N02.1	-	0.14%	0.07%	0.07%	0.62%	0.28%	-	**1.18%**
N02.2	3.54%	-	0.07%	-	-	-	-	**3.61%**
O02	0.69%	-	-	-	-	-	-	**0.69%**
O02.1	2.43%	4.10%	0.35%	0.83%	13.20%	41.49%	0.42%	**62.82%**
O02.12	0.28%	-	-	-	-	-	-	**0.28%**
O02.13	-	0.07%	0.21%	-	-	-	-	**0.28%**
O03.1	0.14%	0.35%	-	0.07%	2.36%	2.08%	-	**5%**
O03.2	-	-	-	0.07%	-	0.07%	-	**0.14%**
O03.3	0.21%	-	-	-	-	-	-	**0.21%**
O06.01	0.35%	0.56%	-	0.07%	-	-	-	**0.98%**
O06.09	2.01%	0.07%	-	-	-	-	-	**2.08%**
O06.10	-	-	-	-	0.14%	0.07%	-	**0.21%**
O06.11	0.28%	-	-	0.07%	-	-	-	**0.35%**
O06.22	-	-	0.14%	-	-	-	-	**0.14%**
O06.91	2.01%	-	-	-	-	-	-	**2.01%**
S03	0.69%	-	-	-	0.62%	0.28%	-	**1.59%**
S04R	0.14%	-	-	-	-	0.07%	-	**0.21%**
W11	-	-	-	-	0.21%	-	-	**0.21%**
W11.2	0.05%	-	-	-	-	-	-	**0.05%**
Total	**13.73%**	**6.75%**	**1.26%**	**1.39%**	**20.90%**	**55.54%**	**0.42%**	**100.0%**
	198	97	18	20	301	799	6	

Appendix B

Appendix B1: Pottery, list of fabrics represented

Common Name	Fabric Code	Green Fabric Code (Metchley Sample No)	Description/references (National Roman Fabric Reference Collection code, Tomber and Dore 1998)/ local code based on the NRFRC system
Black Burnished ware	B02		(DOR BB 1) T&D, 127, pl. 100; Williams 1977; Seager Smith and Davies 1993
Grog-tempered wares	F010	6.3 (S. 14)	Wheelmade, soft. Dark grey (7.5YR 4/1) core with pink (7.5YR 7/4) margins and surfaces. Common, well-sorted and rounded grog (1–2mm), sparse to rare poorly sorted and angular organics (1mm) and sparse, well-sorted and rounded quartz
	F011	(S. 21)	Handmade, soft. Greyish brown (10YR 5/2) core/ external margin/surface with reddish yellow (7.5YR 6/6) internal margin/ surface. Rare, poorly sorted, rounded grog (0.01mm) and abundant, poorly sorted organics (0.3mm). Irregularly fired, poor sorting of inclusions, possibly coil built
Severn Valley ware (Oxidised, plain)	O02		Dump category of oxidised Severn valley wares (used to record very small fragments)
	O02.1	6.2 (S. 4, 5, 33)	(SVW OX 2) T&D, 148–9, pl. 122: plain, unsourced. Variations occur in this fabric: it may include rare, well-rounded grog (0.02mm) as in sample 5, or rare, poorly-sorted and angular grog (1mm) as in sample 33; there may also be variations in the level of micaceousness
	O02.13		Variant with organic and sand inclusions
(Oxidised, organic)	O03.1	7.2 (S. 38)	SVW ORG O: Wheelmade, soft to hard. Pale brown margins, internal surface and core (10YR 6/3) and reddish yellow (7.5YR 6/8) external surface. Abundant, fine, well-sorted, angular organics (charcoal and voids) (0.02mm)
	O03.4		Coarser variant of O03.1
(Reduced, plain)	G04	(S. 35, c.f. 10, 32)	SVW R: Wheelmade, hard. Grey (2.5YR 5/1) core and grey (2.5YR 6/1) margins/ surfaces. Very common, well-sorted and rounded fine quartz (0.01–0.02mm)
(Reduced, organic)	G05	7.2 (S. 1, 2, 4-7)	SVW ORG: Wheelmade, soft. Grey (10YR 6/1) throughout. Abundant, well-sorted organics (charcoal and charcoal voids), 0.02–0.03mm and rare limestone
Misc. oxidised wares	O06.01	6.1 (S.8)	Wheelmade, hard. Reddish yellow (7.5YR 6/6) core, reddish yellow (5YR 6/8) margins/surfaces. Abundant, well-sorted, rounded quartz (0.1mm)
	O06.05		Wheelmade, hard, yellowish red (5YR 5/6) throughout. Common, fine, well-sorted quartz and occasional angular limestone
	O06.09	6.5 (S.17)	Wheelmade, hard. Yellowish red (5YR 5/6) throughout. Moderate well-sorted and rounded quartz (1–mm)
Misc. 'grey' wares	G06.05	7.5 (S. 15)	SAND R1 Wheelmade, soft to hard. Grey (2.5Y 6/1) throughout. Very common, well-sorted, rounded quartz (cf. fabric R52 Bubbenhall, Warks.)
	G06.07	7.6 (S. 18)	Wheelmade, very hard. Dark grey (10YR 4/1) throughout. Very common, well-sorted and rounded quartz (2mm) and rare, poorly sorted and angular quartz (5mm). (cf. fabric R52 Bubbenhall, Warks.)
Greyware with grog	G06.09	7.8 (S. 24)	SAND R5 Wheelmade, soft to hard. Black (5YR 5/1) throughout. Moderate well-sorted and rounded quartz (0.01mm) and rare to sparse, poorly sorted organics (0.02mm)
	G06.10	7.9 (S. 27)	SAND R? Wheelmade, soft to hard. Black (5Y 2.5/1) throughout. Common, well-sorted, angular grog (0.01–0.03mm), common, poorly sorted elongated voids (0.02mm) and very rare well-sorted and rounded quartz. LMARS fabric GW
White wares	W16		Wheelmade
Mortaria, Mancetter - Hartshill	M02		Fabric 3 (normal fabric): A usually fine-textured, cream fabric, varying from softish to very hard, sometimes with pink core. Inclusions usually moderate, smallish, transparent and translucent white and pinkish quartz with sparse opaque orange-brown fragments and occasionally white clay pellets (or re-fired pottery). The range in fabric is, in fact, quite wide, from that with scarcely any inclusions to fabrics with a fair quantity and fabrics with hard, ill-sorted black inclusions. The trituration grit after AD 130/140 consisted of hard red-brown and/or hard blackish, re-fired pottery fragments (Drs D P S.Peacock and D F Williams, pers. comm.) with only very rare quartz fragments. Earlier mortaria usually have a mixed trituration grit in which quartz and sandstone are normal components and some early 2nd-century mortaria probably have entirely quartz trituration grit. (MAH WH) T&D, 189, pl. 157a–d
Oxfordshire white	M04c		Fabric 1: Cowley, Headington, Sandford etc: Young 1977; (OXF WH) T&D, 174–5, pls 145-6a-b. Self-coloured, slightly sandy, off-white fabric, occasionally with pink core. The very distinctive trituration grit, associated with all Oxford fabrics, consists entirely of mixed pink, brownish and transparent quartz. The texture of Fabric 1 varies according to the amount of tempering added; mortaria dated c AD 100–140 often have abundant, well-sorted quartz inclusions and, if the distinctive trituration grit is missing, the fabric can be difficult to distinguish from Fabrics produced in the Verulamium region. Mortaria produced in potteries in the vicinity of Oxford after c AD 140 are mostly, but not invariably, in a fine-textured fabric
'Native' handmade	N02.1	7.1	Malvernian, Group A, handmade (MAL RE A) T&D, 147, pl. 120; Peacock 1967
Samian	S01		South Gaulish, La Graufesenque; (LGF SA) T&D, 28, pl. 17
	S03		Central Gaulish, Lezoux 2 (LEZ SA 2), T&D, 32, pl. 21

Appendix B2: Pottery, vessel classes within assemblage

Form Name	Details
B	Bowl type
BBI	Straight-sided bowl with flange rim (Pudding Pan Rock form 15)
BC	Curving-sided bowl
B	Bowl
BC	Curving-sided bowl (including Drag. 36, 37)
B/D	Bowl or dish
B/DA	Straight-sided bowl or dish (Drag.18/31, 18/31R, 31R)
B/DB	Curving-sided bowl or dish (Drag. 31)
BI	Flanged bowl (includes Drag 38)
B/J	Bowl or jar
DA	Straight-sided dish
DC	Platter (Drag. 15/17)
J	Jar type
JE	High-shouldered, necked jar
JJ	Lid-seated jar
JK	Cooking pot jar
JL	Large storage jar
JN	Narrow-mouthed jar
JW	Wide-mouthed jar
JWS	Wide-mouthed jar (short necked)
MA	Bead and flange mortaria
MB	Hammerhead mortaria
MIG	Colander
NB	Moderately splayed tankard
NC	Very splayed Tankard

Appendix B3: Pottery, occurrence of vessel forms by fabric and phase

Unphased
B02   J
O02.1   B/J19.10, B/J8.33, BI8.41
O02.13   JN1.01, JN20.01
O03.1   BC1.01, JN2.01

Phase 1
S03   B/DA1.01 (Drag. 18/31R)

Phase 2
B02   BI 8.25, DA1.01, JK7.3
F10   JL
F11   JK7.01
G04   JN19.10, JW20.01
G06.9   JJ6.08
M02   MA8.01, MB
M04c   MA8.01
O02.1   JW20.01, JWS20.01
O02.13   BI8.31, BI8.41, J19.10, J7.01, JN2.01, JN7.01, JW19.10, JW2.01, MIG
O03.1   B/J19.10, B/J7.01, BI8.41, J7.01, JN1.01, JW19.10, JW20.01

O06.01   JN7.01, MIG, NC1.01,
O06.09   JN7.01, JW19.10, JW20.01

S03   B/DA1.01 (Drag. 18/31), B/DB1.01 (Drag. 31, 31R)

Phases 2–3
B02   BI8.25, DA1.01, JK7.3
F10   JL10
G04   JN19.1, JW20.01
M02   MA8.01
O02.1   JW20.01, JW7.01
O02.13   B/J7.03, JW20.01, JW7.01, JW7.03, JWS20.01
O03.1   B/J19.1, B/J7.01, B/J7.03, B/J8.33, BC8.04, BC8.33, BI8.41, JN2.01, JW20.01, JW7.01, JWS20.01

O03.4	B/J7.03, JW20.01
O06.09	B/J19.1, BJ8.33, J20.01, JW20.01
	BBI8 (Pudding Pan Rock Type 15)

Phase 3
B02	DA1.01
G05	J19.10, JW20.01
O02.13	NB1.01
S03	DC1.01 (Drag. 15/17)

Phase 4
| O03.1 | J20.01 |

Appendix B4: Pottery, occurrence of fabrics by phase

Fabric	Unphased/Trenching			Phase 1			Phase 2			Phase 2-3			Phase 3			Phase 4		
B02	6	146g	2				8	48g	0	22	303g	61	24	76g	13			
F10							6	376g	0	14	540g	0						
F11							7	24g	18									
G04							1	14g	0	22	216g	33						
G05							8	35g	0	6	62g	0	22	75g	17			
G06.5	2	8g	0				6	173g	0									
G06.7							3	20g	0									
G06.9							35	279g	14									
M02							5	180g	9	4	240g	20						
M04c							3	55g	11									
N02.1	2	24g	0				11	126g	0	2	63g	0						
O02	12	14g	0				139	185g	0	13	12g	0	2	1g	0	2	2g	0
O02.1	43	441g	18	6	37g	0	108	814g	72	41	396g	51	2	4g	0			
O02.13	18	78g	31	10	13g	0	79	629g	139	34	386g	87	29	238g	23			
O03.1	49	313g	51	4	4g	0	120	938g	125	308	1921g	146				1	5g	2
O03.4	4	43g	0				4	8g	0	9	139g	25	1	3g	0	1	8g	0
O06.01							9	53g	27	5	35g	0						
O06.09	5	34g	0	1	1g	0	23	237g	26	8	90g	24	6	26g	0			
O06.10							1	47g	0	1	10g	8						
O06.22							2	17g	0									
O06.05							2	5g	0									
S01	1	1g	0										1	14g	0			
S03	1	5g		1	64g	0	24	281g	64	4	39g							
W16	1	2g	0				12	41g	0	5	17g		1	2g	0			
Total	144	1109g	102	22	119g	0	616	4585g	505	498	4469g	455	88	439g	53	4	415g	2

Appendix C

Appendix C1: List of fabrics represented

Common Name	Fabric Code	Green Fabric Code (Metchley Sample No)	Description/references (National Roman Fabric Reference Collection code, Tomber and Dore 1998)/local code based on the NRFRC system
Black Burnished ware	B02		(DOR BB 1) T&D, 127, pl. 100; Williams 1977; Seager Smith and Davies 1993
Pink Grog-tempered ware	F018		(PNK GT) T&D 210, pl. 175; Booth and Green 1989
Severn valley ware (Oxidised)	O02.1	6.2 (S. 4, 5, 33)	(SVW OX 2) T&D, 148–9, pl 122: Plain, unsourced. Variations occur in this fabric: it may include rare, well-rounded grog (0.02mm) as in sample 5, or rare, poorly-sorted and angular grog (1mm) as in sample 33; there may also be variations in the level of micaceousness
	O02.13		Variant with organic and sand inclusions
(Oxidised, organic)	O03.1	7.2 (S. 38)	SVW ORG O: Wheelmade, soft to hard. Pale brown margins, internal surface and core (10YR 6/3) and reddish yellow (7.5YR 6/8) external surface. Abundant, fine, well-sorted, angular organics (charcoal and voids) (0.02mm)
	O03.4		Coarser variant of O03.1
(Reduced, plain)	G04	(S. 35, cf. 10, 32)	SVW R: Wheelmade, hard. Grey (2.5YR 5/1) core and grey (2.5YR 6/1) margins/surfaces. Very common, well-sorted and rounded fine quartz (0.01–0.02mm)
	G04v		Coarser variant of G04, with common, well-sorted and rounded quartz (0.01mm). Slightly micaceous
(Reduced, organic)	G05	7.2 (S. 1, 2, 4–7)	SVW ORG: Wheelmade, soft. Grey (10YR 6/1) throughout. Abundant, well-sorted organics (charcoal and charcoal voids), 0.02–0.03mm and rare limestone
Misc. oxidised wares	O06.01	6.1 (S.8)	Wheelmade, hard. Reddish yellow (7.5YR 6/6) core, reddish yellow (5YR 6/8) margins/surfaces. Abundant, well-sorted, rounded quartz (0.1mm)
	O06.05		Wheelmade, hard, yellowish red (5YR 5/6) throughout. Common, fine, well-sorted quartz and occasional angular limestone
	O06.07	6.4	Sandy oxidised ware. Wheelmade, hard. Yellow (10YR 7/6) throughout. Moderate well-sorted and rounded quartz (1mm), rare, angular and poorly sorted ironstone and grog
	O06.09	6.5 (S.17)	Wheelmade, hard. Yellowish red (5YR 5/6) throughout. Moderate well-sorted and rounded quartz (1–3mm)
Misc. 'grey' wares	G06.05	7.5 (S. 15)	SAND R1: Wheelmade, soft to hard. Grey (2.5Y 6/1) throughout. Very common, well-sorted, rounded quartz (cf. fabric R52 Bubbenhall, Warks.)
	G06.06	7.4	Wheelmade, hard. Grey (2.5YR 5/1) core, internal surface and margins with strong brown (7.5YR 5/6) external surface. Moderate, well-sorted and rounded quartz (1–3mm). Slightly micaceous (= fabric 7.4, Green et al. 2001)
	G06.07	7.6 (S. 18)	Wheelmade, very hard. Dark grey (10YR 4/1) throughout. Very common, well-sorted and rounded quartz (2mm) and rare, poorly sorted and angular quartz (5mm). (cf. fabric R52 Bubbenhall, Warks.)
	G06.08	7.7	Wheelmade, hard. Dark grey (2.5YR 4/1) core and dark greyish brown (10YR 4/2) margins and surfaces. Very common well-sorted and rounded quartz (0.01–0.02mm) and sparse, poorly sorted and angular organics
White wares	W16		Wheelmade, soft. Pale yellow core ((2.5Y 7/4) with white surfaces (5Y 8/1). Sparse inclusions of moderately sorted brown and black iron rich inclusions <1mm. Distinctive, streaky iron rich inclusions <3mm
Mortaria	M		Wheelmade, pale brown fabric. Dense frequency of fine sub-angular to round quartz sand (<0.5mm) with rare larger sub-angular grains protruding from the surface, along with a scatter of red-brown argillaceous inclusions ranging from fine to <2.5mm. Source uncertain
Mancetter-Hartshill	M02		Fabric 3 (normal fabric): A usually fine-textured, cream fabric, varying from softish to very hard, sometimes with pink core. Inclusions usually moderate, smallish, transparent and translucent white and pinkish quartz with sparse opaque orange-brown fragments and occasionally white clay pellets (or re-fired pottery). Fabric ranges widely, from that with scarcely any inclusions to fabrics with a fair quantity and fabrics with hard, ill-sorted black inclusions. The trituration grit after AD 130/140 consisted of hard red-brown and/or hard blackish, re-fired pottery fragments (Drs D P S Peacock and D F Williams pers. comm.) with only very rare quartz fragments. Earlier mortaria usually have a mixed trituration grit in which quartz and sandstone are normal components and some early 2nd-century mortaria probably have entirely quartz trituration grit. (MAH WH) T&D, 189, pl. 157a–d
'Native' handmade	N02.1	7.1	Malvernian, Group A, handmade (MAL RE A) T&D, 147, pl. 120; Peacock 1967
Samian	S03		Central Gaulish, Lezoux 2 (LEZ SA 2), T&D, 32, pl. 21

Appendix C2: Pottery, vessel classes within assemblage

Form name	Details
BA	Carinated bowl
BC	Curving sided bowl)
B/D	Bowl or dish
BI	Flanged bowl (includes Drag 38)
B/J	Bowl or jar
C/BKC	Cup or bag shaped beaker
DA	Straight-sided dish
JK	Cooking pot jar
JLS	Large storage jar
JN	Narrow-mouthed jar
JW	Wide-mouthed jar
LAA	Conical, concave lid
MA	Bead and flange mortarium
MG	Reeded flange mortarium
MIG	Colander
NC	Very splayed Tankard

Appendix C3: Pottery, occurrence of vessel forms by phase

Form Type	Rim EVE	% Rim EVE
	Phase 1	
B/D1.01	0.05	1.6%
B/J8.33	0.08	2.6%
BC8.33	0.36	11.5%
BI8.22	0.1	3.2%
BI8.25	0.15	4.8%
C/BKC7.01	0.1	3.2%
DA1.01	0.17	5.4%
JK	0.02	0.6%
JK22.05	0.08	2.6%
JLS19.1	0.08	2.6%
JN19.1	0.1	3.2%
JN20.01	0.17	5.4%
JN20.02	0.08	2.6%
JW16.01	0.05	1.6%
JW19.1	0.35	11.2%
JW20.01	0.17	5.4%
LAA16.01	0.06	1.9%
MA8	0.1	3.2%
MG8.01	0.08	2.6%
NC1.01	0.32	10.3%
Total	**2.67**	**85.6%**
	Phase 1/2	
BI8.25	0.03	1.0%
JN1.2	0.08	2.6%
Total	**0.11**	**3.5%**
	Phase 2	
BC8.33	0.11	3.5%
JW20.01	0.21	6.7%
Total	**0.32**	**10.3%**
	Phase 3	
BC8.04	**0.02**	**0.6%**

Appendix C4: Pottery, occurrence of forms by fabric

Form name	B02	G04	G05	G06.05	G06.07	G06.08	M	M02	N02.1	O02.1	O02.13	O03.1	O06.01	O06.09
B/D1.01						0.05								
B/J8.33														0.08
BC8.04										0.02				
BC8.33										0.16	0.31			
BI8.22	0.1													
BI8.25	0.18													
C/BKC7.01											0.1			
DA1.01	0.04			0.09	0.04									
JK	0.02													
JK22.05									0.08					
JLS19.1				0.08										
JN1.2		0.08												
JN19.1											0.1			
JN20.01										0.17				
JN20.02											0.08			
JW16.01											0.05			
JW19.1										0.16	0.05	0.14		
JW20.01			0.05										0.17	0.16
LAA16.01											0.06			
MA8							0.1							
MG8.01									0.08					
NC1.01										0.32				
Total	0.34	0.08	0.05	0.17	0.04	0.05	0.1	0.08	0.08	0.83	0.75	0.31	0.16	0.08

Appendix C5: Occurrence of fabrics by phase (% wt)

Fabric	Un-phased	Phase 1	Phase 1/2	Phase 2	Phase 3	Total
B02	0.3%	4.3%	1.7%	0.6%	-	6.9%
F018	2.2%	3.4%	-	-	-	5.6%
G04	0.7%	5.2%	0.3%	-	0.1%	6.3%
G04v	0.1%	-	-	-	-	0.1%
G05	0.1%	0.5%	-	0.8%	-	1.3%
G06.05	-	4.2%	-	-	-	4.2%
G06.06	0.3%	-	2.8%	-	-	3.1%
G06.07	-	1.0%	-	-	-	1.0%
G06.08	0.4%	-	-	-	-	0.4%
M	-	1.3%	-	-	-	1.3%
M02	-	2.4%	-	-	-	2.4%
N02.1	0.6%	2.6%	-	-	-	3.1%
O02.1	2.6%	12.6%	3.8%	1.3%	1.5%	21.7%
O02.13	0.5%	9.5%	1.2%	3.7%	0.1%	15.0%
O03.1	0.5%	3.9%	1.1%	-	-	5.5%
O03.4	1.0%	0.1%	0.9%	-	-	2.0%
O06.01	-	-	-	2.3%	-	2.3%
O06.05	0.1%	1.5%	-	-	-	1.5%
O06.07	1.8%	-	-	-	-	1.8%
O06.09	-	9.2%	-	4.1%	-	13.3%
P09	0.2%	-	-	-	-	0.2%
S03	-	-	0.2%	-	-	0.2%
W16	-	-	0.6%	-	-	0.6%
Total	**11.2%**	**61.6%**	**12.8%**	**12.8%**	**1.6%**	**100.0%**

www.ingramcontent.com/pod-product-compliance
Lightning Source LLC
Chambersburg PA
CBHW041707290426

44108CB00027B/2878